Tick...Tick...

Hear that clock ticking? It's the countdown to the ASVAB exam, and it'll be here before you know it. Whether you have one year or one day to go, now's the time to start maximizing your score.

The Test Is Just a Few Months Away!

Don't worry—you're ahead of the game! But you should still begin preparing now. Follow the **Strategies for Long-Term Preparation** (page 279) to make the most of your time so you'll be well prepared for test day.

Actually, I Only Have a Few Weeks!

There's still plenty of time for a full review. Turn to the **Comprehensive Strategies and Review** (page 21), where you'll find a **diagnostic test** to help you identify your areas of weakness, **Multiple-Choice Strategies** for advice on how to approach test questions, and in-depth **content review chapters** on each subtest of the ASVAB exam.

Let's Be Honest. The Test Is Tomorrow and I'm Freaking Out!

No problem. Review the **About the ASVAB Exam** chapter (page 5), so you know what to expect when you arrive to take the test. Then take a **practice exam** (pages 287 and 383). Don't worry about the scores— just focus on getting to know the test. Before you go to bed, review the **Quick Test-Taking Tips** (page 17) and keep that list close. It'll walk you through the day ahead.

Relax. Make the most of the tools and resources in th⋯ ⋯ uide, and you'll be ready to earn a top score.

My Max Score

ASVAB: ARMED SERVICES VOCATIONAL APTITUDE BATTERY

Maximize Your Score in Less Time

**Angie Johnston and
Amanda Ross, PhD**

This publication is designed to provide accurate and authoritative information in regard to the subject matter covered. It is sold with the understanding that the publisher is not engaged in rendering legal, accounting, or other professional service. If legal advice or other expert assistance is required, the services of a competent professional person should be sought.—*From a Declaration of Principles Jointly Adopted by a Committee of the American Bar Association and a Committee of Publishers and Associations*

All brand names and product names used in this book are trademarks, registered trademarks, or trade names of their respective holders. Sourcebooks, Inc., is not associated with any product or vendor in this book.

Published by Sourcebooks EDU, an imprint of Sourcebooks, Inc.
P.O. Box 4410, Naperville, Illinois 60567-4410
(630) 961-3900
Fax: (630) 961-2168
www.sourcebooks.com

Library of Congress Cataloging-in-Publication Data

Johnston, Angie
  My max score ASVAB : Armed Services Vocational Aptitude Battery : maximize your score in less time / Angie Johnston and Amanda Ross.
      p. cm.
  1. Armed Services Vocational Aptitude Battery—Study guides. I. Ross, Amanda II. Title. III. Title: Armed Services Vocational Aptitude Battery, maximize your score in less time.
  U408.5.J64 2012
  355.0076—dc23

                           2011045625

Printed and bound in the United States of America.
VP 10 9 8 7 6 5 4 3 2 1

Also Available in the My Max Score Series

AP Exam Study Aids

AP Biology

AP Calculus AB/BC

AP English Language and Composition

AP English Literature and Composition

AP European History

AP U.S. Government & Politics

AP U.S. History

AP World History

SAT Subject Test Study Aids

SAT Literature Subject Test

SAT Math 1 & 2 Subject Test

SAT U.S. History Subject Test

Contents

Introduction

We're not going to lie to you: the *Armed Services Vocational Aptitude Battery* (ASVAB) examination is no walk in the park. The ASVAB is a series of up to ten tests in a wide variety of subject areas. It's used to demonstrate your math, verbal, and science/technical skills as well as your general ability to learn and be trained for different jobs. ASVAB tests can be tough and they require a firm commitment from you in order to achieve a high score.

The ASVAB includes up to ten separate tests in the following subject areas.

- *General Science*—knowledge of Earth and the physical and biological sciences
- *Arithmetic Reasoning*—ability to reason through and solve the calculations in word problems
- *Word Knowledge*—ability to understand words in context and identify synonyms
- *Paragraph Comprehension*—ability to demonstrate understanding of written text
- *Mathematics Knowledge*—knowledge of the principles of high school math
- *Electronics Information*—knowledge of electricity and electronics

- *Auto Information*—knowledge of automotive technology and tools
- *Shop Information*—knowledge of shop terminology and typical shop practices
- *Mechanical Comprehension*—knowledge of mechanical and physical principles, as well as the ability to visualize how illustrated objects are supposed to work
- *Assembling Objects*—spatial orientation, or the ability to visualize how objects will look once assembled

Doing well on the ASVAB is important to different people for different reasons. However, a high score is especially important to those who are interested in enlisting in the U.S. military, because the ASVAB is the "entrance exam" to the armed services. Every branch of the service requires its recruits to take the ASVAB. Your raw scores on the different ASVAB tests are combined in a bunch of ways to calculate what's called your *Armed Forces Qualifying Test Score*, or AFQT. Each branch of the military sets a minimum AFQT score that must be reached in order to enlist for that branch of the service.

Getting into the military is not the only thing the AFQT score is important for, however. What you get to do in the military is also affected by your AFQT score. Different careers and specialties within the military are available only to those individuals who score within predetermined ranges on particular tests. These ranges can vary widely by branch and specialty, so talk to your recruiter to get the specifics in your areas of interest. However, one thing these scores have in common is that they need to be *high*. Doing well is critical for ensuring that the career path you want is open to you.

The good news is, you'll be able to take the ASVAB more than one time if necessary. The bad news is, after the first two tries, you'll be required to wait six whole months before you can test again. If you're taking the ASVAB because you want to enlist, six months can seem like a really long time. So, do yourself a favor and make sure you're really ready when you take the ASVAB.

Don't worry, though, you're on the right path! This book is here to help you maximize your score. By making use of the review information, test tips, and practice tests we've included, you can identify and resolve any problem areas. You're well on the way to maximizing your score.

Visit mymaxscore.com for an additional practice test for the Armed Services Vocational Aptitude Battery, as well as practice tests for the ACT, SAT, and AP exams.

THE ESSENTIALS: A LAST-MINUTE STUDY GUIDE

So, it's a night or two before the exam and you just don't feel ready. Should you panic? No! This is the time to take a deep breath and prepare. If you've been taking an ASVAB prep class, or if you've been preparing in other ways throughout the year, you're just about at your goal. All you need to do now is settle your nerves, review a few strategies to refresh your mind, and get your ducks in a row for test day. It's not too late to maximize your score!

First, take your focus off your nerves and put it on the things you can do to get ready. You don't have much time, so you should make the most of the time you do have. Turn off your phone, your computer, and any other electronic gadgetry. Stop texting and stop surfing the Internet. Ask your family not to disturb you unless it's really important. Close your door and get ready.

Review the Test-Taking Tips

You should already be familiar with the test, but if you're feeling in need of a refresher, start by getting to know the test. The speediest way to do this is to review the **Quick Test-Taking Tips** in this section (page 17). If you have more time, get into more detail in the **Multiple-Choice Strategies** chapter in the next section (page 121).

Take a Practice Test

The only way to *really* get to know the test—and to try out your test-taking strategies—is to take a **practice test** (pages 287 and 383). Time yourself as if the practice test is real, moving on to the next section when time runs out. When you finish, go over your answers, looking particularly for areas where you struggled. (Watch for themes or trends.) If you still have time, go over the sections that cover your problem areas. Use the comprehensive review chapters provided in this book.

Gather Your Materials the Night Before

The last thing you want to have to do on the morning of test day is rush around trying to find everything you need. So, make sure you get everything you need together beforehand. Put together a backpack or small bag with the following items (and anything else you think you need). Have this bag ready so that you can grab it and go in the morning, knowing you're properly equipped. Listed are some things you might put inside your backpack, as well as other suggestions to help you prepare for test day.

- Place your valid photo ID in a side pocket or zippered compartment so you can find it easily. Depending on where you're taking the test, you'll be required to show proof of identity (with a photo). You'll need a valid driver's license or an official government ID.
- Do you need any other identifying information such as your social security number? Make sure you have everything you need beforehand.

- Pack several pencils, a good eraser (test it first to make sure it erases without marking the paper), and several black or blue pens. Use erasable pens if you want, but make sure they aren't going to smudge. There should be a pencil sharpener available in the testing room, but you might want to pack a portable one just in case.

- Include a small, easy-to-eat snack. Test day may be long and you may need nourishment. Depending on where you're taking the test, you probably won't be able to eat during test time, but you might have to wait to test or take a break. Go for a snack that's high in protein with a lower carbohydrate count. Avoid messy substances like chocolate, as it could melt and get on your hands and desk. Avoid loose nuts, as they can trigger allergies in other testers. Some good choices might be an energy or protein bar or drink, an easy-to-eat piece of fruit such as a banana, or some crackers.

- Pack a bottle of water. You'll want something to drink at some point and it's best to avoid substances with a lot of sugar or caffeine. You may think they'll give you energy, but they're more likely to make you jittery.

Other Tips

- Don't stay up all night studying. You're as ready as you'll ever be! Instead, get a good night's sleep, so you'll be alert and ready.

- Eat a light but satisfying meal before the test. Protein-rich foods like eggs, nuts, and yogurt are good choices as they'll fill you up but won't leave you crashing from heavy starches or high sugar content. Don't eat too heavily—you don't want to be sleepy or uncomfortably full. If you must have coffee, don't overdo it.

- Dress in comfortable layers. The testing room might be too hot or it might be too cool. You'll want to be able to easily adjust what you're wearing to the temperature. And, make sure your clothes are of the comfortable variety. The last thing you want is to be annoyed by pants that are too tight or irritated by fabrics that look quite nice but feel really itchy.

Checklist for Test Day

- Avoid bringing things you can't have. For example, cell phones, pagers, and other electronic devices are prohibited in the testing room because they could potentially be used to communicate outside the room.
- As already discussed, bring your valid photo ID.
- Wear or bring a watch. If your watch has any alarms, buzzers, or beepers, turn them off.
- Relax! Once you get to the testing room, take a few deep breaths and try to channel some relaxation. Remind yourself that you're well prepared. It's natural to be nervous, but it's better to channel that anxiety into energy for the test ahead.
- Once the test begins, set your worries aside and do your best. You've done all you can to prepare. Time to make that preparation pay off!

About the ASVAB Exam

What Is the ASVAB?

As its name suggests, the *Armed Services Vocational Aptitude Battery* (ASVAB) is a vocational aptitude test. The ASVAB is designed to measure your likelihood for success in different lines of work. The ASVAB was originally designed—and is still used—as part of the U.S. military recruitment and enlistment process. However, a customized version of the ASVAB is also available to the civilian world at large via the *Career Exploration Program* (CEP).

The ASVAB in all of its forms is the most widely used general aptitude test in the world. Both high school and post-secondary guidance counselors rely on the ASVAB to provide students and job seekers with solid career direction.

The ASVAB is comprised of a series of up to ten tests. Depending on the version of the ASVAB you take, you may be tested in the following subject areas: general science, arithmetic reasoning, word knowledge, paragraph comprehension, mathematics knowledge, electronic information, auto information, shop information, mechanical comprehension, and object assembly.

Who Takes the ASVAB?

The U.S. military uses the ASVAB to determine eligibility for the armed forces. All branches of the armed forces, including the reserves, use the ASVAB to qualify incoming personnel. If you are interested in enlisting, you are required to take the ASVAB and achieve a particular score. Your score will also be used to determine your qualifications for particular military jobs or specialties. In other words, certain kinds of jobs require you to achieve a particular score in one or more content areas.

If you are considering enlistment, you will most likely take the ASVAB at a Military Entrance Processing Station (MEPS) or a Military Entrance Test (MET) site. There is no charge for this test. For more information or to schedule a testing session, contact a recruiter in the branch of service in which you are interested. The recruiter will answer any questions you have and will arrange for you to take the examination at a convenient time and location.

Students and general job seekers may also take a customized version of the ASVAB, the Career Exploration Program (CEP). This version of the ASVAB differs from the U.S. military version in both the content that is tested as well as the number of questions that must be answered. CEP also includes a 90-item career interest inventory called *Find Your Interests*. This interest raises awareness of different careers and helps you identify those career areas that may be of interest. FYI is designed to be used with the OCCU-Find database, a career resource that organizes nearly 500 occupations by title, cluster, interest code, and required skills. This resource helps you to learn about yourself and make better decisions about potential career choices. You will be able to explore a variety of career options using this tool.

The CEP version of the ASVAB is also offered free of charge. If you are interested in taking the ASVAB, contact your guidance counselor or your vocational career counselor.

What Is in the ASVAB?

The ASVAB consists of a series of subtests in a variety of subject areas. Depending on the version of the ASVAB you take, you will be tested in the following:

- *General Science.* The General Science test measures your knowledge of Earth and the physical and biological sciences. All versions of the ASVAB include this test.

- *Arithmetic Reasoning.* The Arithmetic Reasoning test measures your ability to reason through and solve the calculations in mathematical word problems. All versions of the ASVAB include this test.

- *Word Knowledge.* The Word Knowledge test measures your ability to understand words in context. This test also requires you to identify synonyms (words that mean the same as other words) for common terms. All versions of the ASVAB include this test.

- *Paragraph Comprehension.* The Paragraph Comprehension test measures your ability to read short paragraphs of text and demonstrate understanding of what you have read. All versions of the ASVAB include this test.

- *Mathematics Knowledge.* The Mathematics Knowledge test measures your knowledge of the principles of high school mathematics. All versions of the ASVAB include this test.

- *Electronics Information.* The Electronics Information test measures your knowledge of both electricity and electronics. All versions of the ASVAB include this test.

- *Auto Information.* The Auto Information test measures your knowledge of automotive technology and tools. Although all versions of the ASVAB include this test, in some tests, it is combined into a single exam with "Shop Information."

- *Shop Information.* The Shop Information test measures your knowledge of shop terminology and typical shop practices. Although all versions of the ASVAB include this test, in some tests, it is combined into a single exam with "Auto Information."

- *Mechanical Comprehension*. The Mechanical Comprehension exam-ination measures your knowledge of mechanical and physical prin-ciples and your ability to visualize how illustrated objects are supposed to work. All versions of the ASVAB include this test.
- *Assembling Objects*. The Assembling Object test measures your spatial orientation, or the ability to visualize how an object will look once it has been assembled. Only the military version of the ASVAB includes this test.

The ASVAB is available both as a computerized test and in a pencil-and-paper version.

The CAT-ASVAB

If you are interested in joining the military, you will most likely take the ASVAB at a Military Entrance Processing Station (MEPS) or a Military Entrance Test (MET) site. The version of the ASVAB given at these sites is the computerized version, referred to as the *CAT-ASVAB*. The CAT-ASVAB is convenient for a variety of reasons.

First, because the series is computerized, you can navigate through it at your own pace. As you complete each test, you can move on to the next test without waiting until the end of a pre-determined time period. That means your actual testing time can be shortened considerably. (On the other hand, you also can't go back and change your answers, so you should proceed with caution.)

Second, the CAT-ASVAB is an *adaptive* test; that means it's targeted to the test-taker's demonstrated level of ability. It works like this. The first question presented is of medium difficulty (not too easy, not too hard). If you answer this question correctly, your next question will be more difficult. If you answer this question incorrectly, however, the next question will be easier. (And so on, and so forth.) Although this may seem a little unfair, it is actually quite advantageous, because you will not be required to waste your time or feel the frustration of answering a bunch of questions that are either too easy or too difficult for you.

Finally, because the CAT-ASVAB is computerized, your score for each test is immediately available to you. Due to its adaptive nature, the CAT-ASVAB is scored somewhat differently from other versions. Raw scores for each test are not derived just from the number of questions answered; instead, the scores are calculated and adjusted using sophisticated algorithms. The algorithms (basically, computer formulas) consider the relative difficulty level of the questions you actually answered and equate the scoring so that it is fair to all test-takers.

If you take the CAT-ASVAB, your test will break down as shown in the following table.

CAT-ASVAB TEST BREAKDOWN

TEST	NUMBER OF QUESTIONS	TIME LIMIT (IN MINUTES)*
General Science	16	8
Arithmetic Reasoning	16	39
Word Knowledge	16	8
Paragraph Comprehension	11	22
Mathematics Knowledge	16	20
Electronics Information	16	8
Auto Information**	11	7
Shop Information**	11	6
Mechanical Comprehension	16	20
Assembling Objects	16	16
TOTALS	**145 questions**	**154 minutes**

*Remember, this is the maximum amount of time available for the test shown. With the CAT-ASVAB, you will be able to start the next text as soon as you complete the one before it.

**Even though you are tested separately on the automotive and shop sections, your test results will show a single combined score for these subject areas.

The P&P-ASVAB

Students or job seekers taking the ASVAB as part of the Career Exploration Program (CEP) are given the paper-and-pencil version of this exam. This test is referred to as the *P&P-ASVAB* and it is available in high school and post-secondary institutions, among other locations (such as vocational career offices). The P&P-ASVAB also includes a variety of inventory tools designed to help you think about and decide on eventual careers.

If you take the CEP version of the ASVAB, your test will break down as shown in the following table.

P&P-ASVAB TEST BREAKDOWN (CEP VERSION)

TEST	NUMBER OF QUESTIONS	TIME LIMIT (IN MINUTES)*
General Science	25	11
Arithmetic Reasoning	30	36
Word Knowledge	35	11
Paragraph Comprehension	15	13
Mathematics Knowledge	25	24
Electronics Information	20	9
Auto and Shop Information	25	11
Mechanical Comprehension	25	19
TOTALS	**200 questions**	**134 minutes**

Unlike the computerized ASVAB, you cannot shorten the time frame for any of the tests. You will not be able to move to the next section until the end of the time is reached. On the plus side, you will have the opportunity to review your answers and change them up to the end of the designated time period.

How Is the ASVAB Scored?

ASVAB is not a "pass" or "fail" test. Instead, results for each test are calculated individually to obtain a *raw score* (sometimes called a *line score*), then the raw scores are combined in various ways to create *composite scores*. Composite scores are derived by combining different test results together to score your verbal ability, math ability, and general academic ability.

Composite scores are reported as *percentiles* between 1–99. The percentiles indicate the percentage of test-takers from a sample group of testers who scored at or below any given score. For example, if your composite score is 79, that means you scored the same as or better than 79 percent of the people who have taken the test. Likewise, if your composite score is a 32, that means you scored the same as or better than 32 percent of the people who have taken the test.

The military also offers a paper version of the ASVAB, which is used when the CAT-ASVAB is unavailable. Although this version of the test is not adaptable like the CAT-ASVAB, it mimics that test in terms of the type of content and number of questions required. It also includes the Assembling Objects test. Most military recruits take the CAT-ASVAB version of the examination.

Scoring for Military Test-Takers: The AFQT

If you are considering the military as a career, the ASVAB is very important for you. The ASVAB is, essentially, the "entrance exam" to the armed forces. Results on the Word Knowledge, Paragraph Comprehension, Mathematics Knowledge, and Arithmetic Reasoning tests in the ASVAB are combined to compute your *Armed Forces Qualification Test* (AFQT) score.

AFQT results are grouped into five distinct categories based on the percentile score ranges shown in the following table.

AFQT PERCENTILE SCORES AND CORRESPONDING CATEGORIES

AFQT CATEGORY	PERCENTILE SCORE RANGE
1 (I)	93–99
2 (II)	65–92
3A (IIIA)	50–64
3B (IIIB)	31–49
4 (IV)	10–30
5 (V)	1–9

The Department of Defense defines these categories as follows:

- Categories 1 and 2 = Candidate is of above-average ability
- Category 3 = Candidate is of average ability
- Category 4 = Candidate is of below-average ability
- Category 5 = Candidate is not eligible for enlistment

It is the AFQT score that determines if you are qualified for enlistment. The actual AFQT score you need to get into any particular branch of the service varies, so check with your recruiter for more information. Currently, the scores required to get into the U.S. military are as follows:

- Air Force = AFQT score of 36
- Army = AFQT score of 31
- Marine Corps = AFQT score of 32

Even though the ASVAB test is formatted differently in the computerized and pencil-and-paper versions, the tests are statistically equivalent to each other. This is accomplished via a computerized process called *equating*.

- Coast Guard = AFQT score of 40
- Navy = AFQT score of 35

IMPORTANT NOTE: This information is subject to change depending on the needs of the service; check with your recruiter for current requirements.

Your ASVAB scores do not affect your school grades.

Your scores on the ASVAB are also used to determine your eligibility for particular jobs or specialties within the military. These scores are derived from combinations of the different tests and vary by career path or specialty. Again, check with your recruiter to determine which tests you need to focus on in your studies.

Your AFQT score is derived as follows.

First, your Verbal Expression (VE) score is calculated by adding your raw scores for the Paragraph Comprehension (PC) and Word Knowledge (WK) tests. (Raw scores are simply a sum of the number of questions you answered correctly; in this case, your maximum combined raw score is 50.) This sum is then correlated to a VE score.

VE = PC + WK

Next, your VE is multiplied by two and added to the Arithmetic Reasoning and Mathematics Knowledge scores.

AFQT = AR + MK + 2VE

The total score is then correlated to an AFQT percentile and category. For example, a total combined score of 224 is equal to the AFQT percentile of 75, which places the candidate in Category 2 (II), "above average."

How Many Times Can You Take the ASVAB?

Luckily, you can take the ASVAB more than one time. If you aren't happy with your initial score, you can retake the ASVAB in 30 days. After that, you have to wait six months to test again. That is one of the reasons you should study hard to maximize your score your first time through!

> **Q: If I take the ASVAB, am I automatically signed up for the military?**
>
> A: NO! Taking the ASVAB does not obligate you to the armed forces (or anyone else).

ASVAB scores are good for two years. If you take the ASVAB as part of your career exploration in high school and decide to enlist in the military, you can use your original scores (if you are happy with them!) as long as you took the test within the last two years. Students who take the ASVAB as sophomores are required to retake the test before enlisting.

Finally, the military always look to your most recent ASVAB scores. If you have taken the test more than one time, the most recent score may not be your best score. That's another reason it's so important for you to maximize your ASVAB score *every* time you take this test.

Scoring for CEP Test-Takers

The CEP-ASVAB is scored similarly to all other versions of the ASVAB. In addition, composite scores are calculated using different combinations of line scores. These scores help give you a good sense of your verbal, math, science, and technical skills compared to other students in the same grade.

ASVAB Results

Results are presented via the ASVAB Summary Results sheet (see figure below). This report shows line scores and score bands for all eight tests as well as the three composite scores. Your AFQT score is also provided, in case you are considering a career in the military. The ASVAB Summary Results provides appropriate explanations of all scores, as well as suggestions for their use. You will also receive a variety of other career-related documentation designed to help you think about and explore different career paths.

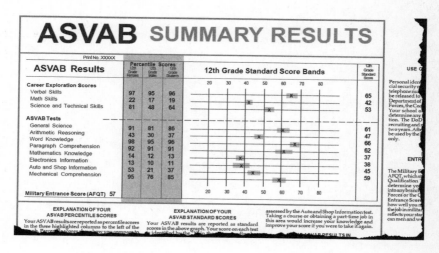

Quick Test-Taking Tips

Your score on the ASVAB is an indicator of your general aptitude as well as specific knowledge of different subject matter. Your score is also an indicator of your ability to do well on this kind of test. Here are a few easy tips to get you started.

- *When practicing for the test, simulate the testing environment as closely as possible.* The smartest way to get comfortable with a particular style of test is to practice taking that test frequently. Each time you test, simulate the testing conditions as closely as possible. For the ASVAB examination, this means testing in a similar environment (a quiet area with no or few distractions), under similar circumstances (closed book exam: just the test, the answer sheet, and you), and within the allotted time frame. It might seem silly to take multiple "pretend" tests, but don't underestimate the comfort level you'll derive in being familiar with the testing circumstances. More importantly, this type of practice will teach you how to pace yourself appropriately for each part of the test.

- *Don't be an island; get others involved.* Other people can help you recognize where you are going wrong on your tests. Don't underestimate how helpful it can be to have at least one knowledgeable person to review and critique your work. It's convenient if this person is also familiar with the ASVAB. Try to be open to feedback.

- *Spread out your studies.* Assuming you have some time before your examination and you aren't cramming for a test next week, it's best if you can spread your studies out over a period of time. Build a formal schedule of study for yourself. Mark off two- or three-hour blocks of time and use that time to review content and take practice examinations. An ideal schedule might utilize two three-hour blocks of time twice per week for a number of weeks prior to the examination.

- *Study different material in different locations.* Recent research suggests that you can actually increase your retention of material simply by choosing to study in different locations. This research suggests that the brain's ability to associate topic areas with unique environments can increase retention.

- *Relax!* As testing day approaches, it's normal to feel nervous and anxious. However, it's important to avoid getting overwhelmed or paralyzed by anxiety. It's true that ASVAB is an important test; however, it is, after all, just a test. Don't waste energy worrying about it. Instead, use that energy to fuel your studies. Focus on testing to the best of your ability.

- *On test day, take care of your body.* That means get a full night's rest the night before the test and eat something nutritious in the morning. If you're hungry, tired, or if you're fueled on sugar and caffeine, it will be much more difficult for you to concentrate.

- *Arrive early.* If you're testing in an unfamiliar location, make sure you know how to get there *before* the day of the test. Regardless, on the day of the test, get to your testing center early. Rushing around will produce adrenaline and fuel anxiety.

- *Take a deep breath and pace yourself.* When the test begins, recognize that this is the moment when all of your studying and practice will pay off. You've worked within the time limits and you know how to best spend that time. Take a deep breath, and do it.

- *Answer the questions in order.* Some test prep materials suggest that you go through a test and answer the questions that seem easy to you. In theory, that might seem like a good idea. However, in practice, this approach is generally a time waster; as you'll have to spend a lot of time later searching for the questions you skipped. Additionally, jumping around on the test increases the possibility that you'll (a) miss questions or (b) fill in the wrong spaces on the answer sheet. (This last option is especially scary and to be avoided at all costs.) Take the questions in order. If you're unsure of an answer, make an educated guess and move on. Flag the question on the test so that you can return to it later if you have time. (For example, you might place a question mark in the margin next to the number of the question.)

- *Don't be afraid to make an educated guess.* Again, try not to leave any questions unanswered as this counts as a wrong answer. Use elimination strategies when you're unsure.

- *If you're taking the pencil-and-paper version of the test, don't be afraid to change your answers.* Some test prep material cautions against changing your answer options, as conventional wisdom suggests your first answer option is usually correct. Although this may be true when you're reasonably sure of the answer, it's not necessarily true when you're unsure. If you've flagged an item, don't be afraid to review your answer option and change it later.

- *If you're taking the CAT version of the test, be careful!* You can't change your responses or return to questions you've answered. Be sure of your answer before moving on.

THE MAIN COURSE: COMPREHENSIVE STRATEGIES AND REVIEW

I f you have a few weeks to go before the exam, there's plenty of time to brush up on your skills. Here's a plan of things to do to prepare in the weeks ahead.

- Go over the chapters in this book to get familiar with the different parts of the exam. Really think how you can best approach the subject matter.

- Assess your knowledge and ability to test by taking the **Diagnostic Test** at the beginning of this section (page 23). As you go through the answers, note any areas of weakness. Read the answers and their explanations. Watch for trends in your answers. If you missed a question, find out why so you can avoid doing so in the future.

- Read through this **Comprehensive Strategies and Review** section. Pay special attention to any areas of weakness you've identified.

- Take at least one more **practice test** before test day. You can download one at www.mymaxscore.com.
- A few nights before the test, go back over the section on **The Essentials** (page 1) for a refresher on **test-taking tips**.
- Do everything on the checklist on page 4.

Pack your materials for the next day, get a good night's sleep, and you'll be ready to earn a top score on the exam.

Diagnostic Test

ASVAB

Part 1

General Science

Time—11 minutes

25 questions

Directions: This test assesses your knowledge of general science principles usually covered in high school classes. Choose the best answer for each question and then mark the space on your answer sheet that corresponds to the question number.

1. What instrument is used to measure weight?

   A. Barometer
   B. Spring scale
   C. Graduated cylinder
   D. Balance beam scale

2. The body gets most of its energy from

    A. water.
    B. protein.
    C. vitamins.
    D. carbohydrates.

3. A sound wave is an example of a _____ wave.

    A. Doppler
    B. reflection
    C. transverse
    D. longitudinal

4. Oceans cover about _____ percent of the Earth's surface.

    A. 16
    B. 33
    C. 71
    D. 92

5. Zero degrees on the Celsius scale is equivalent to what on the Kelvin scale?

    A. –273 K
    B. 0 K
    C. 100 K
    D. 273 K

6. The amount of energy in food is measured in

    A. ATP.
    B. ounces.
    C. Calories.
    D. degrees Celsius.

7. Sound travels fastest in a

    A. gas.
    B. solid.
    C. liquid.
    D. plasma.

8. The four seasons in the Northern Hemisphere are due to the

    A. rotation of Earth.
    B. changing distance between the sun and Earth.
    C. tilt of Earth's axis with respect to its orbital plane around the sun.
    D. All of the above

9. Which of the following electron arrangements requires one less electron to make a stable atom?

    A. 2,6
    B. 2,7
    C. 2,8
    D. 2,8,1

10. The food at the base of a food pyramid includes

    A. vegetables.
    B. milk, yogurt, and cheese.
    C. bread, rice, cereal, and pasta.
    D. meat, fish, eggs, beans, and nuts.

11. An electric current passing through a wire consists of moving

    A. ions.
    B. atoms.
    C. protons.
    D. electrons.

12. The layer of the atmosphere closest to Earth is the

    A. ionosphere.
    B. mesosphere.
    C. troposphere.
    D. stratosphere.

13. An aluminum ion has a charge of +3 and an oxygen ion has a charge of –2. The chemical formula for aluminum oxide is

    A. AlO.
    B. Al_3O_2.
    C. Al_2O_3.
    D. Al_2O_2.

14. All the members of a species that live in one area make up

    A. a biome.
    B. a population.
    C. a community.
    D. an ecosystem.

15. The amount of electric current passing through a wire depends on

    A. only the resistance of the wire.
    B. only the potential difference applied.
    C. both the potential difference applied and the resistance of the wire.
    D. neither the potential difference applied nor the resistance of the wire.

16. If the amount of water vapor in the air remains constant while temperature decreases, then relative humidity

    A.   will increase.
    B.   will decrease.
    C.   will remain the same.
    D.   may increase or decrease.

17. If the atomic number of fluorine is 9, then the valence of fluorine is

    A.   2.
    B.   5.
    C.   7.
    D.   9.

18. Which of the following organisms is a producer?

    A.   Wolf
    B.   Grass
    C.   Antelope
    D.   Mushroom

19. The amount of resistance in an electric circuit is measured in

    A.   volts.
    B.   ohms.
    C.   watts.
    D.   amperes.

20. If an atom loses an electron, it becomes a

    A.   positive ion.
    B.   negative ion.
    C.   new element.
    D.   neutral atom.

21. Which of the following statements about estuaries is NOT true?

    A. Many different habitats exist in and near estuaries.
    B. Estuaries contain a mix of freshwater and saltwater.
    C. The soil in estuaries is poor and contains few nutrients.
    D. Salt marshes and mangrove forests can be part of an estuary.

22. Which of the following is a trait of metals?

    A. They are dull in appearance.
    B. They gain valence electrons easily.
    C. They are gases at room temperature.
    D. They lose their valence electrons easily.

23. Which of the following is a thin, flexible, semi-permeable membrane?

    A. Cell wall
    B. Cytoplasm
    C. Cell nucleus
    D. Cell membrane

24. When similar magnetic poles are brought near one another, they

    A. repel one another.
    B. attract one another.
    C. demagnetize one another.
    D. have no effect on one another.

25. A rock that enters Earth's atmosphere and hits the ground is called

    A. a comet.
    B. a meteor.
    C. an asteroid.
    D. a meteorite.

END OF PART 1

ASVAB
Part 2
Arithmetic Reasoning
Time—36 minutes

30 questions

Directions: This test assesses your skills in arithmetic. Choose the correct answer and then mark the space on your answer sheet. Use scratch paper for any figuring you need to do.

1. Amanda paid a financial strategist $150 to sign on as a client and open a mutual funds account through the bank. She pays $30 per month for the strategist to actively review and make suggestions for her account. How much has she paid the strategist for 2 years of service?

   A. $720
   B. $790
   C. $870
   D. $1,020

2. In 2007, an annual examination at a local veterinarian's office was $85. In 2012, the annual examination cost had increased by $45. Which of the following best represents the percent increase of the examination?

   A. 49 percent
   B. 51 percent
   C. 53 percent
   D. 55 percent

3. Manny draws a card from a 52-card deck, replaces it, and draws another card. What is the probability he draws an ace and then a jack?

    A. $\dfrac{1}{169}$

    B. $\dfrac{4}{663}$

    C. $\dfrac{2}{13}$

    D. $\dfrac{1}{338}$

4. Elaine drinks 15 cups of coffee every 6 days. How many cups of coffee will she drink in 14 days?

    A. 32
    B. 33
    C. 34
    D. 35

5. In a charity run, 22 participants finished 2 miles, 26 participants finished 4 miles, and 18 participants finished 10 miles. Which of the following best represents the average number of miles run by the participants?

    A. 3 miles
    B. 4 miles
    C. 5 miles
    D. 6 miles

67, 67, 94, 99, 87, 97, 78, 72, 73, 99, 85, 93, 94, 81, 67

6. Given the statistics test scores shown above, which of the following has the greatest value?

    A. Mean
    B. Median
    C. Mode
    D. Range

7. Thina owes $39.27 for items she purchased at a bookstore. The total amount of the items, prior to tax, was $35.88. Which of the following best represents the tax rate?

    A. 8.9 percent
    B. 9.2 percent
    C. 9.4 percent
    D. 9.8 percent

8. Four years ago, Richard's annual salary was $24,500. Now his annual salary is $52,000. Which of the following best represents the percent increase in his annual salary?

    A. 102 percent
    B. 106 percent
    C. 112 percent
    D. 119 percent

9. On average, Greta pays $40 per day in rent. Her daily rent is 25 percent of her daily net income. What is her monthly net income, for a 30-day time period?

    A. $4,200
    B. $4,400
    C. $4,600
    D. $4,800

10. James tosses a coin 1,000 times. Based on theoretical probability, how many times can she expect to get tails?

    A. 250
    B. 400
    C. 500
    D. 750

11. Erin spins a spinner with six equally spaced sections, labeled 1 to 6, and then flips a coin. What is the probability the spinner lands on an odd number or she gets heads, when flipping the coin?

    A. $\dfrac{1}{4}$

    B. $\dfrac{1}{2}$

    C. $\dfrac{5}{6}$

    D. 1

12. Tyler purchases a Frappuccino priced at $3.45. He pays $0.39 in sales tax. Which of the following best represents the tax rate?

 A. 10.3 percent
 B. 10.8 percent
 C. 11.3 percent
 D. 11.9 percent

13. An 80-foot long cable must be cut into 8-inch pieces. How many 8-inch pieces can be cut from the cable?

 A. 80
 B. 100
 C. 120
 D. 160

14. Andrew rolls a die. What is the probability that he rolls a number less than 3 or a prime number?

 A. $\dfrac{1}{2}$

 B. $\dfrac{2}{3}$

 C. $\dfrac{3}{4}$

 D. $\dfrac{5}{6}$

15. A traveling sales manager flies 33,600 miles every 6 months. If this trend continues, how many miles will she have flown over the course of 4 years?

    A.   242,400 miles
    B.   246,800 miles
    C.   248,200 miles
    D.   268,800 miles

16. Thus far, Kareem has received the following test scores in his finite math course: 86, 94, 82, and 99. In a course where the grade is based solely on test scores, what is the minimum test score he must receive on the fifth test to receive an A average, which is a score of 90 or higher?

    A.   85
    B.   89
    C.   92
    D.   95

17. On an 8-hour flight, a plane flies at a rate of 510 miles per hour for the first 4 hours and 480 miles per hour for the last 4 hours. What is the average speed of the plane for the 8-hour flight?

    A.   485 miles per hour
    B.   490 miles per hour
    C.   495 miles per hour
    D.   500 miles per hour

18. An office copy machine prints 90 pages per minute. How long will it take to print 1,500 pages?

   A.   17 minutes
   B.   45 minutes
   C.   180 minutes
   D.   1,350 minutes

19. A group of friends orders two appetizers at $6.50 each, three entrees at $11.50 each, and one dessert for $6.00. What is the average price of each item ordered?

   A. $4.00
   B. $8.92
   C. $10.24
   D. $17.84

20. Leon is thinking of two integers that have a sum of −80 and a difference of 46. What are the two integers?

   A.   −17 and −63
   B.   −18 and −64
   C.   −21 and −67
   D.   −52 and −28

21. Carmen drives at 65 miles per hour for 6 hours and 70 miles per hour for 3 more hours. How far does she travel?

   A.   535 miles
   B.   540 miles
   C.   570 miles
   D.   600 miles

22. There are twice as many SUVs in a parking lot as there pickup trucks. If the number of SUVs is 14, how many pickup trucks are in the lot?

    A. 7
    B. 14
    C. 21
    D. 28

23. Last year, Jamie's total computer repair costs were $365. This year, he paid a total of $185 in computer repairs. Which of the following best represents the percent decrease in computer repairs this year?

    A. 32 percent
    B. 37 percent
    C. 49 percent
    D. 56 percent

24. What is the probability of rolling an even number on a die, rolling again, and then rolling a prime number?

    A. $\dfrac{1}{4}$

    B. $\dfrac{3}{10}$

    C. $\dfrac{1}{3}$

    D. 1

25. Carl writes the numbers 1–21 on slips of paper and places them into a bag for a raffle drawing. The probability that Carl will draw an even number at random is

A. $\dfrac{1}{21}$

B. $\dfrac{1}{10}$

C. $\dfrac{10}{21}$

D. $\dfrac{1}{2}$

94, 89, 82, 74, 96, 87, 93, 91, 88, 84, 79, 91

26. Jared's scores for his history class are listed above. Based on this information, what is the range of Jared's history scores?

A. 22
B. 87.3
C. 88.5
D. 91

27. Shauna runs 7.5 miles every 3 days. How many miles does Shauna run in 10 days?

A. 25
B. 30
C. 70.5
D. 225

28. Vince has selected $75.88 worth of merchandise at a sporting goods store, and the sales tax is 6 percent. Which of the following values best represents the total Vince will have to pay?

    A. $75.94
    B. $80.43
    C. $85.97
    D. $121.41

29. Deborah's net income each month is $3,900. Her monthly rent is 15 percent of her net income. What is her monthly rent?

    A. $415
    B. $505
    C. $585
    D. $615

30. Jorge's nephew has 6 red blocks, 4 blue blocks, 9 green blocks, and 5 yellow blocks in a container. What is the probability that Jorge's nephew will randomly draw a red block from the container?

    A. $\dfrac{1}{6}$

    B. $\dfrac{1}{4}$

    C. $\dfrac{1}{3}$

    D. $\dfrac{1}{2}$

END OF PART 2

ASVAB

Part 3

Word Knowledge

Time—11 minutes

35 questions

Directions: This test is about the meanings of words. Each question has an underlined word. You must decide which word in the answer choice has nearly the same meaning as the underlined word. Then mark this space on your answer sheet.

1. After a day at the spa, the tired mother felt <u>regenerated</u>.

   A. Resolved
   B. Renewed
   C. Reserved
   D. Relinquished

2. The <u>benevolent</u> man gave most of his fortune to charity.

   A. Daring
   B. Generous
   C. Malicious
   D. Confounded

3. <u>Malady</u> most nearly means

   A. crypt.
   B. jargon.
   C. sickness.
   D. diagnosis.

4.   My <u>frugal</u> spouse only buys groceries if he has a coupon.

    A.   Thrifty
    B.   Devious
    C.   Fraudulent
    D.   Immaculate

5.   Martina could not <u>visualize</u> her house painted pink.

    A.   Imagine
    B.   Intercede
    C.   Generalize
    D.   Commemorate

6.   <u>Posthumous</u> most nearly means

    A.   after death.
    B.   before birth.
    C.   with assistance.
    D.   with skepticism.

7.   The physician told the patient that her health would improve if she <u>abstained</u> from smoking.

    A.   Reveled
    B.   Resisted
    C.   Ingested
    D.   Alleviated

8. When the teacher told the students they had to stay in for recess, they began to <u>grovel</u>.

   A. Gibe
   B. Emit
   C. Plead
   D. Evoke

9. <u>Chagrin</u> most nearly means

   A. incriminate.
   B. supplement.
   C. emancipate.
   D. disappointment.

10. Because Mark had too many parking tickets, the judge decided to <u>revoke</u> his driver's license for one month.

   A. Invalidate
   B. Formulate
   C. Enunciate
   D. Designate

11. The clown <u>simultaneously</u> juggled balls and rode a bike.

   A. Illogically
   B. Grotesquely
   C. Concurrently
   D. Exceptionally

12. The <u>secluded</u> cabin was miles from the rode and hidden among the trees.

    A. Belated
    B. Isolated
    C. Phenomenal
    D. Reciprocated

13. The <u>laborious</u> job injured many workers, who stood on their feet for ten or more hours a day.

    A. Dominant
    B. Painstaking
    C. Harmonized
    D. Contemptible

14. <u>Depreciate</u> most nearly means

    A. invert.
    B. reduce.
    C. disparage.
    D. reprimand.

15. Even though my sisters are twins, they are <u>dissimilar</u> and don't look at all alike.

    A. Unalike
    B. Unequal
    C. Disheveled
    D. Comparable

16. <u>Pompous</u> most nearly means

    A. discreet.

    B. arrogant.

    C. irrelevant.

    D. indifferent.

17. The living conditions in the house were not luxurious, but they were <u>tolerable</u>.

    A. Endurable

    B. Resplendent

    C. Monotonous

    D. Incomparable

18. <u>Affable</u> most nearly means

    A. genial.

    B. juvenile.

    C. debatable.

    D. melancholy.

19. The store had a going-out-of-business sale to <u>liquidate</u> its contents.

    A. Settle

    B. Relieve

    C. Elevate

    D. Generate

20. <u>Dogmatic</u> most nearly means

    A. intellectual.

    B. intimidated.

    C. treacherous.

    D. opinionated.

21. I don't know why my mother <u>condones</u> my little brother's disre-
    spectful behavior.

    A. Obscures
    B. Tolerates
    C. Necessitates
    D. Impersonates

22. <u>Hypothesis</u> most nearly means

    A. rehearsal.
    B. hindrance.
    C. procedure.
    D. assumption.

23. <u>Disheveled</u> most nearly means

    A. calm.
    B. untidy.
    C. familiar.
    D. dangerous.

24. Because of the <u>ambiguous</u> directions, Enrico became lost and drove
    around town for an hour.

    A. Ludicrous
    B. Perplexing
    C. Enlightening
    D. Economizing

25. My <u>gullible</u> brother actually believed that our dog could fly.

    A. Naïve

    B. Gawky

    C. Virtuous

    D. Innocuous

26. <u>Intuition</u> most nearly means

    A. cynicism.

    B. jubilance.

    C. misgiving.

    D. perception.

27. Our neighbor <u>flaunted</u> his new car by driving it up and down the street.

    A. Qualified

    B. Exhibited

    C. Magnified

    D. Monitored

28. <u>Dissect</u> most nearly means

    A. implore.

    B. separate.

    C. populate.

    D. dissension.

29. The flood washed away <u>invaluable</u> family heirlooms.

    A. Vital

    B. Labyrinth

    C. Precarious

    D. Irreplaceable

30. Maria is <u>bilingual</u> and speaks both Spanish and French.

    A.   Fluent

    B.   Emaciated

    C.   Delinquent

    D.   Perceptive

31. <u>Awry</u> most nearly means

    A.   skewed.

    B.   tasteless.

    C.   conspicuous.

    D.   exaggerated.

32. Marcus <u>explicitly</u> told the girls that they must read the directions before attempting to assemble the bookcase.

    A.   Hastily

    B.   Abruptly

    C.   Precisely

    D.   Transiently

33. He became a pilot because he found the idea of seeing the world <u>alluring</u>.

    A.   Affluent

    B.   Ominous

    C.   Luxurious

    D.   Attractive

34. <u>Hackneyed</u> most nearly means

    A. renewed.

    B. fundamental.

    C. commonplace.

    D. unprecedented.

35. Brian's youthful <u>exuberance</u> often makes his parents tired.

    A. Vigor

    B. Hilarity

    C. Grievance

    D. Indulgence

END OF PART 3

ASVAB

Part 4
Paragraph Comprehension
Time—13 minutes
15 questions

Directions: This test assesses your ability to understand what you read. This section includes reading passages followed by questions or incomplete statements. Read the paragraph and select the choice that best completes the statement or answers the question. Mark your choice on your answer sheet.

In standard airplane flight, propulsion is provided by an engine and lift by rigid wings. Now slow-motion film has revealed how a bird obtains both propulsion and lift from its wings. As the wings flap, both lift and propulsion are produced in the downstroke. With its leading edge tilted down, the wing is at a right angle to the wind and this produces forward thrust. But lift is also provided by the upstroke, as the wing flips to a different position. The drag created during the upstroke is compensated for by the bird partially folding its wings on the way up.

1.   This passage is mostly about how

    A.   birds gain propulsion and lift.
    B.   airplanes gain propulsion and lift.
    C.   a wing produces a forward thrust.
    D.   drag is created during an upstroke.

A wild land of extreme cold, the Yukon Territory is home to Canada's mightiest mountain peaks, Mts. Logan, Kennedy, and Saint Elias. The region was barely inhabited until 1846, when two members of the Tagish Indian tribe stopped for a drink from Rabbit Creek and noticed something glittering in the water. They staked claims and in the next eight years more than a hundred million dollars in gold was taken from the area. Rabbit Creek was given a new name: "Bonanza Creek."

2. According to the passage, what is Rabbit Creek best known for?

A. Gold
B. Money
C. Fresh water
D. Its temperature

The famous American artist Georgia O'Keeffe studied realistic painting while in school at the Art Institute of Chicago. But realism did not interest her. She began to experiment with abstract painting while teaching in Texas. A major influence on her work was a mentor named Arthur Wesley Dow, who convinced her that artists should express their deepest feelings in their work. She later married photographer and art collector Alfred Stieglitz, who promoted her paintings in his New York gallery. After his death, Ms. O'Keeffe moved to New Mexico, where the beauty of the desert became a great influence on her art.

3. According to the passage, Georgia O'Keeffe began painting abstractly

A. while living and working in Texas.
B. during her marriage to Alfred Stieglitz.
C. after moving to the deserts of New Mexico.
D. when a student at the Art Institute of Chicago.

The golden orb-weaving spider is renowned for its ability to spin web strands that are thinner than human hair but stronger than steel. Scientists attach these tiny creatures to silk-gathering machines and study the strands with special instruments. Their goal is not to create spider farms where they can harvest tons of this silk to be used by everyone from surgeons (for sutures) to sky divers (for parachutes). Spiders are too territorial. Because of this, researchers are working on ways to create synthetic spider silk.

4. The passage suggests that spider farms are impractical because spiders

    A. do not produce webs in captivity.
    B. tend to attack and kill each other.
    C. have an extremely short life span.
    D. cannot mate in a laboratory setting.

Chaco Canyon in New Mexico is the former home of "The Lost Civilization," the Anasazi Indian tribe. These people lived in a large and impressive city many hundreds of years before Columbus arrived in America. Pueblo Bonito, one 600-room complex, had five stories of terraced apartments that were constructed to store the sun's heat in the cold months and reflect it when the weather turned hot. From the center of the city, lines radiated out into the desert for miles. Why? The answer is as mysterious as the final fate of these people.

5. From information in the passage, it can be inferred that

    A. the Anasazi race was destroyed by war.
    B. the full history of the Anasazi people is unknown.
    C. Spanish explorers most likely built the Chaco Canyon city.
    D. illness and disease probably caused occupants to abandon the area.

As global warming causes their icy home to shrink around them, polar bears move onto land, which creates another problem. Bears are unused to industrial noises, and this new environment can frighten them, even causing females to abandon helpless cubs. To help solve this problem, scientists have staged experiments to chart the bear's hearing curve to determine at what level a noise disturbs these animals. A test is set up in which bears are trained to touch a target when they hear a certain tone. When they respond correctly, they are given a treat.

6. According to the passage, the main goal of these polar bear experiments is to

    A.   provide a noise-free preserve for all polar bears.
    B.   protect cubs that are abandoned by their mothers.
    C.   learn how to shield these animals from noise pollution.
    D.   create a graph that will depict the bear's hearing curve.

The common cold is the most prevalent viral infection in the world. Colds occur when a virus invades the upper respiratory tract. About 200 known viruses can cause the infection and nearly every adult on Earth suffers two to five colds per year. Colds are passed from one person to another through contact. Children suffer more colds than adults—their rate is six to ten per year. This number is highest during the winter.

7. Based on this information, it can be inferred that children get more colds in winter because

    A.   they do not dress warmly enough.
    B.   they have more contact than adults.
    C.   they are exposed to cold air while playing.
    D.   their immune systems are weaker than adults'.

She was as graceful as a dancer on the court, they say. Suzanne Lenglen was considered France's Queen of Tennis during the 1920s. From 1919 to 1926, she lost only once at Britain's Wimbledon Tournament. Her strokes were extremely accurate, with seldom an error. As the story goes, she was coached by her father, Charles, who taught her to sharpen her drives by placing a handkerchief on the court and paying her every time she hit it. In 1926, she met American champion Helen Wills in what was called "The Match of the Century." Suzanne won it in two hard-fought sets.

8.   Which statement best summarizes the passage?

  A.   Suzanne Lenglen used dancing skills to excel at the sport of tennis.
  B.   Coaching tricks created by Charles Lenglen sharpened his daughter's shots.
  C.   Charles Lenglen was mainly responsible for his daughter's success in tennis.
  D.   Suzanne Lenglen was France's dominant female tennis player for many years.

Wings Away is an amazing documentary film that lets the audience fly along with birds as they migrate. Using ultra-light aircraft, camera operators are able to soar just a few feet from birds of all kinds. It took months of conditioning trips before the birds adapted to these strange companions but the results are spectacular. We feel like flying buddies to geese, cranes, ducks, and pelicans as they migrate from as far as Alaska and all the way to South America.

9.   What is the author's tone in this passage?

  A.   Critical
  B.   Humorous
  C.   Perplexed
  D.   Fascinated

On July 27, 1866, a cable was successfully laid under the Atlantic Ocean that allowed messages to flow between England and the United States. However, the road to this achievement was a long and difficult one. Just previous to the final success, the ship *Great Eastern* had laid down 1,200 miles of cable before it broke. The first four attempts, starting in 1857, also had failed when the cable snapped. On the next try, the job was completed and the continents were linked—for awhile. Then an operator used too high a voltage, and the cable burned out.

10. Which best describes the order of events, from beginning to end?

    A. Four cables snap, 1,200 miles of cable halted by break, operator burns out successful cable, cable succeeds

    B. 1,200 miles of cable halted by break, operator burns out successful cable, four cables snap, cable succeeds

    C. Operator burns out successful cable, four cables snap, 1,200 miles of cable halted by break, cable succeeds

    D. Four cables snap, operator burns out successful cable, 1,200 miles of cable halted by break, cable succeeds

French artist Paul Gaugin was working as a stockbroker and painting on Sundays when two events changed his life. He lost his job in a stock-market crash and one of his landscapes was accepted by the Paris Salon. Tormented by a desire to paint, Gaugin left his wife and five children and began traveling to seek his muse. He eventually landed in Arles and launched an attempt to create a "Studio of the South" with Vincent Van Gogh. The pair did not get along, however, and Gaugin returned to Paris.

11. Which statement best summarizes the passage?

   A. Paul Gaugin was a stockbroker in Paris and lost his job in a stock-market crash.
   B. Paul Gaugin cared more about his art than about those who depended on him.
   C. Paul Gaugin's artistic career began with the loss of a job and the success of a painting.
   D. Paul Gaugin abandoned his family to travel and work with other artists, such as Vincent Van Gogh.

They may live in your furniture. Some are blind and reside in deep ice caves. Others can walk on the undersurface of water, upside down. Beetles: they belong to a family that contains more species than the entire plant kingdom. They range in size from the tiny pest that lives on the mouthparts of bees to the giant four-inch longhorn. Their abilities are legendary. The Whirligig beetle, for example, dives underwater carrying a bubble of air that allows it to breathe. One third of the insect kingdom is composed of beetles.

12. In this passage, the author's primary purpose is to

   A. describe various abilities of beetles.
   B. explain why beetles dominate the insect world.
   C. impress readers with the number and variety of beetles.
   D. convince readers that beetles are pests that must be controlled.

A typical symphony orchestra will have more than one hundred members. Fronting the musicians, the conductor will face the string section—to the left are the violins, to the right are the violas, cellos, and double basses. Behind that section are the woodwinds—flutes, oboes, clarinets, and bassoons. In back of them the brass section sits—trumpets, trombones,

French horns and tubas. In the very back are the percussion instruments—drums, cymbals, piano, etc. If a choir is to be used, it usually is placed on risers behind the orchestra.

13. According to the passage, what is the order of instruments in an orchestra, from back to front?

   A. Woodwinds, brass, percussion, strings
   B. Percussion, brass, woodwinds, strings
   C. Brass, percussion, strings, woodwinds
   D. Strings, woodwinds, brass, percussion

There are many theories that attempt to explain the origin of the term "Texas Leaguer" in baseball. Perhaps the most plausible is one proposed by a player who traveled the Texas circuit between the years of 1907 and 1920. He blamed the Gulf Stream, an ocean current that flowed near many league towns. It caused a strong breeze that would catch a fly ball and cause it to fall between the outfielder and the infielder.

14. According to this passage, the Gulf Stream is

   A. a fly ball.
   B. a strong breeze.
   C. an ocean current.
   D. a baseball player.

From 1894 to 1924, more than twenty million immigrants arrived at Ellis Island in New York Harbor. In a massive project, their records have been digitized and placed on the Internet for free access to all. An army of 12,000 volunteers took on the task, which lasted 5.5 years and cost more than $22 million. A major part of the job was studying 3,700 rolls of microfilm and entering the information into the database.

15. From this passage, you can conclude that

    A.   it was difficult to recruit volunteers for the task.

    B.   digitizing the records took more time than anticipated.

    C.   the microfilm the volunteers read was hard to understand.

    D.   people are interested in accessing the immigrants' records.

END OF PART 4

ASVAB

Part 5

Mathematics Knowledge

Time—24 minutes

25 questions

Directions: This test assesses your ability to solve general mathematical problems. Select the correct answer from the choices given. Mark the corresponding space on your answer sheet. Use scratch paper as needed to solve each problem.

1. What does $(-7x + 6)(3x - 4)$ equal?

   A. $-21x^2 + 7x + 24$
   B. $-21x^2 + 46x - 24$
   C. $-21x^2 - 46x - 24$
   D. $-21x^2 - 10x - 24$

2. Which of the following represents a factor of the polynomial $-30x^3 + 57x^2 - 18x$?

   A. $(6x - 3)$
   B. $(6x - 9)$
   C. $(-5x^2 - 2x)$
   D. $(-5x^2 + 4x)$

3. A rectangle has a length that is 3 times its width, with a perimeter of 104 inches. What is the area of the rectangle?

   A. 507 in²
   B. 509 in²
   C. 512 in²
   D. 514 in²

4. What does $\sqrt[3]{8^4}$ equal?

    A. 12
    B. 16
    C. 18
    D. 24

5. What does $5^{-\frac{1}{2}}$ equal?

    A. $-\sqrt{5}$

    B. $-\dfrac{1}{25}$

    C. $\dfrac{1}{\sqrt{5}}$

    D. 5^2

6. Which of the following represents the simplified product of $7^{\frac{1}{6}}$ and $7^{\frac{2}{3}}$?

    A. $\sqrt[9]{7^2}$
    B. $\sqrt[5]{7^6}$
    C. $\sqrt[6]{7^5}$
    D. $\sqrt[6]{7^3}$

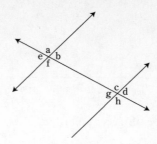

7. Which of the following represents vertical angles in the figure above?

    A. *d* and *f*
    B. *a* and *f*
    C. *c* and *f*
    D. *b* and *h*

8. The sum of the interior angles of a regular polygon is 540°. How many diagonals does the polygon have?

    A. 3
    B. 4
    C. 5
    D. 6

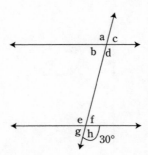

9. What is the measure of ∠b above?

    A. 30°
    B. 60°
    C. 120°
    D. 150°

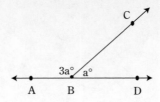

10. What is the measure of ∠ABC above?

    A. 45°
    B. 60°
    C. 108°
    D. 135°

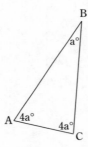

11. Which of the following represents the measure of each base angle in the triangle above?

    A. 72°
    B. 78°
    C. 80°
    D. 88°

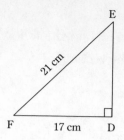

12. Which of the following best represents the length of $\overline{ED}$ in the right triangle above?

    A.   11.8 cm
    B.   12.3 cm
    C.   12.9 cm
    D.   13.2 cm

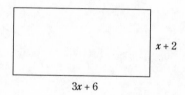

13. Which of the following represents the ratio of the length of the rectangle to its width in the rectangle above?

    A.   2
    B.   3
    C.   4
    D.   6

14. The length of a rectangle with a width of *a* and length of 2*a* is increased by 6 units. Which of the following correctly describes the effect on the area of the rectangle?

   A.   The area is 3 times larger.
   B.   The area is 6 times larger.
   C.   The area is increased by a value equal to 6 times the width.
   D.   The area is increased by a value equal to 12 times the width.

15. A circle has a circumference of approximately 44 inches. The diameter of this circle is about

   A.   7 inches.
   B.   12 inches.
   C.   14 inches.
   D.   17 inches.

16. A ball has a radius of 6 inches. How much air can the ball hold when it is fully inflated?

   A.   904 in^3
   B.   906 in^3
   C.   908 in^3
   D.   912 in^3

17. A can of peas has a diameter of 2 inches and a height of 6 inches. What is the volume of the can?

   A.   9.42 in^3
   B.   18.84 in^3
   C.   37.68 in^3
   D.   75.36 in^3

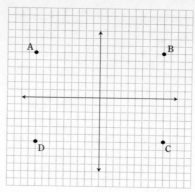

18. Which point above represents the ordered pair (–9, 6)?

    A. Point *A*
    B. Point *B*
    C. Point C
    D. Point *D*

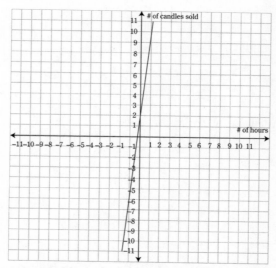

19. The number of candles sold per hour at a candle-making shop is shown in the graph above, where *x* represents the number of hours. According to the graph, how many candles are sold per hour?

    A. 6
    B. 8
    C. 10
    D. 12

20. A line containing the point (3, −13) has a slope of −3. Which pair of points is also found on the line?

    A. (8, −28)
    B. (6, −24)
    C. (10, −32)
    D. (12, −42)

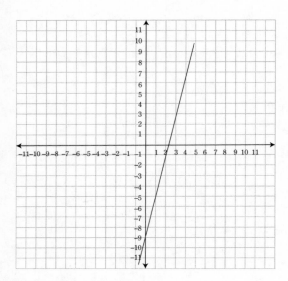

21. What is the slope of the line above?

    A. −4
    B. −2
    C. 2
    D. 4

22. A cube has a surface area of 294 square inches. What is the length of each edge of the cube?

    A. 4 inches
    B. 6 inches
    C. 7 inches
    D. 8 inches

$$y \geq 3x - 5$$
$$y < -2x - 8$$

23. Which of the following points represents a possible solution of the system of inequalities shown above?

   A. (−8, −5)
   B. (−3, −3)
   C. (1, 2)
   D. (4, 3)

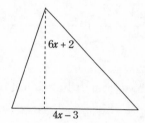

24. Which of the following expressions represents the area of the triangle above?

   A. $12x^2 - 5x - 3$
   B. $24x^2 - 10x - 6$
   C. $24x^2 + 13x - 6$
   D. $24x^2 - 13x - 3$

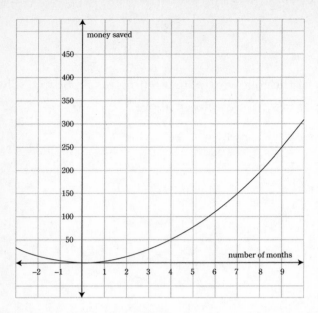

25. The amount of money Hannah has saved over a number of months is shown in the graph above, where x represents the number of months she has been saving money. Approximately how much money has she saved after 8 months?

   A. $147
   B. $192
   C. $243
   D. $300

END OF PART 5

ASVAB

Part 6

Electronics Information

Time—9 minutes

20 questions

Directions: This section assesses your knowledge of electrical, radio, and electronics information. Choose the correct answer and mark the corresponding space on your answer sheet.

1. An electromagnetic wave consists of two main components,

    A. a radioactive wave and an antenna.
    B. an electrical current and an antenna.
    C. an electric field and a magnetic field.
    D. a magnetic field and a radioactive field.

2. Devices that produce or use light during operation are called

    A. triac waveforms.
    B. light-emitting SCRs.
    C. optoelectronic devices.
    D. common anode displays.

3. A device that converts light energy into electrical energy is called

    A. a battery.
    B. a solar cell.
    C. a solar coupler.
    D. an optical coupler LED.

4. How many terminals would you expect to find on a unijunction transistor (UJT)?

   A. 1
   B. 2
   C. 3
   D. 4

5. Which diagram shows a unijunction transistor (UJT)?

   A.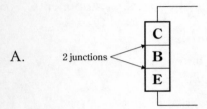

   B.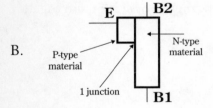

   C.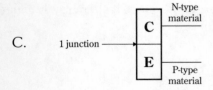

   D. None of the above

6. Which diagram shows a common transistor?

A.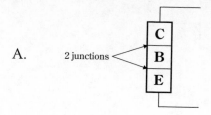

B.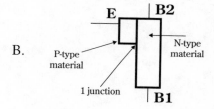

C.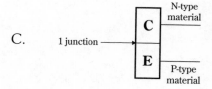

D. None of the above

7. The Zener effect explains electrical breakdown below _____ volts, while the Avalanche effect explains electrical breakdown above this number.

A. 3

B. 5

C. 7

D. 10

8. Which diagram correctly shows the depletion region?

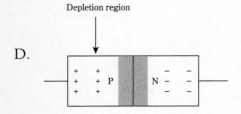

A.

Depletion region

B.

Depletion region

C.

Depletion region

Depletion region

D.

9. Using Ohm's law, determine the current produced by a 1.5-volt battery and a light bulb with a resistance of 5 ohms.

A.   .03 ampere
B.   .3 ampere
C.   3 ampere
D.   None of the above

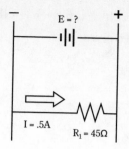

10. What is the voltage in the circuit above?

    A. 0.01 volt
    B. 22.5 volts
    C. 90 volts
    D. None of the above

11. Power rating is measured in

    A. volts.
    B. ohms.
    C. watts.
    D. amperes.

12. The amount of power converted by an electrical device can be calculated by using which formula?

    A. Power = work × watts
    B. Power = work × watts × hours
    C. Power = work × ohms × hours
    D. Power = watts × hours × volts

13. Calculate the power converted by a 10HP motor that runs continuously for a 40-hour workweek.

    A.   2,984 watt-hours
    B.   29,840 volts
    C.   298,400 watt-hours
    D.   298,400 horsepower

14. When a break interrupts a complete conducting pathway, a circuit is considered

    A.   open.
    B.   short.
    C.   closed.
    D.   transferred.

15. All of the following statements about Ohm's law are true EXCEPT

    A.   a series circuit has only one path for current.
    B.   Ohm's law applies to series and parallel circuits.
    C.   Ohm's law tells us that the current in a circuit is inversely proportional to the circuit resistance.
    D.   according to Ohm's law, currents will cause short circuits when subjected to cold temperatures.

16. Which diagram shows a series circuit?

A.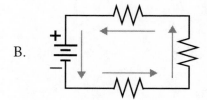

B.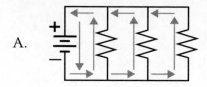

C.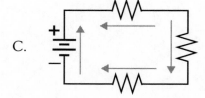

D.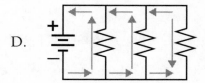

17. Which diagram shows a parallel circuit?

A.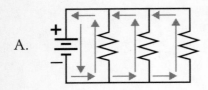

B.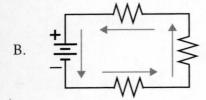

C.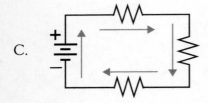

D. None of the above

18. Which course of action is NOT correct when leak testing a battery?

A. Choose a DC voltage scale at or above the battery's voltage.
B. Connect the negative meter lead to the negative battery post.
C. Measure the voltage leaking across the two terminals with a multimeter.
D. Apply grease to the battery terminal to use as a preservative when the test is complete.

19. Two transistors paired together to achieve high current gain are called a

    A.   double pair.

    B.   PN junction.

    C.   Darlington pair.

    D.   None of the above

20. The act of introducing impurities into a pure semiconductor is called

    A.   doping.

    B.   appealing.

    C.   conducting.

    D.   degenerating.

END OF PART 6

ASVAB
Part 7
Auto and Shop Information
Time—11 minutes
25 questions

Directions: This test assesses your knowledge of automobiles, shop practices, and tools. Choose the correct answer to each question and then mark the corresponding space on your answer sheet.

1. What is used in new vehicles in place of carburetors in internal combustion engines?

    A. Throttles
    B. Atomizers
    C. Fuel injectors
    D. Oxygen sensors

2. Which tool would you be most likely to use to cut a padlock?

    A. Jigsaw
    B. Hacksaw
    C. Bolt cutters
    D. Sledgehammer

3. Which of the following statements is true?

    A. A saw with 40 TPI provides a smoother cut than one with 80 TPI.
    B. A saw with 80 TPI provides a smoother cut than one with 40 TPI.
    C. A saw with 40 TPI provides a smoother cut than one with 120 TPI.
    D. A saw with 80 TPI provides a smoother cut than one with 120 TPI.

4. What item would you use to measure angles?

   A. Billhook
   B. Hex key
   C. Protractor
   D. Carpenter's ruler

5. The part of a drill bit held by the chuck is known as the

   A. spur.
   B. shank.
   C. trigger.
   D. selection ring.

6. Which of the following is part of a car's suspension system?

   A. Muffler
   B. Spark plugs
   C. Shock absorber
   D. Catalytic converter

7. All of the following are parts of an antilock braking system EXCEPT

   A. valves.
   B. pistons.
   C. a pump.
   D. speed sensors.

8. The process of joining two pieces of metal with molten metal is known as

   A. wicking.
   B. wetting.
   C. soldering.
   D. None of the above

9. A car's battery may occasionally require the addition of

    A. oil.
    B. oxygen.
    C. distilled water.
    D. All of the above

10. An oscilloscope can be used to measure

    A. voltage.
    B. frequency.
    C. Both A and B
    D. Neither A nor B

11. Which type of hammer has a hollow head filled with steel shot?

    A. Claw hammer
    B. Ball peen hammer
    C. Fiberglass hammer
    D. Dead-blow hammer

12. A two-stroke engine fires after ___ revolution(s) of the crankshaft.

    A. 1
    B. 2
    C. 3
    D. 4

13. When referring to oil viscosity, what does the "W" represent?

    A. Wear
    B. Work
    C. Winter
    D. Weight

14. A vehicle's tachometer displays

    A. speed.

    B. fuel level.

    C. temperature.

    D. revolutions per minute.

15. The process of enlarging a hole that has already been cut is called

    A. boring.

    B. lathing.

    C. barreling.

    D. None of the above

16. What does the octane rating of gasoline represent?

    A. The horsepower the gasoline is used to achieve

    B. The percentage of chemicals the gasoline contains

    C. How many miles a vehicle can travel per gallon of the gasoline

    D. How much the gasoline can be compressed before spontaneously igniting

17. Which of the following statements is true?

    A. Antifreeze raises the boiling point of water in an engine.

    B. A radiator allows outside air to cool heated water in an engine.

    C. A water pump circulates water through water jackets in an engine.

    D. All of the above

18. In a disc brake system, the wheels are attached to

    A. rotors.
    B. calipers.
    C. brake pads.
    D. None of the above

19. A manual transmission requires the operator to use

    A. a clutch.
    B. a gearshift.
    C. Both A and B
    D. Neither A nor B

20. The main function of a muffler is to

    A. reduce engine noise.
    B. remove pollutants from exhaust.
    C. assist the car's suspension system.
    D. All of the above

21. Which of the following parts of the coil sends a spark to the distributor?

    A. Primary winding
    B. Secondary winding
    C. Both A and B
    D. Neither A nor B

22. The catalytic converter is part of the

    A. ignition system.
    B. exhaust system.
    C. computer system.
    D. transmission system.

23. The cylinders in an engine can be arranged

    A. vertically.
    B. horizontally.
    C. Both A and B.
    D. Neither A nor B

24. During the compression stroke in a four-stroke internal combustion engine

    A. the air-fuel mixture is ignited.
    B. the exhaust valve begins to open.
    C. the gases inside the cylinder become hotter.
    D. low pressure creates a vacuum in the cylinder.

25. Which type of saw would most likely be used to cut metal?

    A. Ripsaw
    B. Hacksaw
    C. Coping saw
    D. Crosscut saw

END OF PART 7

ASVAB
Part 8
Mechanical Comprehension
Time—19 minutes
25 questions

Directions: This test assesses your knowledge of mechanics. Choose the correct answer to each question and then mark the corresponding space on your answer sheet.

1. The mechanical advantage of a gear train is also known as

   A. gear ratio.
   B. torque ratio.
   C. angular velocity.
   D. None of the above

2. Units of work are measured in

   A. joules.
   B. torque.
   C. meters.
   D. newtons.

3. According to Newton's second law of motion, how much net force is required to accelerate a 500kg boat at 10 m/s²?

   A. 500 J
   B. 500 N
   C. 5,000 J
   D. 5,000 N

4. Which of the following is NOT a third-class lever?

    A. Tongs
    B. Broom
    C. Fishing pole
    D. Wheelbarrow

5. A marble rolls along a concrete sidewalk. The marble will eventually stop because of

    A. inertia.
    B. gravity.
    C. velocity.
    D. None of the above

6. Using a block and tackle with eight ropes to lift a load ten feet, without friction, what is the mechanical advantage gained?

    A. 4:1
    B. 4:5
    C. 8:1
    D. 10:1

7. A 5-kilogram box requires less force to begin moving than a 10-kilogram box because it has

    A. less inertia.
    B. less velocity.
    C. more weight.
    D. more momentum.

8.   Which of the following is NOT part of a planetary gear set?

   A.   Sun gear
   B.   Ring gear
   C.   Moon gear
   D.   Planet gears and carrier

9.   "For every action, there is an equal and opposite reaction" is

   A.   Newton's first law of motion.
   B.   Newton's second law of motion.
   C.   Newton's third law of motion.
   D.   Newton's fourth law of motion.

10. All of the following formulas involving work are true EXCEPT

   A. $W = Fd$.

   B. $F = \dfrac{W}{d}$.

   C. $d = \dfrac{W}{F}$.

   D. $W = \dfrac{d}{W}$.

11. If 150 pounds of force are applied to an area of 5 square inches, the pressure is

   A.   0.3 psi.
   B.   30 psi.
   C.   750 psi.
   D.   None of the above

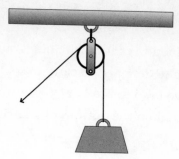

12. Which of the following is true regarding the above diagram?

    A. The pulley is fixed.
    B. The mechanical advantage is 1.
    C. There is no multiplication of force.
    D. All of the above

13. Which of the following statements is false?

    A. Spur gears have straight teeth.
    B. Worm gears are used to change directional forces.
    C. Worms can turn gears, but gears cannot turn worms.
    D. Large gears complete fewer revolutions than smaller ones within the same system.

14. In a first-class lever, the fulcrum is

    A. between the applied force and the load.
    B. always in the center of the lever.
    C. beside the applied force and opposite the load.
    D. None of the above

15. A caster is a

    A. coating designed to reduce friction.
    B. simple machine designed to carry loads.
    C. type of wedge used to hold objects in place.
    D. wheel mounted on the bottom of a large object.

16. What is the formula for weight?

    A. $W = mg$

    B. $W = \dfrac{g}{m}$

    C. $W = \dfrac{m}{g}$

    D. $W = Fd$

17. The energy stored in an object is considered

    A. inertia.
    B. pressure.
    C. kinetic energy.
    D. potential energy.

18. Which of the pendulums in the diagram below will take the longest to complete one swing, barring friction and assuming each pendulum weighs the same amount?

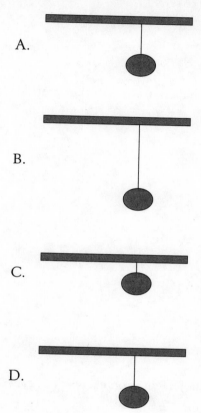

A.

B.

C.

D.

19. What is used between a wheel and an axle to reduce friction?

    A. Nuts
    B. O-rings
    C. Bearings
    D. Force compressors

20. What term describes the opposite of acceleration?

    A. Inertia
    B. Friction
    C. Deceleration
    D. Negative velocity

21. A wheel with teeth that engage a chain, a track, or other material is a

    A. gear.
    B. lever.
    C. pulley.
    D. sprocket.

22. The brakes on a vehicle use _____ to stop.

    A. friction
    B. momentum
    C. deceleration
    D. All of the above

23. The place on an object where equal weight is on each side is called its

    A. pivot.
    B. fulcrum.
    C. center of gravity.
    D. centrifugal force.

24. On which pole does the weight press harder?

A.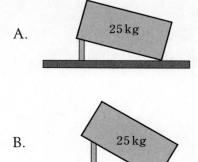

B.

C.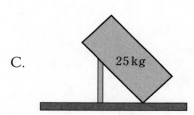

D. The weight is equal on all the poles.

25. A gear differs from a pulley because it

A. rotates clockwise.
B. is not designed to bear weight.
C. is not designed to transmit motion.
D. engages other gears and toothed objects.

END OF DIAGNOSTIC TEST

Diagnostic Test Answers and Explanations

Answer Key

PART 1: GENERAL SCIENCE

1. B
2. D
3. D
4. C
5. D
6. C
7. B
8. C
9. D
10. C
11. D
12. C
13. B
14. B
15. C
16. A
17. C
18. B
19. B
20. A
21. C
22. D
23. D
24. A
25. B

PART 2: ARITHMETIC REASONING

1. C
2. C
3. A
4. D
5. C
6. B
7. C
8. C
9. D
10. C
11. D
12. C
13. C
14. B
15. D
16. B
17. C
18. A
19. B
20. A

21. D

22. A

23. C

24. A

25. C

26. A

27. A

28. B

29. C

30. B

PART 3: WORD KNOWLEDGE

1. B

2. B

3. C

4. A

5. A

6. A

7. B

8. C

9. D

10. A

11. C

12. B

13. B

14. B

15. A

16. B

17. A

18. A

19. A

20. D

21. B

22. C

23. B

24. A

25. A

26. D

27. B

28. B

29. D

30. A

31. A

32. C

33. A

34. C

35. A

PART 4: PARAGRAPH COMPREHENSION

1. A

2. A

3. A

4. C

5.	B	14.	C
6.	C	15.	C
7.	B	16.	A
8.	D	17.	B
9.	D	18.	A
10.	D	19.	B
11.	C	20.	A
12.	C	21.	D
13.	D	22.	C
14.	C	23.	A
15.	D	24.	A
		25.	B

PART 5: MATHEMATICS KNOWLEDGE

1. B
2. B
3. A
4. B
5. C
6. C
7. B
8. C
9. D
10. C
11. C
12. B
13. B

PART 6: ELECTRONICS INFORMATION

1. B
2. C
3. B
4. C
5. B
6. A
7. B
8. C
9. B
10. B
11. C
12. D

13. C

14. A

15. D

16. B

17. A

18. D

19. C

20. A

17. D

18 A

19. C

20. A

21. B

22. B

23. C

24. C

25. B

PART 7: AUTO AND SHOP INFORMATION

1. C

2. C

3. B

4. C

5. B

6. C

7. B

8. C

9. C

10. C

11. D

12. A

13. C

14. D

15. A

16. D

PART 8: MECHANICAL COMPREHENSION

1. B

2. A

3. D

4. D

5. A

6. C

7. A

8. C

9. C

10. D

11. B

12. D

13. B

14. A

15. D

16. A   21. D

17. D   22. A

18. B   23. C

19. C   24. A

20. C   25. D

Answer Explanations

PART 1: GENERAL SCIENCE

1. **B**. You should use a spring scale to measure weight, which is the pull of gravity on a given mass. A balance beam, on the other hand, is used to measure mass, or the amount of matter in an object.

2. **D**. The body uses carbohydrates (starches and sugars) for energy. Proteins provide the body with amino acids needed for growth and repair. Vitamins are needed in only small amounts and are used for enzyme-catalyzed chemical reactions. Water is one of the most important nutrients; it keeps the body hydrated.

3. **D**. A sound wave is a longitudinal wave. In this type of wave, the medium vibrates back and forth in the direction of the wave. In a transverse wave, the medium moves back and forth at right angles to the direction of the wave.

4. **C**. Oceans cover about 71 percent of Earth's surface.

5. **D**. Zero degrees on the Celsius sale is the freezing point of pure water, which is 273 K. The Kelvin scale is a scale of temperature on which absolute zero is equal to 0 K.

6. **C**. The amount of energy in food is measured in Calories (with a capital C). A food Calorie is the amount of energy needed to increase the temperature of a kilogram of water and is equivalent to 1,000 calories (with a small c).

7. **B**. The transmission of sound is simply the vibration of molecules back and forth, that is, the bumping together and moving apart of the

molecules of the medium through which the sound wave travels. Sound waves travel fastest in a solid because solids are denser than liquids, gases, or plasmas. The distances between molecules in a solid are very small. Because the molecules are so close, they can collide with each other very quickly. In other words, it takes less time for a molecule of a solid to bump against its neighbors.

8.   **C.** The four seasons are due to the tilt of Earth's axis with respect to its orbital plane around the sun. In winter, the northern hemisphere is tilted away from the sun, so the days are shorter and the sun's rays hit the earth at a more oblique angle. In summer, the northern hemisphere is tilted toward the sun, so the days are longer and the sun's rays hit the earth at a more direct angle.

9.   **D.** A stable atom has a full outer electron shell. The second electron shell can hold 8 electrons. The atom that has an electron arrangement of 2,8,1 would become stable if it loses one electron.

10. **C.** The base of the food pyramid consists of foods that have the greatest number of recommended servings per day: bread, rice, cereal, and pasta. You should eat 6–11 servings from this group daily. The recommended servings for the other food groups are vegetables (3–5); meat, fish, eggs, beans and nuts (2–3); milk, yogurt, and cheese (2–3).

11. **D.** An electric current is made up of moving electrons.

12. **C.** The troposphere starts at Earth's surface and goes up to a height of 7 to 20 km above sea level. About 75 percent of the atmosphere is in the troposphere, and almost all weather occurs within this layer. The other layers of the atmosphere, from lowest to highest, are stratosphere, mesosphere, and ionosphere.

13. **B.** A chemical formula consists of the symbols of the elements present in the molecule, plus a number behind and below the symbol to show how many atoms of that element are in the molecule. You need to use the correct combination of ions to produce a compound with a net charge of zero. In this case, two aluminum ions with a net

charge of 2 × 3 = +6 will cancel out 3 oxygen ions with a net charge of 3 × (–2) = –6.

14. **B.** All the members of a species that live in one area make up a population. A biome is an environment that has a characteristic climax community. A community comprises all the populations of organisms living in an area. An ecosystem comprises all the biotic and abiotic factors in an area.

15. **C.** The amount of current (measured in amps) that runs through a wire depends on both the potential difference (measured in volts) and the resistance of the wire (measured in ohms). The formula for current is amps = volts/ohms.

16. **A.** Relative humidity is the ratio of the current humidity to the highest possible humidity at that air temperature. A reading of 100 percent relative humidity means that the air is completely saturated with water vapor and cannot hold any more. Cooler air cannot hold as much water vapor as warmer air. Therefore, if the amount of water vapor in the air remains constant while temperature decreases, then the relative humidity will increase.

17. **C.** The valence of an atom is the number of electrons in the outer shell. Fluorine has two electrons in the first shell and 7 in the second shell. Therefore, the valence is 7.

18. **B.** Grass is a producer. Producers carry on photosynthesis to make their own food. A wolf and an antelope are consumers because they feed on producers or other consumers. A mushroom is a type of consumer called a decomposer because it feeds on the remains of dead organisms.

19. **B.** Resistance, or the conditions that limit the flow of electrons in a circuit, is measured in ohms. Amperes is a measure of the number of electrons moving past a point in an electric circuit in a second. A volt is a measure of the amount of work done in moving electrons between two points in an electric circuit. Watts is a measure of power, which is voltage × amps.

20. **A.** If an atom loses an electron, it becomes a positive ion with a charge +1. Gaining an electron would give an atom a charge of –1.

21. **C.** An estuary is a body of water along the coast where freshwater from rivers and streams meets and mixes with saltwater from the ocean. Estuarine environments are among the most productive on Earth. Thousands of species of birds, mammals, fish, and other wildlife depend on estuarine habitats as places to live, feed, and reproduce. Because they contain decaying plants and animals, the soil in estuaries is rich with nutrients and good for growing Therefore, Choice D is correct.

22. **D.** Metals that lose electrons lose their valence electrons easily. Metals usually have the following properties: They have one, two, or three electrons on the outside electron shell. The outside electrons make it more likely that the metal will lose electrons, making positive ions. Non-metals usually have four, five, six, or seven electrons in the outer shell. When they join with other elements, non-metals can either share electrons in a covalent bond or gain electrons to become a negative ion and make an ionic bond.

23. **D.** The cell membrane is a thin, flexible, semi-permeable membrane. The cell wall is a rigid structure that supports the cell membrane and is found in plant, algae, and some bacterial cells. The cytoplasm is the region between the cell nucleus and cell membrane. The cell nucleus is the organelle that is the control center of the cell.

24. **A.** Similar magnetic poles repel one another while opposite poles attract one another.

25. **B.** A meteorite is a small mass of matter that has fallen to Earth's surface from outer space. A meteor is a small body of matter from outer space that enters Earth's atmosphere, appearing as a streak of light. It burns up in the atmosphere before reaching the ground. An asteroid is a small rocky body orbiting the sun. Large numbers of these are found between the orbits of Mars and Jupiter. A comet is a celestial object

consisting of a nucleus of ice and dust and, when near the sun, a "tail" of gas and dust particles pointing away from the sun.

PART 2: ARITHMETIC REASONING

1. **C.** The linear relationship can be represented by the equation $y = 30x + 150$. Substituting the number of months of service for the variable x will show the amount Amanda paid over the course of two years, or y. Substitute 24 for x: $y = 30(24) + 150$, which simplifies to $y = 870$. Thus, Amanda paid the strategist $870 for two years of service.

2. **C.** The amount of the increase is equal to the product of the original cost and some percent, x.

The percent increase can be determined by setting up the following equation: $45 = 85x$. Solving for x gives $x \approx 0.53$. The percent increase in the examination is approximately 53 percent.

3. **A.** The probability of these mutually exclusive events occurring can be determined using the formula, $P(A \text{ and } B) = P(A) \cdot P(B)$. The probability of drawing an ace on the first draw is $\frac{4}{52}$. The probability of drawing a jack on the second draw considering the first card was replaced is also $\frac{4}{52}$. Thus, the probability of drawing an ace, replacing the card, and then drawing a jack can be written as $\frac{4}{52} \cdot \frac{4}{52}$, which simplifies to $\frac{1}{169}$.

4. **D.** The following proportion can be used to solve the problem: $\frac{15}{6} = \frac{x}{14}$. Solving for x gives $6x = 210$ or $x = 35$. Elaine will drink 35 cups of coffee in 14 days.

5. **C.** The problem represents a weighted average. The following ratio can be written: $\frac{22(2) + 26(4) + 18(10)}{66}$, which simplifies to $\frac{44 + 104 + 180}{66}$ or $\frac{328}{66}$. This is approximately 5. The participants ran an average number of approximately 5 miles.

6. **B.** The mean is approximately 83.5. The median, mode, and range

of the given test scores are 85, 67, and 32, respectively. The median has the greatest value in this data set.

7.   C. The amount of sales tax is \$3.39. This amount is equal to the product of the cost of the items prior to sales tax and some tax rate, x. The following equation can be written $3.39 = 35.88x$. Solving for x gives $x \approx 0.094$. The sales tax rate is approximately 9.4 percent.

8.   C. The amount of the increase is equal to the product of his original salary and some percent x. The following equation can be written and solved: $27,500 = 24,500x$. Solving for x gives $x \approx 1.12$. The percent increase in his annual salary is approximately 112 percent.

9.   D. Greta's daily rent is equal to the product of 25 percent and some daily net income, x. The following equation can be written and solved for x: $40 = 0.25x$, which simplifies to $x = 160$. Her monthly net income for a 30-day time period is equal to the product of \$160 and 30, or \$4,800.

10. C. Theoretical probability states there is a 1 in 2 chance of getting tails. Thus, James can expect to get tails $\frac{1}{2}(1000)$ times, or 500 times.

11. D. The probability of mutually exclusive events A or B occurring can be determined using the formula, $P(A \text{ or } B) = P(A) + P(B)$. The probability of the spinner landing on an odd number is $\frac{3}{6}$. The probability of getting heads when flipping a coin is $\frac{1}{2}$. Thus, the probability of the spinner landing on an odd number or the coin landing on heads can be written as $\frac{3}{6} + \frac{1}{2}$, which equals 1.

12. C. The amount of the sales tax is equal to the product of the pre-taxed cost of the Frappuccino and some tax rate, x. The following equation can be written $0.39 = 3.45x$. Solving for x gives $x \approx 0.113$. The sales tax rate is approximately 11.3 percent.

13. C. To determine the number of 8-inch pieces that can be cut from the cable, first convert the length of the cable to inches: 8 ft × 12 in/ft =

96 in. Next, divide this total length by the length of each piece: 96 in ÷ 8 in = 12.

14. **B.** The probability of non-mutually exclusive events A or B occurring can be determined using the formula, $P(A \text{ or } B) = P(A) + P(B) - P(A \text{ and } B)$. The probability of rolling a number less than 3 is $\frac{2}{6}$. The probability of rolling a prime number is $\frac{3}{6}$. The probability of rolling a number less than 3 and a prime number is $\frac{1}{6}$. Note: 2 is less than 3 and a prime number. Thus, the probability of rolling a number less than 3 or a prime number can be written as $\frac{2}{6} + \frac{3}{6} - \frac{1}{6}$, which equals $\frac{4}{6}$ or $\frac{2}{3}$.

15. **D.** The following proportion can be used to solve the problem: $\frac{33,600}{6} = \frac{x}{48}$. Solving for x gives $6x = 1,612,800$ or $x = 268,800$. If this trend continues, the sales manager will have flown 268,800 miles in four years.

16. **B.** The following equation can be used to determine the minimum value required on Kareem's fifth test: $\frac{86 + 94 + 82 + 99 + x}{5} = 90$. The equation can be simplified as $\frac{361 + x}{5} = 90$. Multiplying both sides of the equation by 5 gives $361 + x = 450$. Solving for x gives $x = 89$. Kareem must make at least an 89 on his fifth test in order to receive an A in the course.

17. **C.** The problem represents a weighted average. The following ratio can be written: $\frac{4(510) + 4(480)}{8}$, which simplifies to $\frac{3960}{8}$ or 495. The average speed of the plane for the 8-hour flight is 495 miles per hour.

18. **A.** Divide the total number of pages by the number of pages printed per minute: 1500 pages ÷ $\frac{90 \text{ pages}}{\text{minute}}$. Flip and multiply the second term: 1,500 pages × min/90 pages = 1500 pages × $\frac{\text{minute}}{90 \text{ pages}}$ ≈ 17 minutes.

19. **B.** The average price of each item ordered is a weighted average: two appetizers were orders, at \$6.50 each, totaling \$13.00; three entrees at \$11.50 totals \$34.50; and the dessert is weighted just once, at \$6.00. The total of all the items is \$53.50. Dividing by the total number of items, 6, yields \$8.92 with rounding.

20. **A.** The integers can be determined by writing and solving the following system of equations:

$$x + y = -80$$
$$x - y = 46.$$

Solving for x gives $2x = -34$, where $x = -17$. Substitution of the x-value of -17 into the first equation gives $-17 + y = -80$; $y = -63$.

21. **D.** Distance is the product of speed and time. Thus, for the first 6 hours, Carmen drove 390 miles. For the last 3 hours, she drove 210 miles. In all, she drove 600 miles.

22. **A.** If there are 14 SUVs, and this number is twice the number of pickup trucks, then there are half as many pickup trucks as SUVs. One half of 14 is 7. There are 7 pickup trucks in the lot.

23. **C.** The decrease in computer repair costs, or \$180, is equal to the product of last year's repair costs and some percent, x. This situation can be represented by the equation $180 = 365x$. Solving for x gives $x \approx 0.49$. Thus, the percent decrease in computer repair costs was approximately 49 percent.

24. **A.** The probability of these mutually exclusive events occurring can be determined using the formula $P(\text{A and B}) = P(A) \cdot P(B)$. The probability of rolling an even number is $\frac{3}{6}$. The probability of rolling a prime number is also $\frac{3}{6}$. Thus, the probability of rolling an even number and then rolling a prime number can be written as $\frac{3}{6} \cdot \frac{3}{6}$, which simplifies to $\frac{1}{4}$.

25. **C.** The range of numbers from 1 through 21, inclusive, consists of 21 numbers. Of these, 10 are even and 11 are odd. The chances of choosing an even number is therefore $\frac{10}{21}$.

26. **A.** In a series of numbers, the range is the difference between the highest and lowest numbers. In this case, it is the difference between 96 and 74: $96 - 74 = 22$. Therefore, the range is 22.

27. **A.** Dividing 7.5 by 3 yields the number of miles Shauna runs each day: 7.5 mi ÷ 3 = 2.5 mi. Therefore, Shauna runs 2.5 miles each day. To determine how many miles she runs in 10 days, multiply 2.5 miles by 10: 2.5 mi × 10 = 25 mi.

28. **B.** To determine the amount of the sales tax in dollars, first convert 6 percent to a decimal by dividing 6 by 100: $6 \div 100 = 0.06$. Then, multiply 0.06 by the amount of the merchandise: $\$75.88 \times 0.06 \approx \$4.55$. Then, add this amount to the amount of the merchandise: $\$75.88 + \$4.55 = \$80.43$.

29. **C.** To determine Deborah's monthly rent, first convert 15 percent to a decimal by dividing 15 by 100: $15 \div 100 = 0.15$. Next, multiply Deborah's net income by 0.15: $\$3,900 \times 0.15 = \$585$. Therefore, Deborah's monthly rent is $585.

30. **B.** To determine the probability, first determine the total number of blocks in the container: $6 + 4 + 9 + 5 = 24$. Next, create a ratio to determine the number of red blocks (6) in comparison to the total number of blocks (24): $6 : 24$ or $\frac{6}{24}$. Then, simplify by dividing both the numerator and the denominator by 6: $\frac{6}{24} \div \frac{6}{6} = \frac{1}{4}$. Therefore, the probability that Jorge's nephew will randomly draw a red block is $\frac{1}{4}$.

PART 3: WORD KNOWLEDGE

1. **B.** *Regenerated* most nearly means *renewed*. *Resolved* means determined, *reserved* means shy or distant, and *relinquished* means gave away.

2. **B.** *Benevolent* most nearly means *generous*. *Daring* means brave. Someone who is *malicious* is mean, and *confounded* means confused.

3. **C.** *Malady* most nearly means *sickness*, as in "The woman suffered from some terrible malady." A *crypt* is a tomb, *jargon* is a specialized language, and a *diagnosis* is a decision about an illness.

4. **A.** *Frugal* most nearly means *thrifty*. *Devious* means tricky, *fraudulent* means deceitful, and *immaculate* means spotless.

5. **A.** *Visualize* most closely means *imagine*. To *intercede* means to intervene or negotiate. To *generalize* mean to simplify or oversimplify, and to *commemorate* means to celebrate or honor.

6. **A.** *Posthumous* most nearly means after death, as in "The writer's novel was published posthumously."

7. **B.** *Abstained* most nearly means *resisted*. *Reveled* means celebrated, *ingested* means digested, and *alleviated* means relieved.

8. **C.** *Grovel* most nearly means *plead*. *Gibe* means to taunt or tease, *emit* means to release or produce, and *evoke* means induce.

9. **D.** *Chagrin* most nearly means *disappointment*, as in "Much to my father's chagrin, my sister said she would not go on the camping trip with us." To *incriminate* means to implicate, to *supplement* means to add to, and to *emancipate* means to set free.

10. **A.** *Revoke* most nearly means *invalidate*. *Formulate* means to convey, *enunciate* means to pronounce, and *designate* means to appoint.

11. **C.** *Simultaneously* most nearly means *concurrently*. *Illogically* means not logically, *grotesquely* means ugly, and *exceptionally* means very well.

12. **B.** *Secluded* most nearly means *isolated*. *Belated* means delayed, *reciprocated* means given back to or returned, and *phenomenal* means outstanding.

13. **B.** *Laborious* most nearly means *painstaking*. *Dominant* means leading, *harmonizing* means blending, and *contemptible* means despised.

14. **B.** *Depreciate* most nearly means *reduce*, as in "After only two

years, the car's value depreciated significantly." *Invert* means to flip-flop or reverse, *disparage* means to criticize, and *reprimand* means to find fault with.

15. **A**. *Dissimilar* most nearly means *unalike*. *Unequal* means not equal, *disheveled* means unkempt, and *comparable* means similar.

16. **B**. *Pompous* most nearly means *arrogant*. *Discreet* means not obvious or inconspicuous, *irrelevant* means unimportant, and *indifferent* means uninterested.

17. **A**. *Tolerable* most nearly means *endurable*. *Resplendent* means dazzling, *monotonous* means repetitive and boring, and *incomparable* means unique.

18. **A**. *Affable* most nearly means *genial*. *Juvenile* means young, *debatable* means controversial or arguable, *melancholy* means sad.

19. **A**. *Liquidate* most nearly means *settle*. *Relieve* means to alleviate, *elevate* means to raise, and *generate* means to create.

20. **D**. *Dogmatic* most nearly means *opinionated*, as in "The dogmatic professor would not change his outdated policies regarding class attendance." *Intellectual* means intelligent, *intimidated* means scared or dominated, *treacherous* means dangerous.

21. **B**. *Condones* most closely means *tolerates*. *Obscures* means to make unclear, *necessitates* means needs, and *impersonates* means to pretend to be someone else.

22. **C**. *Hypothesis* most nearly means an *assumption* or a guess. *Rehearsal* means to practice, a *hindrance* is an interference, and a *procedure* is a process.

23. **B**. *Disheveled* most closely means *untidy*, or messy. *Calm* means peaceful, *familiar* means easily recognized, and *dangerous* mean risky or unsafe.

24. **A**. *Ambiguous* most nearly means *perplexing*, or confusing. *Ludicrous* means absurd, *enlightening* means clarifying, *economizing* means frugal.

25. **A.** *Gullible* most nearly means naïve. *Gawky* means clumsy or awkward, *virtuous* means honorable, and *innocuous* means harmless.

26. **D.** *Intuition* most closely means *perception*, as in "The teacher's intuition was correct; the bus had broken down." *Cynicism* means pessimism, *jubilance* means joy, and *misgiving* means suspicion.

27. **B.** *Flaunted* most closely means *exhibited*, or shown off. *Qualified* means competent, *magnified* means made larger, and *monitored* means supervised.

28. **B.** *Dissect* most closely means separate, or dismember. *Populate* means inhabit, *implore* means beg, and *dissension* means disagreement.

29. **D.** *Invaluable* most nearly means *irreplaceable*. *Vital* means necessary, a *labyrinth* is a maze, and *precarious* means risky.

30. **A.** *Bilingual* most nearly means *fluent*. *Emaciated* means gaunt or scrawny, *delinquent* means criminal or wrong, and *perceptive* means insightful.

31. **A.** *Awry* most nearly means *skewed*. *Tasteless* means cheap or flashy, *conspicuous* means noticeable, and *exaggerated* means overemphasized.

32. **C.** *Explicitly* most nearly means *precisely*. *Hastily* means quickly, *abruptly* means unexpectedly, and *transiently* means briefly.

33. **A.** *Alluring* most nearly means *attractive*. *Affluent* means wealthy, *ominous* means threatening, and *luxurious* means lush and comfortable.

34. **C.** *Hackneyed* most nearly means *commonplace*, as in, "My grandfather loves that hackneyed phrase, 'what's good for the goose, is good for the gander.'" *Renewed* means to make new again, *fundamental* means basic, and *unprecedented* means unique or first time.

35. **A.** *Exuberance* most nearly means vigor. *Hilarity* means humor, *grievance* means complaint, and *indulgence* means leniency.

PART 4: PARAGRAPH COMPREHENSION

1. **A.** Most of the passage explains how birds gain propulsion and lift. The other answer choices give details in the passage.

2.   **A.** This question asks you to recall a detail from the passage. You can look back at the passage to find the answer. Rabbit Creek is best known for the gold found there. According to the passage, more than a hundred million dollars in gold was discovered in the creek.

3.   **A.** This question asks you to recall a detail in the passage. You can look back at the passage to find the answer. O'Keeffe began painting abstractly while she was teaching in Texas.

4.   **C.** To answer this question, you have to use the information in the passage to draw a conclusion.

The passage says that scientists are not creating spider farms where they can harvest tons of this silk because spiders are too territorial. This suggests that the spiders might attack and kill each other.

5.   **B.** To answer this question, you have to make an inference based on the information in the passage. The last line of this passage says that the final fate of these people is mysterious, meaning it is not known. Therefore, you can infer that the full history of the Anasazi people is unknown.

6.   **C.** The author of the passage says that industrial noises frighten polar bears so much that females sometimes abandon helpless cubs. They are conducting these experiments to help solve this problem. Therefore, the main goal of the experiments is to learn how to shield these animals from noise pollution.

7.   **B.** The passage says that colds are passed from one person to another through contact and that children suffer from more colds than adults do. Therefore, you can infer that children have more contact than adults do.

8.   **D.** This question asks you to choose the best summary of the passage. You need to choose the statement that tells what the passage is mostly about. Choice D gives the best summary: Suzanne Lenglen was France's dominant female tennis player for many years. The other answer choices give details in the passage.

9.   **D.** The author's tone in the passage is fascinated. The words "the results are spectacular" clue you in to the correct answer.

10. **D.** This question asks you to identify the sequence of events in the order in which they occurred. If you look back at the passage, you'll see that Choice D is correct.

11. **C.** This question asks you to choose the sentence that best summarizes the passage, or states what the entire passage is about. The best choice is C: Paul Gaugin's artistic career began with the loss of a job and the success of a painting.

12. **C.** Choice C best states the author's purpose in writing this passage: to impress readers with the number and variety of beetles. The author says one third of the insect kingdom is composed of beetles and that beetles range in size from the tiny pest that lives on the mouthparts of bees to the giant four-inch longhorn.

13. **D.** This question asks you to recall details in the passage in the order in which they are presented. Choice D is correct. According to the passage, the order of instruments in an orchestra from back to font is strings, woodwinds, brass, and percussion.

14. **C.** The passage says that the Gulf Stream is an ocean current that flowed near many league towns. This current caused a strong breeze that caught fly balls.

15. **D.** The best conclusion based on the information in the passage is that people are interested in accessing the immigrants' records. If they weren't, this difficult task should not have been undertaken.

PART 5: MATHEMATICS KNOWLEDGE

1. **B.** The product of the two binomials can be written as $-21x^2 + 28x + 18x - 24$, which simplifies to $-21x^2 + 46x - 24$.

2. **B.** The factor given for Choice B divides into the given polynomial evenly. The factors of the polynomial are $(6x - 9)$ and $(-5x^2 + 2x)$. The product of the factors can be written as $-30x^3 + 12x^2 + 45x^2 - 18x$, which reduces to $-30x^3 + 57x^2 - 18x$.

3. **A.** The width of the rectangle can be represented by w, and the

length of the rectangle can be represented by $3w$. Thus, the perimeter can be represented by the equation $3w + 3w + w + w = 104$, which simplifies to $8w = 104$, where $w = 13$. Therefore, the width of the rectangle is 13 inches, whereas the length of the rectangle is 3 times that number, or 39 inches. The area of the rectangle can be determined by calculating the product of the length and the width. Doing so gives an area of 507 square inches.

4. **B.** The number under the radical can be rewritten as 4,096. Thus, the radical expression can be rewritten as $\sqrt[3]{4096}$. The cubed root of 4,096 can be evaluated by rewriting the expression as $4096^{\frac{1}{3}}$, which equals 16.

5. **C.** The rules of exponents state that an expression in the form $a^{-\frac{1}{b}}$ can be rewritten as $\frac{1}{a^{\frac{1}{b}}}$. Thus, the expression $5^{-\frac{1}{2}}$ can be rewritten as $\frac{1}{5^{\frac{1}{2}}}$, which equals $\frac{1}{\sqrt{5}}$.

6. **C.** The rules of exponents state that $a^x \cdot a^y = a^{x+y}$. Thus, $7^{\frac{1}{6}} \cdot 7^{\frac{2}{3}} = 7^{\frac{1}{6}+\frac{2}{3}}$, or $7^{\frac{5}{6}}$. The rules of exponents also state that $a^{\frac{x}{y}}$ can be equivalently written as $\sqrt[y]{a^x}$. Thus, $7^{\frac{5}{6}}$ can be rewritten as $\sqrt[6]{7^5}$.

7. **B.** Vertical angles are opposite angles formed by a transversal that intersects two parallel lines. Angles a and f are opposite angles.

8. **C.** The number of sides of the polygon can be determined from the given sum of interior angles. The following equation can be written $(n - 2) \cdot 180 = 540$. Solving for n gives $n = 5$. The number of diagonals of a polygon can be determined from the number of sides of the polygon, using the expression $\frac{n(n-3)}{2}$. Substituting 5 for n gives $\frac{5(5-3)}{2}$, or $n = 5$. Thus, a regular polygon with a sum of its interior angles equal to 540 degrees has 5 diagonals.

9. **D.** Angles f and h are supplementary. Since angle h measures 30°,

angle f measures $150°$. Angles f and b are alternate interior angles. Such angles are congruent, so the measure of angle b is $150°$.

10. **C.** Since the two angles are supplementary, the following equation can be written: $4a = 180$. Solving for a gives $a = 45$. The $m\angle ABC = 3(45)$ degrees, or 135 degrees.

11. **C.** Since the sum of the interior angles of a triangle equals 180 degrees, the following equation can be written: $4a + 4a + a = 180$, where $a = 20$. Substituting 20 for a in the expression, $4a$, gives the measure of each base angle: $4(20)$ or 80. Thus, the measure of each base angle of the isosceles triangle is 80 degrees.

12. **B.** The Pythagorean Theorem states $a^2 + b^2 = c^2$, where a and b are the lengths of the legs of a right triangle and c is the length of the hypotenuse. Substituting a leg of length 17 and the hypotenuse of length 21 into the equation gives $17^2 + b^2 = 21^2$. Solving for b gives $b^2 = 152$ or $b = \sqrt{152}$, which is approximately 12.3. Therefore, the length of the hypotenuse of the given right triangle is approximately 12.3 cm.

13. **B.** The ratio of the length of the rectangle to its width can be written as $\dfrac{3x + 6}{x + 2}$, which can be rewritten as $\dfrac{3(x + 2)}{x + 2}$, or 3. The ratio of the length of the rectangle to its width is 3.

14. **C.** The area of the original rectangle is equal to $2a \cdot a$ or $2a^2$. The area of the increased rectangle is equal to $(2a + 6)a$ or $2a^2 + 6a$. Therefore, the area of the rectangle is increased by a value equal to the product of 6 and the width.

15. **C.** The circumference of a circle can be determined using the formula $C = \pi d$, where C represents the circumference and d represents the diameter of the circle. Substitute the given circumference for C: $44 = \pi d$. Then solve for d: $d \approx 14$. Therefore, the diameter of the circle is approximately 14 inches.

16. **A.** The volume of a sphere is determined using the formula, $V = \dfrac{4}{3}\pi r^3$, where r represents the radius of the sphere. Substituting a radius of 6

inches gives the following: $V = \frac{4}{3}\pi(6)^3$, which is approximately 904. The fully inflated ball holds approximately 904 cubic inches of air.

17. **B.** The volume of a cylindrical can is determined using the formula $V = \pi r^2 h$, where r represents the radius and h represents the height. Substitute 1 inch for the radius and 6 inches for the height: $V = \pi(1)^2(6)$ or $V = 6\pi$, which is approximately 18.84. The can has a volume of approximately 18.84 cubic inches.

18. **A.** The coordinates of the given ordered pair represent an x-value of −9 and a y-value of 6. Point A correctly represents these values.

19. **B.** The slope of the line represents the number of candles sold per hour. The slope is the ratio of the change in y-value per the change in the corresponding x-value. The slope can be determined by substituting the corresponding x- and y-value of any two points found on the line. Choosing the points, (0, 2) and (1, 10) gives $\frac{10-2}{1-0}$ or 8. The slope of the line is 8, which means that 8 candles are sold per hour.

20. **A.** The slope of −3 and the x- and y-values from the point (3, −13) can be substituted into the point-slope form of an equation ($y - y_1 = m(x - x_1)$) to find the equation of the line. Doing so gives $y - (-13) = -3(x - 3)$ or $y + 13 = -3(x - 3)$, which can be rewritten as $y + 13 = -3x + 9$ or $y = -3x - 4$. If you substitute the x- and y-values from Choice A into this equation, you'll see that (8, −28) is a point on the line.

21. **D.** The slope can be determined by substituting the corresponding x- and y-value of any two points found on the line. Choosing the points, (0, −9) and (1, −5) gives $\frac{-5+9}{1-0}$ or 4, which is the slope of the line. Since the slope of the line is positive, you can eliminate Choices B and C.

22. **C.** The surface area of a cube can be represented using the formula $SA = 6a^2$, where a represents the length of each edge of the cube. Substituting the surface area of 294 square inches into the formula gives

$294 = 6a^2$. Solving for a gives $49 = a^2$, where $a = 7$. Therefore, the length of each edge of the cube is 7 inches.

23. **A.** The solution area is the overlapping area found below the line, $y = -2x - 8$ and above the line, $y = 3x - 5$. The point $(-8, -5)$ is located in the solution region.

24. **A.** The area of the triangle can be written as $A = \dfrac{1}{2}(4x - 3)(6x + 2)$, which simplifies to $A = \dfrac{1}{2}(24x^2 - 10x - 6)$ or $A = 12x^2 - 5x - 3$.

25. **B.** The graph reveals an approximate y-value of 196 for an x-value of 8; $192 is closest to $196, so it best represents the amount of money she has saved after 8 months.

PART 6: ELECTRONICS INFORMATION

1. **B.** Electromagnetic waves are composed of both an electric field and a magnetic field. The electric field is created by the application of voltage, and the magnetic field is a direct result of current flow.

2. **C.** The first optoelectronic device was the light-emitting diode (LED). Optoelectronic devices either produce or use light during operation; some when they are forward biased, and others when they are reverse biased.

3. **B.** When exposed to light, solar cells can produce electrical energy. Like batteries, their current capacity is determined by their size; the larger the solar cell, the more current it can produce.

4. **C.** A unijunction transistor (UJT) has three terminals. It differs from a common transistor in that a common transistor has a collector, and the UJT has two bases and no collector.

5. **B.** The UJT transistor has one PN junction and three terminals. The area between the two bases acts as a resistor, and there is no collector.

6. **A.** A common transistor has two PN junctions, a collector and a base, and two terminals. The diagram in Choice A is correct.

7. **B.** The Zener effect explains electrical breakdown below 5 volts

because the electrons are not triggering chain reactions. The Avalanche effect ruptures covalent bonds, increases heat, and in turn ruptures more bonds. Therefore, electrical breakdown above 5 volts is a result of the Avalanche effect.

8. **C.** A PN junction is surrounded by a thin area where no positive or negative current carriers rest. All charge carriers near the depletion region are forced away by the electric field.

9. **B.** Ohm's law states that current is inversely proportional to resistance. The equation $I = E/R$ represents Ohm's law. I represents the current, in amperes; E represents the voltage in volts; and R represents the resistance in ohms.

To solve for I, divide 1.5 by 5. The answer is .3 ampere.

10. **B.** Since Ohm's law can be modified to solve for different variables, you can determine the voltage (E) with the equation $E = I \times R$. Since $I = .5$ amperes and $R = 45$ ohms, multiply .5 by 45. The product is 22.5. Therefore, the circuit produces 22.5 volts.

11. **C.** Power rating is measured in watts, which is the rate at which something converts electrical energy into light, heat, or other forms of energy. Light bulbs are an example of a power rating: a 60-watt light bulb converts less electrical energy into light than a 100-watt light bulb; 100-watt light bulbs are far brighter than 60-watt bulbs.

12. **D.** You can calculate power if you know the input power (in horsepower) and the amount of time a device has been operated. You must also know that 1 horsepower equals 746 watts. Power is expressed in watt-hours.

13. **C.** First, determine the horsepower in watts. Since 1 horsepower equals 746 watts, 10HP equals 7,460 watts (10 x 746 = 7,460).

Multiply 7,460 by the number of hours. In this case, the motor runs continuously for 40 hours, so multiply 7,460 by 40 (7,460 x 40 = 298,400).

The power the motor converts equals 298,400 watt-hours during a 40-hour workweek.

14. **A.** An open circuit does not allow current to complete its cycle. A flashlight with an "Off/On" switch is an example of a basic circuit. When the switch is turned "On," the circuit is closed; this means power can circle around the circuit and the bulb can illuminate. When the switch is turned "Off," the circuit is broken, or open, and the power cannot go all the way around, and the light stays off because it has no power.

15. **D.** Ohm's law simply states, "The current in a circuit is inversely proportional to the circuit resistance." Ohm's law can be expressed by the equation $I = V/R$. I is the current (measured in amperes); V is the potential difference across the conductor (measured in volts); and R is the resistance of the conductor (measured in ohms). Ohm's law applies to both series and parallel circuits.

16. **B.** A series circuit has only one path that electrons can use. The direction of electron flow is indicated by the arrows; note that there is only one path.

17. **A.** A parallel circuit provides more than one path for electrons to flow. Choices B and C show series circuits.

18. **D.** Grease is not a good preservative for battery terminals because heat often causes it to melt and coat the casing and terminals. Dust and debris can easily stick to the battery when grease is used as a preservative.

19. **C.** A Darlington pair is a combination of two transistors to achieve high current gain. Darlington pairs are used to make touch switches that are activated by the very small electrical current running through human fingertips.

20. **A.** Doping is the process of introducing impurities into a semiconductor, and it is done for the express purpose of changing the semiconductor's performance. The materials introduced are called "dopants."

PART 7: AUTO AND SHOP INFORMATION

1. **C.** Carburetors were used in the 1980s and earlier as the primary fuel-delivery system in internal combustion engines. Fuel-injection

systems replaced carburetors because they are more efficient, produce fewer emissions, and cost less than carburetors.

2. **C.** Bolt cutters are the most efficient tool for cutting padlocks. The long handles and short blades of bolt cutters allow you to exert less energy to cut the padlock than if you attempted to saw through a padlock.

3. **B.** TPI means "teeth per inch" on a saw blade. Generally, the more TPI a saw blade has, the smoother the cut it makes.

4. **C.** A protractor measures angles and circles in degrees. Protractors can be circular or semicircular and are frequently used in woodworking and metalwork.

5. **B.** The chuck of a drill is a clamp designed to hold a drill bit. The portion of a drill bit that fits inside the chuck is known as the shank, and the shank is opposite a drill bit's cutting edge.

6. **C.** A car's suspension system utilizes shock absorbers to create a smoother ride. Shock absorbers dissipate the energy coming from bumps in the road.

7. **B.** There are four main components in an antilock braking system: the pump, valves, speed sensors, and a controller. The pump replaces pressure in a brake line after a valve releases it, and the speed sensors provide information on when the brakes are about to lock. The controller is the computer that monitors the speed sensors and sends signals to the valves and pumps. Pistons are not part of an antilock braking system.

8. **C.** Soldering is the act of connecting two pieces of metal by melting a different type of metal between them. Generally, the metal that is used for soldering has a lower melting point than the types of metal being connected. Soldering differs from welding because in welding, the connected pieces are melted together.

9. **C.** When a battery is overcharged, or when it is charged at a very high voltage for a long period of time, some of the water it contains can break down into hydrogen and oxygen. This exposes the plates inside

and can cause irreparable damage, so the occasional addition of distilled water may be necessary.

10. **C.** An oscilloscope uses an electron beam to measure voltage and frequency. When an input signal is added to an oscilloscope, the signature it leaves allows the user to determine its voltage and duration.

11. **D.** A dead-blow hammer is a type of hollow-headed mallet that is used when it is necessary to minimize the hammer's rebound. Mechanics often use dead-blow hammers for chassis work, hubcap installation, and other work that requires them to avoid damaging nearby parts.

12. **A.** A two-stroke engine fires after each revolution of the crankshaft. For this reason, two-stroke engines are generally more powerful than four-stroke engines of a comparable size.

13. **C.** The Society of Automotive Engineers (SAE) created a system to grade motor oil. The "W" stands for *winter* and is used to represent the oil's cold-start viscosity.

14. **D.** A vehicle's tachometer displays its crankshaft's revolutions per minute, or RPM. Most tachometers display a "safe zone" of operation, and RPMs exceeding the recommended number for that vehicle can cause engine damage.

15. **A.** Boring is the process of using a cutting tool to enlarge a hole. Boring can also be done to create a tapered hole. Objects such as gun barrels and funneled pipes are often bored.

16. **D.** Gasoline's octane rating represents how much the gasoline can be compressed before spontaneously igniting. Some engines require gasoline to be able to withstand high amounts of compression, while others tolerate much less.

17. **D.** In a vehicle's cooling system, a water pump pushes water around the hottest parts of an engine. The water circulates through the radiator, where it is cooled by outside air. Antifreeze is added to the water to raise its boiling point so it does not evaporate.

18 **A.** Disc brakes use rotors, or metal discs, attached to the wheels. The rotors spin until the calipers clamp down to slow the speed of the rotors and wheels.

19. **C.** A manual transmission leaves the operation of the clutch and the gearshift up to the driver. Depressing the clutch disengages the transmission so the driver can shift gears. An automatic transmission does that work itself.

20. **A.** The muffler is the final component of an engine's exhaust system. While it does remove some of the pollutants from exhaust, its main job is to quiet the noise coming from the engine.

21. **B.** The secondary winding of the coil is the part that sends the spark to the distributor. The primary winding is the part of the coil that takes energy from the battery and increases its charge.

22. **B.** The catalytic converter is part of the exhaust system. The catalytic converter changes harmful carbon monoxide and hydrocarbons into water and carbon dioxide. Then, those waste products enter the muffler and are expelled through the tailpipe.

23. **C.** The cylinders in an engine can be arranged either horizontally or vertically. Engines typically have four, six, or eight cylinders.

24. **C.** During the compression stroke, the gases inside the cylinder are compressed into a smaller and smaller space. As the gases compress, they become hotter.

25. **B.** Hacksaws have thinner blades and are generally used to cut metal. Ripsaws, crosscut saws, and coping saws are handsaws that are used to cut wood.

PART 8: MECHANICAL COMPREHENSION

1. **B.** Torque ratio and mechanical advantage are synonymous when used in the context of a gear train. Torque ratio is dependent on the gear ratio.

2. **A.** Work is measured in joules. One joule is the work done by a force of one newton acting over one meter.

3.   **D.** Newton's second law of motion states that acceleration is directly proportional to the net force and inversely proportional to the mass. Using the equation $F = ma$, where F represents force, m represents mass and a represents acceleration, you can determine the force necessary in this problem by multiplying 500 kg by 10 m/s². Force is measured in newtons (N), so the answer is 5,000 N.

4.   **D.** A wheelbarrow is second-class lever. Second-class levers are characterized by a fulcrum at one end of the lever, with the load between the fulcrum and the applied force. Third-class levers are characterized by a fulcrum at one end of the lever and the load at the other; force is applied between the fulcrum and the load. Fishing poles, brooms, tongs, tweezers, shovels, and baseball bats are all third-class levers.

5.   **A.** Inertia is an object's resistance to a change in its motion or rest. According to Newton's first law of motion (the law of inertia), an object with no external forces acting on it will continue moving indefinitely. However, the marble in this problem is subject to external forces such as the friction from irregularities in the concrete.

6.   **C.** In a block and tackle system, the number of ropes supporting the moving block determines the mechanical advantage. If you used a block and tackle with four ropes to lift the same load, the mechanical advantage would be 4:1. The height of the lift is irrelevant.

7.   **A.** Inertia refers to an object's resistance to change. A heavier, denser object has more inertia than a lighter object. A bicycle is easier to move than a motorcycle because it has less inertia.

8.   **C.** A planetary gear set consists of a ring gear, the planet gears and their carrier, and a sun gear. A planetary gear set allows one gear (the sun gear) to engage other gears (the planets) at the same time. The planet gears can engage the inside of a ring gear.

9.   **C.** Newton outlined three laws of motion. Newton's first law of motion states that every object in a state of uniform motion tends to stay that way unless acted upon by an external force. His second law of motion

states that mass is directly proportional to acceleration. The third law states that for every action, there is an equal and opposite reaction.

10. **D.** Work is calculated by multiplying force by displacement. W represents work, F represents force, and d represents displacement. The formula for work is $W = Fd$. Using that formula as a base, force can be calculated by dividing work by displacement ($F = \dfrac{W}{d}$), and displacement can be calculated by dividing work by force ($d = \dfrac{W}{F}$). Work cannot be calculated by dividing displacement by work ($W = \dfrac{d}{W}$).

11. **B.** The formula to calculate pressure is $P = \dfrac{F}{A}$, where P represents pressure, F represents force in pounds, and a represents area in square inches. In this problem, divide 150 pounds (the force) by 5 square inches (the area) to determine the pressure in pounds per square inch (psi). The correct answer is 30 psi.

12. **D.** The figure depicts a fixed pulley (it is anchored in place). A fixed pulley provides no mechanical advantage or multiplication of force, so its mechanical advantage is 1. A fixed pulley's main purpose is to change the direction of force, not to provide a mechanical advantage.

13. **B.** Worm gears are not used to change directional forces. Worm gears are used to create large gear reductions.

14. **A.** A first-class lever is characterized by the location of its fulcrum. First-class levers have a fulcrum between the applied force and the load, like a seesaw on a playground. The rider pushing up with his feet is the applied force, and the rider being lifted is the load. The center pivot point is the fulcrum.

15. **D.** A caster can be a single, double, or compound wheel. Casters are designed to make movement of a large object easier. Wheeled office chairs and other furniture often use casters, as do shopping carts and tow lines.

16. **A.** The formula for weight is $W = mg$, where W represents weight, m represents mass, and g represents acceleration due to gravity. On earth, the average acceleration due to gravity is 9.8 m/s². Mass and weight cannot be confused. $W = Fd$ is the formula for calculating work.

17. **D.** The energy stored in an object is considered its potential energy. For example, if you hold a wrecking ball at a diagonal and do not release it, the energy in the wrecking ball is potential energy. The energy stays there until you release the wrecking ball, and then it becomes kinetic energy. Kinetic energy is the energy of motion.

18. **B.** The pendulum with the longest pivot (or string) will take the longest to complete one swing. A pendulum that is displaced from its resting position is acted upon by a force that tries to bring it back to its resting position. A pendulum's resting position is also known as its equilibrium position.

19. **C.** Bearings are used to reduce friction between points of contact. A bearing is designed to force the friction generated to act over a shorter distance.

20. **C.** Deceleration is the act of slowing down, while acceleration is the act of speeding up. When an object encounters friction, it decelerates according to Newton's first law of motion.

21. **D.** A sprocket is a wheel with teeth that can grip a chain, a track, or other material. Unlike a gear, a sprocket never engages another sprocket. While pulleys fulfill a similar function, pulleys are smooth; sprockets have distinct teeth with which to engage other indented materials.

22. **A.** Brakes are equipped with pads that create friction by gripping a disc attached to the wheel. The friction slows the motion of the disc and eventually forces the vehicle to stop.

23. **C.** An object's center of gravity is located in the spot where equal amounts of weight are on each side. For example, a straight board's center of gravity is very near the middle. A baseball bat's center of gravity is closer to the wide end and farther from the handle.

24. **A.** The pressure on each pole is affected by both the weight and the distance between the resting point and pressure point. Since the distance between the resting point and pressure point is longest in figure A, and more of the weight is held by the shortest pole, the pole in figure A is receiving more pressure than those in the other figures.

25. **D.** Gears are designed to engage other gears, whereas pulleys do not engage one another. Pulleys engage ropes, belts, and strings. Gears can rotate in any direction, they can transmit motion, and some gears are designed to bear weight.

Multiple-Choice Strategies

The ASVAB is totally multiple choice. You are presented with a question and four answer options. You must answer ALL questions on each test within a set time frame. Make the most of the time that's available to you. The following list details multiple-choice test-taking strategies.

- *Don't be afraid to mark up your test booklet.* If you are answering on paper, your answer sheet needs to be kept clean and free from any stray markings. However, your test booklet can be marked up as much as needed. Don't be afraid to flag the questions you want to return to, or underline or otherwise mark any part of the question or answer option that you think needs to be reviewed more carefully. If you're taking the exam online, use scrap paper to work through calculations (which will be provided to you at the test center; you can't bring your own with you).

- *First, mentally answer the question.* Read the full question, and then mentally answer it *before* you look at the answer choices. Sometimes answer options are intentionally distracting. (That's why they're called "distracters.") If you already have an idea of the answer you're looking for, you'll be less confused by the answer options.

- *Pay attention to the wording.* Some questions include the words NOT or EXCEPT. For those questions, you're looking for the answer that is NOT true or does NOT apply. These can be tricky, so make sure you're aware.

- *Review all answer options before making a selection.* Make sure you review *all* of the answer options before making your answer choice. Sometimes, more than one answer is correct; one choice might be "more correct" than another.

- *Does your answer choice* completely *address the question? Is it qualified in some way?* If an answer is only partially true, or if it's qualified with narrow conditions (look for words like *never, always, only*), it's probably not the right answer.

- *Use elimination strategies.* If you don't know an answer, start by eliminating answer choices. See if you can eliminate one or two of the choices. Look for clueing words like *always, only, never*, and so on. Once you've eliminated answer choices you believe are wrong, guess from those that remain. The more answer choices you eliminate, the better your chances of getting the correct answer.

- *Take a guess!* If you're lost on a question or don't feel like you have enough time to analyze it as deeply as you'd like, take a wild guess. Fill in an oval at random if you must. There's no penalty for guessing (but there is one for leaving a question unanswered), and you just might get lucky.

- *On the paper test, flag difficult questions.* Answer them on the answer sheet, but flag them on the test. Come back to them after you've gone through the entire test.

- *On the paper test, be careful on the answer sheet!* Don't make mistakes. Make sure your question and answer numbers correspond. Also, be sure you have penciled in the answer space completely and have no stray pencil marks in other spaces.

Review Chapter 1:
General Science

Homeostasis and Life Functions

All living things require and use energy to grow and develop, respond to the environment, and regulate internal states. At least some organisms in a species must also reproduce.

The state of internal balance an organism maintains is called **homeostasis**. For example, a human being's body regulates temperature and blood glucose levels as needed. Homeostasis is achieved through feedback loops. A **negative feedback loop** functions like a thermostat, sensing and adjusting to achieve a set point.

The Cell

The cell is the basic unit of life. All living things are composed of cells, which may be **unicellular** or **multicellular**. Organisms are divided into two major categories based on cell type: **prokaryotes** and **eukaryotes**. Prokaryotes include **eubacteria** and **archaea**. Eukaryotes include protists, fungi, plants, and animals.

Prokaryotic cells are smaller and simpler than eukaryotic cells. Both cell types have a **cell membrane**, **cytoplasm**, and genetic material in the form of **DNA**. Only eukaryotic cells, however, contain membrane-bound

organelles. Either cell type may have a rigid **cell wall** surrounding the cell membrane.

Eukaryotic Cell Structure

Eukaryotic cells feature the following structures:

STRUCTURE	DESCRIPTION	FUNCTION
Plasma membrane	Phospholipid bilayer with floating protein channels	Surrounds cell and determines which molecules may enter
Cytoplasm	Fluid that contains membrane-bound organelles and ribosomes	A **cytoskeleton** provides structure and support
Centrosome	Present in animal cells	Organizing center of **microtubules**
Nucleus	The **nuclear envelope** contains the **chromosomes** and **nucleolus**	The "control center" of the cell
Ribosomes	Small particles composed of RNA and protein; may be free or bound to organelles	Synthesize proteins from mRNA
Endoplasmic reticulum (ER)	A complex network of membrane folds and sacs continuous with the nuclear envelope	Synthesis and metabolism of biological molecules
Golgi apparatus	A stack of membrane sacs, from which small vesicles bud off	"Processing center" for molecules made in the ER; Vesicles transport proteins to other parts of cell
Vacuole	A water-filled organelle; plant cells contain a large, central vacuole	Water storage

STRUCTURE	DESCRIPTION	FUNCTION
Mitochondria	Small organelles surrounded by two membranes; the inner membrane is intricately folded	Cellular respiration; Present in both plant and animal cells
Chloroplasts	Organelles containing connected stacks of **thylakoids (grana)** in a fluid called **stroma**	Sites of **photosynthesis**; Thylakoids contain **chlorophyll**; Present only in plants and algae
Cell wall	Plant cell walls are made of **cellulose**, while fungi cell walls are made of **chitin**; animal cells lack cell walls	Provide structure and rigidity

Plant and Animal Cells

These illustrations show the major components and organelles of plant and animal cells.

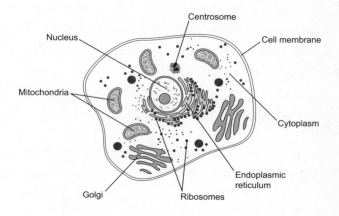

Animal cell

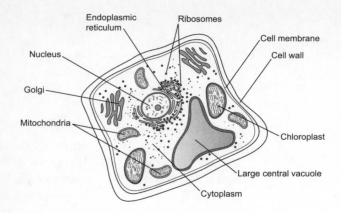

Plant cell

Cell Division

A parent cell divides to produce two new daughter cells. Prokaryotes divide by **binary fission**, while eukaryotes undergo the much more complicated process of **mitosis**. Mitosis consists of a series of stages in which the chromosomes replicate, align, and are pulled apart, and two identical nuclei are formed. Mitosis is part of the **cell cycle**.

Sexually reproducing organisms must create **haploid** gametes (sperm and egg cells) through **meiosis**. In meiosis, pairs of **homologous** chromosomes separate to form nuclei with half the **diploid** number of chromosomes.

Classification

In addition to the prokaryote-eukaryote division, the three-domain system and the five-kingdom system are used to classify living things.

Three-Domain System

- *Eubacteria*—"True" bacteria, which are simple prokaryotic cells.
- *Archaea*—These prokaryotes share many features with eukaryotes. Many are **extremeophiles** found in extreme temperature, salinity, pH, or pressure.

- *Eukarya*—Includes both unicellular and multicellular organisms (protists, fungi, plants, animals).

Five-Kingdom System

The **five-kingdom system** is an older system that is still widely used.

- *Prokaryotes*—Includes archaea and eubacteria.
- *Protists*—Any eukaryote that does not belong to any of the kingdoms below is considered a protist. Most are single-celled, but algae are multicellular protists.
- *Fungi*—May be unicellular (yeasts) or multicellular (mushrooms). Fungi digest food outside the cell and then absorb it. Many fungi are saprophytes or decomposers.
- *Plants*—Multicellular organisms that carry out photosynthetic organisms.
- *Animals*—Multicellular organisms that filter or ingest food from the environment.

Taxonomic classes divide kingdoms into smaller categories or **taxa**. These are, from largest to smallest: **Kingdom, Phylum, Class, Order, Family, Genus, Species**.

Binomial nomenclature ensures that every species has a unique name by assigning it a genus and a species name (e.g., *Homo sapiens*).

Human Body Systems

The human body consists of cells, tissues, and organs that make up body systems that function to keep all the cells in the body healthy. The major body systems, and their components and functions, are listed below.

SYSTEM	FUNCTION	ORGANS AND TISSUES
Digestive	Take in and break down food into basic molecules, which are absorbed into the body	Mouth, teeth, tongue, salivary glands, esophagus, stomach, liver, pancreas, gall-bladder, small intestine, large intestine, rectus, anus
Respiratory	Take in, warm, and moisturize air; absorb oxygen into and expel carbon dioxide from the bloodstream	Nasal cavity, pharynx, trachea, bronchioles, lungs, alveoli
Circulatory	Transport oxygen-poor blood from tissues to the heart and then to the lungs; transport oxygen-rich blood from the lungs to the heart and then to tissues	Heart, arteries (e.g., aorta), veins, blood vessels, capillaries
Endocrine	Glands produce and secrete **hormones** into the bloodstream, which regulate body states and metabolism; hormones affect only specific tissues	Adrenal, thyroid, parathyroid, and pituitary ("master") glands; hypothalamus, gonads, liver, and pancreas
Excretory	Filter and eliminate wastes from bloodstream	Kidneys, ureters, bladder, urethra
Reproductive	Produce gametes (eggs and sperm); allow fertilization; nourish and protect embryo	Female: ovaries, Fallopian tubes, uterus, vagina, vulva, placenta Male: testes, epidydimus, prostate gland, penis
Sensory	Receive information from the environment	Eyes, ears, skin, taste buds, olfactory bulb

SYSTEM	FUNCTION	ORGANS AND TISSUES
Nervous	Process information from the environment; control voluntary and involuntary movement	**CNS:** Brain and spinal cord **PNS:** Nerves between spinal cord and body; involuntary; sympathetic, parasympathetic, and enteric divisions **Somatic:** Voluntary movements
Muscular	Muscles attached to bone allow locomotion; muscles move by contraction only and are in opposing pairs	Striated muscle (voluntary) Smooth muscle (involuntary) Cardiac muscle (heart) Ligaments
Skeletal	Structure, support, protection, and movement (via attached muscles)	Bones and joints; tendon, cartilage
Immune	Specific and nonspecific defense against **pathogens**	Skin and mucous membranes; bone marrow, spleen, thymus; immune system cells (lymphocytes, phagocytes, etc.)

Genetics

Genetics describes *how* traits are inherited. Most traits are the result of many different **genes**, but some are due to single genes. One parent passes on a copy of each gene to offspring. Different versions or **alleles** of a gene may be inherited. Some alleles are **dominant**, masking the trait specified by a **recessive** allele. The combination of alleles of a gene is the **genotype**, while the trait that results is the **phenotype**.

Health and Nutrition

Nutrition

A healthy diet provides not only energy but also the substances needed to repair the body and ensure that cells function properly. The energy provided by food is measured in **calories**. Besides providing energy, the components of a healthy diet have other functions.

- **Carbohydrates** (starches and sugars) are broken down into simple sugars, such as in digestion. Glucose is converted to energy by cells in the process of cellular respiration.

- **Fats** are a more-concentrated form of energy, providing more calories per gram than carbohydrates.

- **Proteins** are broken down into their components, **amino acids**, and used for growth, repair, and the synthesis of important molecules.

- **Minerals** are simple, inorganic elements, including sodium, potassium, calcium, and iron. Cells need proper concentrations of minerals to function, and some biological molecules also include a mineral component (e.g., the iron ion associated with **hemoglobin**, the oxygen-binding protein in blood).

- **Vitamins** are small molecules that allow cells to function and that the body cannot make on its own.

- **Water** is needed to carry out the chemical reactions inside cells. The human body is about 62 percent water.

- **Fiber** is not absorbed into the body during digestion, but it keeps the digestive tract healthy by making it easier to eliminate digestive waste.

Disease

A **disease** is a condition that disrupts homeostasis and/or impairs function. Diseases may be classified in various ways, but one major distinction is between **infectious** and **non-infectious** diseases. Infectious (contagious) diseases are caused by pathogens (viruses, bacteria, protists, or parasites) and can be transmitted between people and/or animals. Non-infectious diseases have various causes. They may be genetic or caused by lifestyle factors such as smoking. Some non-infectious diseases, such as heart disease or depression, may have a variety of causes.

Ecology

Ecology is the study of organisms in relation to their physical environment. The organisms of a single species, found in a particular ecosystem, make up a **population**. The populations of all species living in the same ecosystem make up a **community**. The community and the abiotic factors surrounding it make up the **ecosystem**.

A species' role in an ecosystem is understood by its mode of nutrition: **Producers** harness the energy of the sun to convert carbon dioxide and water to food (mainly carbohydrates) that **consumers** can eat. Finally, **decomposers** break down dead and decaying organisms, returning a portion of their components to the soil, where they can be used by plants. Consumers may be may be herbivores, omnivores, or carnivores, and can be further classified as predators, browsers, grazers, filter feeders, or scavengers. All consumers, however, derive energy by eating other organisms.

Where does the energy in an ecosystem ultimately come from? The sun provides energy in the form of light, which is then harnessed by producers and converted to the chemical energy in plant matter. A small percentage of this energy is then consumed by herbivores or **primary consumers**, which are in turn eaten by organisms at higher **trophic levels**. At each level, energy is lost as heat or in life processes; only about 10 percent of the energy at one trophic level is passed on to the next higher level. This results in the energy distribution shown below.

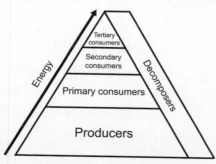

The Solar System

Earth, Sun, and Moon

The patterns of day and night, the phases of the moon, the changing of the seasons—even the tides—are all due to the periodic motions of the earth and moon in relation to the sun. Earth **rotates** on its **axis** once every 24 hours, leading to periods of daylight and darkness. However, because Earth's axis is tilted 23.5 degrees, not all locations experience equal periods of daylight. (Note that the location marked by the star will receive more hours of daylight than darkness.)

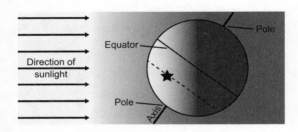

How much daylight a given location receives varies with the seasons. Earth completes one **revolution** around the sun every 365 days, and the tilt of its axis in relation to the sun changes over the course of Earth's **orbit**. The northern tip of the axis is tilted maximally toward the sun on about June 22, when summer begins in the Northern Hemisphere. It is tilted maximally away from the sun on about December 22, the winter **solstice** in the Northern Hemisphere. (The seasons are reversed for the Southern Hemisphere.) On the **equinoxes**, the axis is tilted parallel to the sun and all locations experience the same period of daylight.

The Moon and Tides

The moon completes one revolution around Earth in approximately 28 days. One half of the moon always faces the sun and is therefore lit. However, because of its changing position, viewers on Earth see different portions of the lit face as **phases**. When the moon casts a shadow on Earth, blocking the sun, a **solar eclipse** occurs. When Earth casts a shadow on the moon, a **lunar eclipse** results.

High and low tides are due to the moon's gravitational pull on Earth's waters. **High tides** occur in the areas closest and farthest from the moon. **Low tides** occur in intermediate areas.

Planets and Other Celestial Bodies

Earth is only one of eight planets that orbit the sun. The inner four **rocky planets** are Mercury, Venus, Earth, and Mars. The outer four **gas giants** are Jupiter, Saturn, Uranus, and Neptune. Between Mars and Jupiter lies the **asteroid belt**, a large band of irregular objects too small to be planets. **Meteoroids** are smaller than asteroids and may enter the atmosphere as meteors. Finally, **comets** orbit the sun in long, elliptical orbits. A tail or **coma** forms when the comet is near the sun, due to the melting of ices.

Geology

Earth's Layers

- **Inner core:** Solid, high-pressure center up to 5000°C
- **Outer core:** Hot, high pressure; composed of liquid iron and nickel
- **Mantle:** Largest layer; hot (870–2200°C), dense molten rock; convection currents
- **Crust or Lithosphere:** Thinnest, outermost layer; 8–32 km thick; composed of granite (continental crust) or basalt (oceanic crust)

Plate Tectonics

Plate tectonic theory explains why the shapes of Earth's continents and oceans have changed over geologic time. Earth's crust is divided into **plates** that shift, collide, and rip apart. Earthquakes and volcanic activity may result. The boundaries between plates may be **convergent** or **divergent**. Plate movement is caused by convection currents in Earth's outer mantle.

Rocks

- **Sedimentary** rock forms as small particles, or sediment, are cemented together under high pressures.
- **Igneous** rock forms as **magma** enters Earth's surface and cools.
- When sedimentary or igneous rock is subject to high heat and pressure, **metamorphic** rock forms as a result.

Fossils, the preserved remains of organisms, are found only in sedimentary rock.

Meteorology

Meteorology is the study of weather and climate. **Weather** is described by air temperature, pressure, humidity, precipitation, wind, and cloud conditions. The usual weather in a region is its **climate**.

Earth's Atmosphere

The **atmosphere** is a mixture of gases consisting of about 78 percent nitrogen, 21 percent oxygen, and 1 percent other gases (including carbon dioxide and ozone). Air becomes "thinner" with altitude. The atmosphere is divided into layers:

LAYER	MAX. ALTITUDE (KM)	DESCRIPTION
Thermosphere	600	temperature increases with height
Mesosphere	120	temperature decreases with height
Stratosphere	85	temperature increases with height; ozone forms in this layer
Troposphere	50	temperature decreases with height; most weather occurs in this layer

Measurement

The **International System** (SI) of units, used in science, includes base units (e.g., gram, liter, meter). Combined prefixes indicate a factor of ten times the base unit. For example, a kilometer is equal to 1,000 meters, while a milliliter equals one-thousandths of a liter.

PREFIX	FACTOR	EXAMPLE
kilo-	1000	kilogram
deka-	10	dekaliter
centi-	1/100	centimeter
milli-	1/1000	milligram
micro-	1/1,000,000	microliter

Other SI units include the joule (J, energy), newton (N, force), watt (W, power), and volt (V, electrical potential).

Science also uses the Celsius and Kelvin scales, rather than the Fahrenheit scale, to measure temperature. Common values for the three scales are shown in the table.

	FAHRENHEIT	CELSIUS	KELVIN
BOILING POINT OF WATER	212°	100°	373 K
HUMAN BODY TEMPERATURE	98.6°	37.0°	310
ROOM TEMPERATURE (APPROX.)	77°	25°	298 K
FREEZING POINT OF WATER	32°	0°	273 K
ABSOLUTE ZERO	–460°	–273°	0 K

Matter

The Atom

All matter is composed of **atoms**, basic building blocks of fundamental types called **elements**. An atom consists of a dense nucleus composed of uncharged **neutrons** and positively charged **protons**. Nearly massless, negatively charged **electrons** orbit the nucleus. When an atom consists of different numbers of protons and neutrons, it has a charge and is called an **ion**.

The elements are arranged in the **periodic table** so that the columns, or **groups**, share chemical properties. Elements increase in **atomic number**, or number of protons, across rows. The **atomic mass** is the average mass of all **isotopes** of an element (versions with different numbers of neutrons).

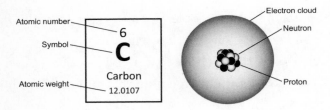

Atoms of different elements may be chemically bonded to form **compounds** such as water (H_2O), table salt (NaCl), or carbon dioxide (CO_2). A bond may be **ionic**, when electrons are exchanged between atoms, or **covalent**, when electrons are shared. (In **polar** covalent bonds, electrons are shared, but unequally.) Only covalent bonds form **molecules**.

Matter can change physically (volume, color, shape) or chemically. A **chemical change** requires that bonds between atoms be broken or formed, changing the identity of the compounds. This is called a **chemical reaction**.

Chemical Reactions and Conservation of Matter

Reactions are described by **chemical equations**. The original substances, the **reactants**, appear on the left side of the equation. The resulting substances, the **products**, appear on the right. The equation must be balanced, meaning that the number of atoms *of each element* in the reactants must equal those in the products. The equation below is balanced by **coefficients** (bold).

If the masses of the products and reactants were to be carefully measure, they would be found to be identical. This is because matter is conserved in chemical reactions.

$$CH_4 + 2O_2 \rightarrow CO_2 + 2H_2$$

Reactants   Products

Acids and Bases

Some substances, when dissolved in water, act as acids or bases. An acid increases the number of protons or hydrogen ions (H^+) in the solution, while a base increases the number of hydroxide ions (OH^-).

Acidity (or basicity) is measured on the **pH** scale, which ranges from 1 to 14. A pH of 1 indicates an extremely acidic substance, while a pH of 14 indicates a very strong base. The scale is not linear: A substance with a pH of 4 is ten times more acidic than one with a pH of 5. Neutral substances have pH levels around 7.

Energy

Energy can be understood as the power to do work. Energy comes in various forms and from various sources, such as:

- **Light:** electromagnetic radiation (from the sun)
- **Heat:** the amount of molecular motion
- **Sound:** mechanical waves (vibration through air)
- **Mechanical:** the energy of position and motion; includes **gravitational potential** energy and **kinetic** energy
- **Electrical:** the energy produced by the movement of charges in a circuit
- **Chemical:** the energy associated with the breaking and forming of bonds; includes **chemical potential energy**, such as that stored in fuel or food
- **Kinetic:** the energy of velocity or speed

Energy can be converted from one form to another (for example, a ball rolling down a hill gains speed as it loses potential energy associated with height). However, some energy is always lost as heat when energy is converted (some of the ball's potential energy is converted to heat due to friction). The percentage of energy that is successfully converted is referred to as **efficiency**.

In an isolated, closed system, energy is conserved; the amount of energy does not change. Earth is not an isolated system. Energy continuously streams in from the sun and is continuously lost to the universe as heat.

Electricity and Circuits

Electrical energy is due to the continuous movement of charged particles (electrons) through a **circuit** (closed loop) of **conductive** material; this movement is a **current**. Current can be stopped by opening the loop, such as by opening the loop with a **switch** or by inserting an **insulating** (non-conducting) material into the loop. As long as current flows, power is supplied to any **load** on the circuit (such as a light bulb).

The charges flowing through the circuit are supplied by a battery or other electron source; they return to the same battery. Because the direction of current is considered that of the movement of (hypothetical) positive charges, the electrons in an actual circuit move in the opposite direction as the current.

The Laws of Motion

Newton's laws of motion describe how the velocity and acceleration of objects are influenced by forces. **Velocity** refers to speed and direction. **Acceleration** is any change in velocity, including slowing, coming to rest, or altering direction.

- **Newton's first law:** An object at rest will tend to remain at rest and an object in constant, straight-line motion will tend to remain in motion unless it is acted on by an unbalanced force. Because objects tend to resist acceleration, they are said to have **inertia**.

- **Newton's second law:** A force acting on an object results in an acceleration proportional to the magnitude of the force, but inversely proportional to the mass of the object. Often expressed as $F = ma$.
- **Newton's third law:** When an object exerts a force on a second object, the second object exerts an equal and opposite force on the first. (Note that the effects of the forces may be different: one object may move while the other does not.)

Gravity, Weight, and the Normal Force

All objects exert a **gravitational force** that varies with mass. Earth, being much larger than the moon, exerts a greater gravitational force. Weight results from Newton's Second Law: the acceleration due to gravity (g) acting on a mass (m) results in a force or weight pulling the mass toward Earth's center. This is why weight is less on the moon (relative to Earth) while mass remains the same.

For an object at rest on Earth's surface, the downward force of gravity is balanced by the equal and opposite force exerted by the surface: the **normal force**. (If these forces where not balanced, the object would not be at rest.)

Light, Sound, and Waves

Waves are periodic motions that transmit energy and range from the electromagnetic to mechanical. **Electromagnetic radiation** consists of many types of light in addition to the visible light that we perceive. These include infrared radiation, gamma rays, microwaves, and broadcast frequencies, and do not need a medium in which to travel. **Mechanical waves** (vibration, ocean waves, sound) require a medium.

All waves have:

- **Amplitude:** The height from the midline to the highest or lowest point
- **Crests and troughs:** The maximum and minimum points on a wave, respectively

- **Wavelength (λ):** The distance between one point of a wave and the next corresponding point; the length of one complete wave cycle
- **Frequency (f):** The number of complete wave cycles to pass a fixed point in a given period of time; measured in cycles per second, or hertz (Hz)
- **Period (T):** Time required for one complete wave cycle to pass a fixed point; period and frequency are inversely related ($f = 1/T$ and $T = 1/f$)
- **Propagation velocity (v):** Speed at which a given point on a wave travels; the product of frequency and wavelength ($v = f\lambda$). For electromagnetic waves, the propagation velocity (in a vacuum) is always the speed of light (3×10^8 m/s). For mechanical waves, the propagation velocity depends on the medium through which the wave is traveling. The speed of sound waves through air is about 340 m/s.

The relationships among wavelength, frequency, period, and speed allow any of these physical properties to be determined from one or more of the others.

The **Doppler Effect** results when the source of a wave is moving toward or away from the viewer or listener.

Practice Questions

1. Which of the following substances is a compound?

    A. Argon gas (Ar)
    B. Hydrogen flouride (HF)
    C. Graphite carbon (C)
    D. Oxygen gas (O_2)

2. Which body system is responsible for eliminating the carbon dioxide produced by cells?

    A. Excretory
    B. Digestive
    C. Respiratory
    D. Endocrine

3. Which of the following is *closest* to 100°F?

    A. 0°C
    B. 37°C
    C. 65°C
    D. 200°C

4. Which of the following is present in animal cells but *not* in bacteria cells?

    A. Cell membrane
    B. Cell wall
    C. Cytoplasm
    D. Nucleus

5. A single-celled organism is found to have cell walls made of chitin and contain a membrane-bound nucleus. Which group does this organism most likely belong in?

    A. Fungi
    B. Plant
    C. Prokaryote
    D. Protist

6. Vinegar has a pH of about 3. Black coffee has a pH of about 5. What is the difference in the concentration of hydrogen ions (H^+) between the two liquids?

   A. Coffee has about one hundred times more hydrogen ions than vinegar.
   B. Coffee has about one and a half times more hydrogen ions than vinegar.
   C. Vinegar has about one hundred times more hydrogen ions than coffee.
   D. Vinegar has about one and a half times more hydrogen ions than coffee.

7. Which group of organisms in an ecosystem, combined, contains the *most* energy?

   A. Plants and algae
   B. Bacteria and fungi
   C. Fast-moving predators
   D. Large grazing mammals

8. An athlete eats a large breakfast before running a marathon. This energy conversion is *best* described as

   A. light energy to chemical energy.
   B. kinetic energy to potential energy.
   C. chemical energy to mechanical energy.
   D. potential energy to gravitational energy.

9. A stack of books rests on a table. Book 1 weighs 20 newtons (N) and Book 2 weighs 30 N. Which describes the normal forces acting on the books?

    A. A normal force of 20 N acts on Book 1 and a normal force of 30 N acts on book 2.
    B. A normal force of 30 N acts on Book 1 and a normal force of 20 N acts on book 2.
    C. A normal force of 20 N acts on Book 1 and a normal force of 50 N acts on book 2.
    D. A normal force of 30 N acts on Book 1 and a normal force of 50 N acts on book 2.

10. Weather balloons are sent into the atmosphere to observe and record weather phenomena. Which is the *lowest* atmospheric layer at which a weather balloon could observe most weather *from above*?

    A. The mesosphere
    B. The stratosphere
    C. The thermosphere
    D. The troposphere

Answer Explanations

1. **B.** A compound is a substance composed of two or more types of elements. Hydrogen fluoride is composed of the elements hydrogen (H) and fluorine (F); it is therefore the only compound. Oxygen gas, while consisting of O_2 molecules, is not a compound because both of its atoms are of the same type; it is a molecular element.

2. **C.** The carbon dioxide produced as a result of cellular respiration is passed into the bloodstream and transferred to the alveoli of the lungs during gas exchange. It is eliminated from the body by the respiratory system.

3. **B.** Normal human body temperature is close to 100°F. In the Celsius scale, normal human body temperature is 37°C. To convert 100°F to degrees Celsius, subtract 32 from the Fahrenheit temperature and divide the result by 1.8.

4. **D.** Animals are eukaryotes while bacteria are prokaryotes. All eukaryotic cells contain a membrane-bound nucleus. Both prokaryotic and eukaryotic cells have a cell membrane and cytoplasm. Animal cells do not have cell walls.

5. **A.** The presence of a membrane-bound nucleus indicates that the organism is a eukaryote rather than a prokaryote. Cell walls made of chitin are a characteristic of fungi.

6. **C.** A lower pH level indicates a more acidic substance. Because the pH scale is logarithmic, a substance with a pH of 3 will have 10^2 or 100 times more hydrogen ions than a substance with a pH of 5.

7. **A.** The producers in an ecosystem, such as plants, algae, and other photosynthesizers, will contain more energy than consumers or decomposers. Producers convert the energy reaching Earth as sunlight into chemical energy. Some of this energy is consumed by primary consumers when they feed on the producers, but much of it is lost and not transferred to higher trophic levels.

8. **C.** Food provides energy in the form of chemical energy, as the bonds

between glucose molecules (from digested food) are broken to make energy in the process of cellular respiration. This converts the chemical energy form food into the mechanical energy of the runner's motion.

9.   **C**. The weight of Book 1 on Book 2 is 20N. Therefore, according to Newton's third law of motion, Book 2 exerts a reactive force of 20 N on Book 1. The weight of both books combined on the table surface is 50 N. Therefore, the table exerts a normal force of 50 N on the bottom of the stack, Book 2.

10. **B**. Most weather phenomena occur in the lowest atmospheric layer, the troposphere. Therefore, a weather balloon would need to be at the next highest layer, the stratosphere, in order to observe the weather from above.

Review Chapter 2:
Arithmetic Reasoning

Types of Numbers

Positive and Negative Numbers

Numbers can be thought of as being arranged in order, on a line with zero at the center. The line extends to infinity to the right, where numbers are increasingly larger. It also extends forever to the left, with the negative numbers. Although the **absolute value** of negative numbers also increases, the negative sign in front of them means that they reach values that are increasingly smaller.

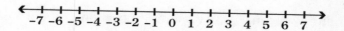

Think of positive numbers as money in a bank account and negative numbers as debt. If your account is at –850, you need +850 to erase the debt and be at 0. If your account is at +850, you can spend up to this much before going into debt again.

Rules for Negative Numbers

- To add two negative numbers, simply add the values of the two numbers. The answer will be negative.

- To add a negative number to a positive number, subtract the value of the negative number from the positive number.
- To subtract a negative number from a positive number, change the sign of the negative number and add the two numbers together.
- To subtract a positive number from a negative number, simply add the values of the two numbers together. The answer is a negative number.

Integers, Decimals, and Place Value

The numbers shown on the number line are **integers**, or whole numbers. Between each consecutive integer lie the **decimals**. The decimal 1.5 is exactly halfway between the integers 1 and 2. The digit 5 in 1.5 is in the tenths place, meaning that it has one-tenth the value of the same digit in the ones place (the number 5). The decimal 1.6 is one-tenth closer to 2. Exactly halfway between 1.5 and 1.6 lies the decimal 1.55. Decimals can be infinitely long, but the ASVAB will only ask you to work with up to three or four decimal places.

Rules for Decimals

- To add or subtract decimals, align the decimal points. "Missing" values should be treated as zeros.
- To multiply decimals, carry out multiplication as you would for integers. Then, count the number of decimal places in the numbers you multiplied, add these together, and count that many places from the right of the answer. This is where you insert the decimal point.

Prime Numbers

A prime number is a number that can be evenly divided only by itself and the number 1. (Oddly, the number 1 is not considered prime.) The prime numbers include 2, 3, 5, 7, 11, 13, etc.

Squares and Square Roots

A number multiplied by itself gives a **square** or squared number. The original number is the **root** of the square. When the square root is an integer, the square is a **perfect square**. The numbers 4, 9, 16, 25, and 36 are all perfect squares (and more can be found by squaring the integers. In contrast, the number 5 is not because its square root is 2.2360679...

Fractions

A fraction is simply a place on the number line between two integers (whole numbers). A fraction has two parts: a numerator (top) and a denominator (bottom). Think of a fraction as a part of a whole: The denominator tells you how many equal parts the whole is divided into, and the numerator tells you how many of those parts there are.

In a **proper** fraction, the numerator (the parts) is less than the denominator (the whole). Because there are less parts than one whole, the value of the fraction is less than 1. You will often see a fraction as part of a mixed number: an integer followed by a fraction. This fraction represents a number greater than the integer but less than the next integer. A fraction in which the numerator and the denominator are the same is equal to exactly 1.

Reducing Fractions

The fractions below represent parts of a pizza cut into different numbers of equal parts. Notice that they all specify exactly one half of each pizza.

Fractions can be reduced by dividing both the numerator and the denominator by a common factor, until they can no longer be evenly divided.

$$\frac{60}{96} \xrightarrow{\text{Divide by 3}} \frac{20}{32} \xrightarrow{\text{Divide by 4}} \frac{5}{8}$$

Converting Improper Fractions

Sometimes, you will see a fraction in which the top number (the numerator) is larger than the bottom number (the denominator). How can there be more parts than in a whole? An **improper fraction** represents a number greater than one. For example, if there are 16 parts in the numerator, but only 8 parts in the whole, this means that there are enough parts to make up two whole pizzas.

An improper fraction can be converted to a mixed number by dividing the numerator (top) by the denominator (bottom). Sometimes, this will result in a remainder, which will be the numerator of the proper fraction.

$$\frac{30}{7} \quad \boxed{\text{Divide by 7}} \quad 4\frac{4}{7}$$

Multiplying and Dividing Fractions

Multiplying fractions is easier than adding or subtracting them: Simply multiply the numerators of the two fractions and their denominators.

$$\frac{3}{8} \times \frac{2}{3} \quad \boxed{\begin{array}{c}\text{Multiply}\\\text{Multiply}\end{array}} \quad \frac{6}{24}$$

To divide one fraction by a second fraction, invert the second fraction and multiply.

$$\frac{3}{8} \div \frac{2}{3} = \frac{3}{8} \times \frac{3}{2} \quad \boxed{\begin{array}{c}\text{Multiply}\\\text{Multiply}\end{array}} \quad \frac{9}{16}$$

Adding and Subtracting Fractions

How can $\frac{5}{8}$ and $\frac{2}{6}$ be added together?

A fraction indicates the number of parts in a whole. If two fractions specify wholes made up of equal-sized parts, then they can be added together simply by adding the number of parts, or the numerators:

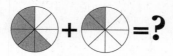

But what if the wholes are divided into parts of different size, as in the first example? In order to add and multiply fractions, you must convert them so that they have equal-sized parts. To do this, multiply the top and bottom of each fraction by the denominator of the other fraction. Don't worry, this won't change the value of the fractions. Remember that a fraction with the same number in the top and bottom is equal to 1, and any number multiplied by 1 is equal to itself.

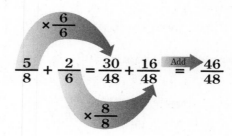

Converting Fractions to Decimals

Simply divide the numerator (top) of the fraction by the denominator (bottom). If it is a proper fraction, the numerator will be smaller than the denominator and the resulting decimal will have a value between 0 and 1.

$$\frac{6}{7} \xrightarrow{\text{Divide by 7}} 0.85714...$$

Percentages

A percent can be thought of as the numerator (top) of a fraction in which the denominator (bottom) is 100. A percent can be converted to a fraction simply by placing the number over 100 and reducing. A percent can also be converted to a decimal by moving the decimal two places to the left (in other words, dividing by 100).

$$75\% = \frac{75}{100} = \frac{3}{4}$$

$$75\% = 0.75$$

Like fractions and decimals, percents express part-whole relationships. Percents are often used to describe how much something has increased or decreased, or what fraction of the total cost of an item is the sales tax or discount. To calculate a certain percent of a given value:

- Convert the percent to a decimal.
- Multiply the decimal by the value.
- If the problem asks for a percent increase or decrease, add or subtract this result from the original value.

Example: The number of customers at a restaurant is 560 one month, and this number increases by 20 percent the next month. To calculate the new number of customers, multiply the original number (560) by the percent converted to decimal form (0.20). Add this result to the original number of customers.

$$20\% \times 560 = 0.20 \times 560 = 112$$

$$560 + 112 = 672$$

You may also be given a final value after a percent increase or decrease has been applied and asked to calculate the original value. For example, you may be told the final price of a sweater after a given sales tax has been added and asked to find the original price. In this case, the final price consists of 100 percent of the original price plus the sales tax percent of that price. The steps below show how to quickly determine the original price. This method also works if you are asked to find the original value after a discount or percent reduction has been applied.

- Final price = 100% of original price + tax % on original price = $45.00

- Sales tax = 5%
- Final price = original price × (100% + 5%) = original price × 105% = original price × 1.05
- Original price = final price ÷ 1.05 = $45 ÷ 1.05 = $42.86

Check your answer: The original price of the sweater must be less than the price plus tax.

Averages

To many people, the term *average* means "somewhere in the middle." However, in math there are three different types of averages with very specific meanings:

- **Mean:** This is the usual meaning of the word *average*. (If you are asked for simply the *average*, you are usually being asked for the mean.) To find the mean of a set of values, add the values together and divide by the number of values. For the set of values 47, 44, 49, 39, and 48, the sum of those values is 227. This number, divided by 5, is 45.4.
- **Median:** When the set of values is ordered from least to greatest, the value that falls in the middle is the median. Of the remaining values, half are greater than the median and half are less. If the set has an even number of values, there will be two values in the middle. The median is the mean of these two values. For the set of values 47, 44, 49, 39, and 48, the median is 47 (39 and 44 are less than 47, and 48 and 48 are greater than 47).
- **Mode:** The mode is the value that occurs most often in the set of values.

In addition, the **range** of a set of values is the difference between the highest and lowest value. For the set of values 47, 44, 49, 39, and 48, the range is 49 – 39 = 10.

Rates and Ratios

A rate is a description of how one thing changes with another. A rate is similar to a ratio. For example, a speed is the ratio of distance traveled to units of time. Other rates may include the amount of work done per person, number of tasks accomplished per hour, cost per number or items, etc.

Questions about rate most often involve simple multiplication or division. A good way to tell which is required is to think of rates as fractions. For example, a speed of 60 miles per hour is the fraction $\dfrac{60 \text{ miles}}{\text{hour}}$ (the term in the denominator actually means 1 hour). The unit on the bottom will cancel if you multiply the fraction by the same unit. Multiplying $\dfrac{60 \text{ miles}}{\text{hour}}$ by 2 hours gives you 120 miles: the hour units cancel out. When solving rate problems, canceling units should leave you with the units being asked for.

Ann writes 5 letters per month. How many letters does she write in 6 months?

$$\frac{5 \text{ letters}}{\text{month}} \times 6 \text{ months} = 30 \text{ letters}$$

Water bottles cost $3.00 each. How much do 12 water bottles cost?

$$\frac{\$3.00}{\text{water bottle}} \times 12 \text{ water bottles} = \$36.00$$

A vehicle gets 30 miles per gallon of gasoline. How many miles can the car travel on 11 gallons of gasoline?

$$\frac{30 \text{ miles}}{\text{gallon}} \times 11 \text{ gallons} = 33 \text{ miles}$$

A vehicle gets 30 miles per gallon of gasoline. How much gasoline is required for a 1000 mile trip?

$$\frac{\text{gallon}}{30 \text{ miles}} \times 1000 \text{ miles} = 33.33 \text{ gallons}$$

Ratios and Proportions

A ratio is similar to a rate in that it describes a relationship between two things: Either a part to a whole or a part to a second part of the same whole. The examples below are ratios:

- In a class of 17 students, 11 are girls. The ratio of girls to students is 11:17.

- In a class of students, 11 are girls and 6 are boys. The ratio of girls to boys is 11:6.

A proportion is similar to a ratio, except that it compares continuous quantities (height, width, time) instead of discrete quantities.

- For a line of computer monitors the height is two-thirds of the width. The proportion of height to width for these monitors is 2:3.

A question may give values and ask for a ratio. Example: If 280 A-line stereos are sold in a month, and 1,380 B-line stereos are sold in the same month, what is the ratio of A-line stereos to B-line stereos? To find the ratio, think of the two values as parts of a fraction, with the first part (A-line) on top: $\frac{280}{1400}$. Then, reduce this fraction: $\frac{1}{5}$. The ratio is 1:5. Note that if the question had asked for the ratio of B-line stereos to A-line stereos sold, the ratio would be reversed (5:1).

A question may also ask for a value, given the ratio. Example: If the same ratio (1:5) holds for the next month, and a total of 1800 stereos are sold, how many B-line stereos are sold? Note that the total, 1800, represents the A-line and B-line stereos combined. Divide this number by the sum of 1 and 5: $1800 \div 6 = 300$. This is the value of a single unit in the ratio. Multiply this value by the number of units of B-line stereos sold: $300 \times 5 = 1500$.

Probability

A probability is the chance or likelihood of something occurring. Probabilities describe events that have happened or may predict the chances that something will happen. The questions you are likely to encounter will ask you to predict outcomes using probabilities.

- When there are a number n possible outcomes, all equally likely, the chance of any one outcome is $\dfrac{1}{n}$. For example, if you roll a six-sided die, the chances of it coming up on any one side are equal. Therefore, the probability of rolling a 5 is 1 in 6, or $\dfrac{1}{6}$.

- When asked about the probability of a range of outcomes, add the probabilities of each outcome alone. For example, the probability of rolling an even number is the sum of the probabilities of rolling a 2, 4, or 6, and the probability of each of these is $\dfrac{1}{6}$. It is therefore $\dfrac{1}{6} + \dfrac{1}{6} + \dfrac{1}{6} = \dfrac{3}{6} = \dfrac{1}{2}$. Half the time, an even number comes up.

- When asked about the probability of two or more outcomes occurring, multiply the probabilities of each outcome alone. For example, the probability of rolling a 1 and then, immediately after, rolling a 2 is the product of the probability of each event alone $\dfrac{1}{6}$. It is therefore $\dfrac{1}{6} \times \dfrac{1}{6} = \dfrac{1}{36}$.

Practice Questions

1. Sarah swam a lap around her pool in 2.16 minutes. The next day, she completed the lap in 1.9 minutes. How much more time did Sara take to complete the lap on the first day than on the second day?

    A.   2.35 minutes
    B.   1.97 minutes
    C.   1.07 minutes
    D.   0.26 minutes

2. A thermos fits one half-cup of liquid. How many thermoses are needed to hold 4.5 cups of liquid?

   A. 2
   B. 3
   C. 5
   D. 9

3. A summer camp enrolls 64 students. If the ratio of boys to girls at the camp is 9:7, how many girls are enrolled?

   A. 28
   B. 32
   C. 36
   D. 42

January	February	March	April	May	June
$40.00	$45.00	$65.00	$80.00	$55.00	$90

4. Juan records the amount he spends on gas for his car each month. What is the average amount he spent on gas for the months shown in the table?

   A. $47.50
   B. $55.00
   C. $62.50
   D. $65.00

5. June and Keisha open a car wash in their driveway. June can wash 3 cars in one hour, and Keisha can wash 4 cars in the same amount of time. If they charge $5 per wash, what is the most June and Keisha could earn in 6 hours?

   A. $210
   B. $240
   C. $300
   D. $360

6. Jerome spent $340.78 on his credit card account in a single month. In the same month, he returned a pair of boots that he had bought previously. The price of the boots, $66.44, was credited to his account. What will be Jerome's credit card balance for that month?

   A. −$274.34
   B. −$286.74
   C. −$396.92
   D. −$407.22

7. What is the next prime number after 47?

   A. 49
   B. 51
   C. 53
   D. 57

8. A car costs $15,540 after an end-of-year discount is applied. If the discount is 15 percent, which is the closest to the original price of the car before the discount?

   A. $16,355
   B. $16,985
   C. $17,870
   D. $18,280

9. The storage capacity of a digital device increases 80 percent per year. If this rate holds steady, which is closest to the storage capacity of a 1-gigabyte device after 5 years?

   A. 3 Gb
   B. 4 Gb
   C. 10 Gb
   D. 18 Gb

10. Champagne glasses can safely hold 100 milliliters of liquid. If there are 12 bottles of champagne, each containing 750 milliliters, how many champagne glasses can be filled?

   A. 62
   B. 90
   C. 120
   D. 144

Answer Explanations

1. **D.** The time difference between the first and second days can be found by subtracting the time required to complete the lap on the second day from the time required on the first day. When adding decimals, align the decimal point. $2.16 - 1.9 = 0.26$.

2. **D.** To determine the number of thermoses needed, divide the total amount of liquid by the amount held in a single thermos.

$$4.5 \text{ cups} \quad \frac{\frac{1}{2}\text{cup}}{\text{thermos}} = 4.5 \text{ cups} \times \frac{\text{thermos}}{\frac{1}{2}\text{cup}} = 9 \text{ thermoses}$$

3. **A.** First, determine the ratio of girls to total students. If the ratio of boys to girls is 9:7, then the ratio of girls to total students is 7:(9+7) = 7:16. Next, convert the ratio to find the number of girls. Dividing 64 by 16 yields 4. Multiply the ratio of girls by 4 to find the number of girls: 28.

4. **C.** First, sum the amounts spent each month: $40 + $45 + $65 + $80 + $55 + $90 = $375. Next, divide this sum by the number of values that were summed: $375 \div 6 = $62.50.

5. **A.** To determine the amount that June and Keisha could earn by washing cars for 6 hours, begin by finding the number of cars per hour that they can, working together, wash in an hour: $3 + 4 = 7$. Multiply this number by the number of hours (6) and the amount earned per car ($5):

$$\frac{7 \text{ cars}}{\text{hours}} \times \frac{\$5}{\text{car}} \times 6 \text{ hours} = \$210$$

6. **A.** To determine Jerome's balance, subtract the amount he spent ($340.78) from the amount credited to the account for the returned item: $66.44 - $340.78 = -$274.34.

7. **C.** A prime number is evenly divisible only by 1 and itself. The number 51 is not prime because it is a multiple of 17 and 3. The next prime number is 53.

8. **D.** To find the original price of the car before the discount is applied,

divide the final price ($15,540) by the total percent after the discount (100% – 15% = 85%). $15,540 ÷ 0.85 = $18,282.

9. **D**. Apply the percent increase to the starting size year by year: After 1 year, the storage capacity will increase to 1 Gb + (0.8)(1 Gb) = 1.8 Gb. After two years, applying the percent increase to the new capacity, it will increase to 1.8 Gb + (0.8)(1.8 Gb) = 3.24 Gb. After three years, it will be 3.24 Gb + (0.8)(3.24 Gb) = 5.832 Gb. After four years, it will be 5.832 Gb + (0.8)(5.832 Gb) = 10.4976 Gb. Finally, after five years, the capacity will have increased to 10.4976 Gb + (0.8)(10.4976 Gb) = 18.89568 Gb.

10. **B**. To determine the number of glasses needed, first find the total amount of champagne by multiplying the number of bottles by the amount of champagne in each. Then divide this total amount by the amount of champagne that can safely be held in each glass. This is shown below using the "invert-and-multiply" rule.

$$12 \text{ bottles} \times \frac{750 \text{ mL}}{\text{bottle}} \times \frac{\text{glass}}{100 \text{ mL}} = 90 \text{ glasses}$$

Review Chapter 3: Word Knowledge

What Is Word Knowledge?

In terms of the ASVAB, Word Knowledge is one of four subtests that make up the Armed Forces Qualification Test, or AFQT. The Word Knowledge subtest includes 35 questions that must be answered in 11 minutes. Your score on the Word Knowledge subtest is factored into your overall AFQT score. Your AFQT score is important, because it determines your eligibility for the military service of your choice. The higher your score, the more choices you'll have. Therefore, word knowledge is also important; but what does it mean?

The phrase *word knowledge* means "knowing words." More specifically, it means understanding the definitions, or meanings, of words. To gain more knowledge of words, you have to build your vocabulary, and to build you vocabulary, you have to start with the basics.

Parts of Words

Think of a word as a salad. A salad is composed of many different vegetables—for example, lettuce, tomatoes, cucumbers, and carrots. Similarly, a word is composed of different word parts known as roots, prefixes, and suffixes. By identifying the meanings of word parts, you can identify the meanings of unknown words.

Roots

A **root** is the main part of a word. It may be a word that can stand on its own, such as *graph*, which means "write," or it may be a group of letters that serves as the base upon which other words are built, such as *nov*, which means "new." The following table includes a list of a hundred common roots and their meanings. Learning these root words will help you figure out the meanings of many unfamiliar words.

ROOT	MEANING	ROOT	MEANING
act	do	ject	throw
aer(o)	air	junct	join
agri	farming	jur(e)	swear
anim	life	liber	free
ann(u)	year	lingu	language
anthro(p)	man	lith	rock, stone
aqua	water	lum	light
astro	star	magn	large
aud	hear	mal	bad
bene	good	man(u)	hand
bibli(o)	book	mar	sea
bio	life	mater	mother
brev	short	ment	measure
cardio	heart	micro	small
cas	fall	mit	send
ced(e)	go	mono	one
cid(e)	kill	mort	death
chrom(o)	color	mot	move
chron	time	multi	many
circum	around	nom	name
clud(e)	close	nov	new
cogn(o)	know	oper	work

ROOT	MEANING	ROOT	MEANING
corp	body	ortho	straight
cred	believe	pater	father
crypto	hidden	pat(h)	suffer, feel
curr	run	ped	foot
dem	people	phon	sound
derm	skin	pod	foot
dic(t)	say	port	carry
domin	rule	press	squeeze
duc(t)	lead	psych(o)	mind
dyna	power	pyro	fire
erg(o)	work	rupt	break
equ(i)	equal	scrib, script	write
fer	carry	sens, sent	think, feel
fin	end	sol	alone
flect	bend	spect	look
flu(x)	flow	sphere	ball
form	shape	struct	build
frac, frag	break	techno	skill
frater	brother	tele	far
geo	earth	temp	time
graph	write	terra	land
gress	step, go	therm(o)	heat
helio	sun	tract	pull, drag
herbi	grass	vert	turn
hetero	different	vic(t)	conquer
homo	same	vis(io)	see
hydr(o)	water	voc, vok	voice, call
icon(o)	image	zoo	animal life

Prefixes

A **prefix** is a group of letters added to the beginning of a word that changes the overall meaning of the word, such as *trans-*, which means "across." For example, adding the prefix *trans-* to the root word *fer* creates the word *transfer*. You know that the root word *fer* means "carry," so you can conclude that *transfer* means "carry across." This meaning is pretty close the definition included in the dictionary—"to convey or carry from one person, place, or situation to another." The following table includes a list of common prefixes.

PREFIX	MEANING	PREFIX	MEANING
a-	not	intra-	within
ab(s)-	away, from	mis-	wrong
ante-	before	omni-	all
anti-	against	over-	above
bi-	two	poly-	many
con(tra)-	against	post-	after
de-	from, away	pre-	before
ex-	out of	re-	again
extra-	beyond	semi-	half
fore-	before	sub-	under
hyper-	above	super-	above
hypo-	below	syn-	together
il-, im-, in-	not	trans-	across
in-	into	un-	not
inter-	between	under-	below

Suffixes

A **suffix** is a group of letters added to the end of a word that, like a prefix, changes the overall meaning of the word, such as *-ful*, which means, "full of." For example, adding the suffix *-ful* to the word *regret* creates the word *regretful*. Based on your understanding of suffixes, you can conclude that *regretful* means "full of regret." The following table includes a list common suffixes

SUFFIX	MEANING	SUFFIX	MEANING
-able, -ible	capable of	-itis	inflammation
-age	action, result	-ize	cause, treat, become
-al	characterized by	-less	without
-ance	instance of an action	-let	version of
-cracy, crat	government, rule	-log, -logue	speech
-en	made of	-man	relating to humans
-er	more, one who	-mania	craving, strong desire
-est	most	-ness	possessing a quality
-ful	full	-oid	similar to
-ic	consisting of	-or	one who
-ical	related to	-ous	full of, having
-ion	action or process	-phobe, -phobia	fear
-ish	relating to	-scope, -scopy	visual exam
-ism	state, quality	-ty	state, condition, quality
-ist	characteristic of	-y	made up of, characterized by

It's important to note that the lists of roots, prefixes, and suffixes provided here are by no means comprehensive, but they do provide good building blocks for expanding your vocabulary. In addition, keep in mind that these lists can sometimes overlap. A word included in the roots list may show up as a prefix in some words. For example, the word *bibliography* includes two roots—*biblio* and *graph*—and the suffix *-y*. In this case, *biblio* is serving as a prefix to the root *graph*. Regardless, the same rule applies: Break the word into its parts to figure out its meaning. *Biblio* means "book," *graph* means "write," and *-y* means "made up of." Therefore, the definition of *bibliography*—"a list made up of books consulted by an author while writing"—makes total sense.

Synonyms and Antonyms

Some questions on the Word Knowledge portion of the ASVAB ask you to identify the synonym of another word. **Synonyms** are words that have the same, or nearly the same, meaning. For example, some synonyms for the word *hot* are *boiling, blistering, burning, scorching, sizzling,* and *warm*. Other questions on the ASVAB ask about the meanings of words in a sentence. When a word is used in a sentence, you can look for context clues about its meaning. **Context clues** are words or phrases around the unknown word that help you figure out its meaning. Consider the following sentence:

> The <u>startled</u> girl jumped and screamed when everyone yelled, "Surprise!"

If you didn't know the meaning of the word *startled* in this sentence, context clues such as *jumped and screamed* and *Surprise* would help you determine that *startled* means *shocked* or *surprised*. In this case, a synonym for *startle, surprise,* appears in the sentence.

Sometimes antonyms can provide context clues about the meanings of unknown words, too. **Antonyms** are words that have opposite, or nearly opposite, meanings. For example, some antonyms for the word *hot* are *arctic, cold, cool, freezing,* and *icy*. Consider the following sentence:

> The absence <u>tarnished</u> the boy's otherwise perfect attendance record.

If you didn't know the meaning of the word *tarnished* in this sentence, context clues such as the phrase *otherwise perfect* would help you determine that *tarnished* means *flawed* or *imperfect*. In this case, an antonym for *tarnished*, *perfect*, appears in the sentence.

Word Knowledge Resources

When it comes to learning new words, don't rule out old standbys such as dictionaries and thesauruses. A **dictionary** is a comprehensive list of words and their meanings. A **thesaurus** is a comprehensive list of words and their synonyms and antonyms. You should also consider creating a **vocabulary notebook**, which is a notebook in which you record unfamiliar words. For example, if you encounter a new word while reading—a newspaper, a website, a magazine, etc.—underline it or jot it in your vocabulary notebook, so you can remember to look up the meaning of the word later.

To study for the Word Knowledge portion of the ASVAB, consider making flash cards. A **flash card** is a small slip of paper or an index card that contains a word on one side and its definition (and/or its synonyms and antonyms) on the other. Create flash cards for words you have trouble remembering, so you can quickly study them whenever you have free time.

Practice Questions

Directions: For each question, select the answer choice that contains the word that most nearly matches the meaning of the underlined word.

1. The assembly line manufacturing process developed by Ford Motor Company in the early twentieth century was an <u>innovative</u> way to mass-produce cars at a lower cost for consumers.

   A. Difficult
   B. Expensive
   C. New
   D. Strange

2. The music had an upbeat <u>tempo</u> that kept everyone dancing.

    A. Change
    B. Pace
    C. Step
    D. Volume

3. <u>Fraternal</u> most nearly means

    A. brotherly.
    B. carrying.
    C. collegiate.
    D. identical.

4. <u>Incognito</u> most nearly means

    A. corporate.
    B. knowledgeable.
    C. undercover.
    D. victorious.

5. When the candidate was elected, her opportunities to enact change seemed <u>infinite</u>.

    A. Achievable
    B. Beneficial
    C. Devious
    D. Endless

6. <u>Preface</u> most nearly means

    A. excerpt.
    B. introduction.
    C. praise.
    D. scope.

7. The sight of gray clouds and dead leaves did nothing to brighten her <u>somber</u> mood.

    A. Anxious
    B. Calm
    C. Gloomy
    D. Smug

8. The man was <u>meticulous</u> when shelving his movie collection, separating the films by genre and arranging them in alphabetical order.

    A. Careful
    B. Divisive
    C. Erratic
    D. Frugal

9. The firefighter faced a <u>perilous</u> situation as he climbed down the face of the steep cliff to rescue the missing hiker.

    A. Exciting
    B. Notable
    C. Risky
    D. Timid

10. The team of underdogs showed an <u>indomitable</u> spirit during the game and emerged victorious.

    A. Determined
    B. Indifferent
    C. Sympathetic
    D. Unbelievable

Answer Explanations

1. **C.** The word *innovative* includes the prefix *in-*, which means "into," and the root word *nov*, which means "new." These two clues suggest that *innovative* means "into something new." Therefore, the word closest in meaning to *innovative* is *new*.

2. **B.** The word *tempo* includes the root word *temp*, which means "time." This clue suggests that the correct answer is associated with the timing of the music. Therefore, the word closest in meaning to *tempo* is *pace*, which is the rate at which something moves.

3. **A.** The word *fraternal* includes the root word *frater*, which means "brother." Therefore, the word closest in meaning to *fraternal* is *brotherly*, which means "like brothers" or "in a brotherly way."

4. **C.** The word *incognito* includes the prefix *in-*, which means "not," and the root word *cogn*, which means "know." These two clues suggest that *incognito* means "not known." Therefore, the word closest in meaning to *incognito* is *undercover*, which means "hidden" or "secret."

5. **D.** The word *infinite* includes the prefix *in-*, which means "not," and the root word *fin*, which means "end." These two clues suggest that *infinite* means "no end." Therefore, the word closest in meaning to *infinite* is *endless*, which means "without end."

6. **B.** The word *preface* includes the prefix *pre-*, which means "before." This clue suggests that the correct answer is associated with something that comes before something else. Therefore, the word closest in meaning to *preface* is *introduction*, which is the part of a book or article that comes before the main body of text.

7. **C.** Context clues such as the phrases *gray clouds*, *dead leaves*, and *did nothing to brighten* suggest that the word *somber* means "grave" or "sad." Therefore, the word closest in meaning to *somber* is *gloomy*, which means "dismal" or "depressed."

8. **A.** Context clues such as the phrases *separating…by genre* and *arranging…in alphabetical order* suggest that the word *meticulous* means

"painstaking" or "particular." Therefore, the word closest in meaning to *meticulous* is *careful*, which means "with much care."

9.   **C.** Context clues such as the phrase *climbed down the face of the steep cliff* suggest that the word *perilous* means "dangerous." Therefore, the word closest in meaning to *perilous* is *risky*, which means "characterized by risk" or "unsafe."

10. **A.** The word *indomitable* includes the prefix *in-*, which means "not," the root word *domin*, which means "rule," and the suffix *-able*, which means "capable of." These three clues suggest that *indomitable* means "not capable of being ruled." Therefore, the word closest in meaning to *indomitable* is *determined*, which means "strong" or "dogged."

Review Chapter 4:
Paragraph Comprehension

Reading for Understanding

Like Word Knowledge, Paragraph Comprehension is one of four subtests that make up the ASVAB's Armed Forces Qualification Test, or AFQT. The Paragraph Comprehension subtest includes 15 questions that must be answered in 13 minutes. Your score on the Paragraph Comprehension subtest is factored into your overall AFQT score, which determines your eligibility for the military service of your choice. A higher AFQT score means more choices.

To comprehend a paragraph is to read it and consider what it says and what it means. In other words, paragraph comprehension is basically reading for understanding. Paragraph Comprehension questions focus on a variety of different aspects of paragraphs, such as main idea, details, and organizational structure.

Main Idea

The **main idea** of a paragraph is a phrase or statement that captures the most important point in that paragraph. A main idea can be stated or implied. A **stated** main idea is a topic sentence that presents the most important point in the paragraph. The topic sentence often appears at the beginning or end of the paragraph, but it can appear elsewhere in the paragraph, too. Consider the following paragraph:

> A concussion is one of the most common types of traumatic brain injuries. Often caused by a blow to the head, a concussion can cause a temporary loss of brain function and must be taken seriously. To treat a concussion, physicians recommend plenty of rest and time for the injury to properly heal itself. In a few weeks' time, concussion symptoms typically subside, though complications do arise on occasion.

In this paragraph, the stated main idea is "A concussion is one of the most common types of traumatic brain injuries." The rest of the paragraph provides details to support this idea, such as the causes and effects of a concussion and the recommended treatment.

Unlike a stated main idea, an **implied** main idea is not stated directly in the paragraph. To determine an implied main idea, you have to figure out how the individual details in a paragraph tie together—the idea that unites all of them. Consider the following paragraph:

> The Atlantic region saw an above-average number of tropical storms in 2005, with a record fifteen reaching hurricane status. The same year, a record four hurricanes reached Category 5 status, the highest ranking on the scale used to measure hurricane strength. The high number of strong hurricanes resulted in the most damage ever recorded in a single season. In addition, the season refused to end until January 6, 2006, which made it the latest end to a hurricane season.

Though it is not stated directly in the paragraph, the details in this paragraph imply the main idea: "The 2005 Atlantic hurricane season broke many records." Each detail in the paragraph supports this main idea.

Details

Details, as suggested previously, are statements that support the main idea. Each detail in a paragraph provides additional information about the main topic. The following are some examples of details that you may encounter when reading:

- **arguments**—statements intended to persuade others to agree with a particular way of thinking or believing
- **definitions**—statements that provide meaning
- **descriptions**—statements that appeal to the senses by explaining how things taste, feel, look, sound, or smell
- **examples**—models that serve to represent a whole group
- **facts**—statements that provide objective information
- **opinions**—personal beliefs or judgments
- **statistics**—a collection of numbers, figures, percentages, or other data

Some questions on the Paragraph Comprehension subtest of the ASVAB may ask about individual details in a paragraph (or a group of paragraphs), while others may require you to use the given details to figure out main ideas, make inferences, or draw conclusions.

Inferences and Conclusions

If you enjoy solving puzzles, then inference and conclusion questions will be a snap for you. When authors write, they don't always tell you everything they want you to know; they leave it up to you to figure out certain pieces of information. They provide you with the pieces of the puzzle—facts and details. Then, you have to fit the facts and details together to solve the puzzle and see the big picture—in other words, to make inferences and draw conclusions.

Inferences and conclusions are similar, but they do have some minor differences. An **inference** is an assumption made based on given facts and prior knowledge. Consider the following sentence:

Before stepping outside, Jeremy donned a ski jacket, a wool hat and mittens, and a pair of waterproof snow boots.

What can you infer from this sentence?

- **Given facts:** Jeremy has bundled up in warm clothes.
- **Prior knowledge:** Warm clothes are typically worn in cold weather.
- **Inference:** The weather outside is very cold.

By combining the given facts with your prior knowledge, you can infer that wherever Jeremy is, it's cold outside.

A **conclusion** is an assumption made by combining a number of given details. Consider the following sentences:

Before trying to sink a putt during a game of golf, consider the distance between your ball and the hole. Next, examine the green to determine if a break will cause your ball to roll one way or the other, so you can adjust the direction of your swing. Then, take a few practice swings to determine how hard you need to tap the ball.

Based on the paragraph, what can you conclude about putting?

- **Detail:** You have to consider the distance between your ball and the hole.
- **Detail:** You have to examine the green and adjust the direction of your swing.
- **Detail:** You have to practice your swing.
- **Conclusion:** Putting requires great skill and concentration.

By combining the given details, you can conclude that putting is more than just tapping a golf ball into a hole; it requires great skill and concentration.

Understanding how to make inferences and draw conclusions is an important skill when reading for understanding. These skills can help you determine main ideas and even figure out the meanings of vocabu-lary words.

Vocabulary

While the ASVAB devotes the entire Word Knowledge subtest to under-standing vocabulary, it's not uncommon for a few vocabulary questions to pop up in the Paragraph Comprehension subtest. When answering vocabulary questions, it's important to look for **context clues**, which are words or phrases in the paragraph that help you figure out the meaning of a particular word. In some cases, you'll need to choose the correct definition of a word. In others, you'll need to choose the word that best replaces a given word in the paragraph. These types of questions often involve **homonyms**, which are words that sound the same and are spelled the same but that have different meanings. An example of a homonym is the word *bark*. Consider the following sentences:

The dog has a very loud *bark*. (the sound a dog makes)

The *bark* on the white birch tree is peeling. (the outer covering of a tree)

The instructor's *bark* is worse than his bite. (an angry tone of voice)

To determine the correct meaning of the word *bark* in a paragraph, you would have to look for clues that suggest its meaning. Now read this sentence and consider the question that follows:

My brother-in-law is skilled in the carpentry trade and often helps to build homes for Habitat for Humanity.

The word *trade* is closest in meaning to

    A. practice.
    B. exchange.
    C. occupation.
    D. publication.

While all four answer choices are meanings of the word *trade*, only one matches the meaning of *trade* within the context of the sentence: *occupation*. You could replace the word *trade* with the word *occupation* and it wouldn't change the meaning of the sentence: My brother-in-law is skilled in the carpentry *occupation* and often helps to build homes for Habitat for Humanity.

Organization

Some questions on the Paragraph Comprehension subtest of the ASVAB may ask about a paragraph's organizational structure. **Organizational structure** is the way in which the ideas in a paragraph relate to each other. Consider the following sentence:

> Shark attacks on humans sometimes occur in recreational swimming areas because sharks mistake brightly colored swimsuits, sparkling jewelry, and contrasting tan lines for their usual prey.

This sentence uses a cause-and-effect organizational structure to explain how two ideas relate to each other. The cause explains why something happens, and the effect explains the result. In this case, "sharks mistake brightly colored swimsuits, sparkling jewelry, and contrasting lines for their usual prey" is the cause and "Shark attacks on humans sometimes occur in recreational swimming areas" is the effect.

The following table identifies some of the most common organizational structures that authors use to connect their ideas and some key words associated with each type of organization.

ORGANIZATIONAL STRUCTURE	EXPLANATION	KEY WORDS
Cause and effect	Cause-and-effect organization explains why something happens (the cause) and the result of what happens (the effect).	• as a result • because • consequently • due to • hence • since • therefore • thus
Chronological (sequential) order	Chronological, or sequential, order lists steps in the order in which they should occur or explains events in the order in which they happened.	• after • before • eventually • finally • first • following • last • later • meanwhile • next • previously • then
Comparison and contrast	Comparison-and-contrast organization explains the similarities and/or differences between two subjects.	• although • both • conversely • differ • different • however • instead • like • likewise • on the contrary • same • similarly • unlike • whereas
Problem and solution	Problem-and-solution organization describes a problem and then develops a possible solution to the problem.	• a possible solution • if…then • the answer is • the problem is • therefore

ORGANIZATIONAL STRUCTURE	EXPLANATION	KEY WORDS
Spatial organization	Spatial organization presents information in terms of direction or physical location.	• above • below • behind • down • east • in front of • left • near • next to • north • right • south • under • up • west

Paragraph Comprehension Tips

On other reading tests, you were likely told to read passages carefully before answering the questions. When it comes to the Paragraph Comprehension subtest of the ASVAB, however, you simply won't have time to carefully consider each paragraph before answering the questions—after all, you have less than a minute to answer each question! Instead, practice active reading.

- Read the question or questions *before* you read the paragraph. This helps you determine exactly what information you need to find as you read. Don't read the answer choices, however, as this could cause confusion.

- As you read the paragraph, be on the lookout for the information that you think answers the question.

- When you find this information, try to think of an answer to the question in your own words.

- Then, scan the answer choices for an option similar to the one you developed.
- If you can't find a matching answer choice, try eliminating answers that you know are incorrect. Then, focus on the best possible answer from your remaining choices.

Practice Questions

Directions: Read each paragraph and answer the question or complete the statement that follows it. Select the answer choice that best answers the question or completes the statement.

In the water cycle, heat from the sun warms water on Earth's surface, which causes it to turn into a gas, water vapor, in a process known as evaporation. As water vapor rises into the air, it begins to cool. As a result, the water vapor changes back into a liquid—a process called condensation—and forms clouds. Eventually, so much water condenses that the clouds become too heavy for the air to hold, and the water begins to fall back to the earth as precipitation. The water collects in rivers, lakes, and oceans, or it soaks into the soil and becomes groundwater. When the sun reemerges after the rain, hail, sleet, or snow, the whole cycle begins again.

1. During condensation, water vapor changes from a gas to a liquid because it

   A. cools as it rises into the air.
   B. is too heavy for clouds to hold.
   C. is warmed by heat from the sun.
   D. falls to the earth as precipitation.

Raindrops pelted the window even harder as I made the turn onto Pine Street. "Charlie, why are you doing this to me?" I asked the empty car. I scanned the deserted sidewalks for any sign of him. Despite the driving rain, I rolled down the window and called his name at the top of my lungs: "Charlie!" I was about to give up hope and return home when I caught movement out of the corner of my eye. *There!* I could see him sitting near a lamppost, his dejected gaze cast toward the ground. A wave of relief washed over me as I slowed the car to a stop. I grabbed my umbrella and Charlie's leash from the seat and dashed across the street.

2.   Which of the following can be inferred from the paragraph?

A.   The narrator's dog had run away from home.
B.   The narrator had broken down during a storm.
C.   The narrator had been searching for a lost child.
D.   The narrator's evening drive had been ruined by rain.

Ernest Henry Shackleton was an explorer who led an expedition to cross Antarctica. Unfortunately, before Shackleton and his crew could reach the frozen continent, their ship, the *Endurance*, became trapped in pack ice in the Weddell Sea. Eventually, the crew was forced to abandon the ship and set up camp on a large ice floe for several months. When land finally came into view, Shackleton and his men piled into three lifeboats and sailed to Elephant Island. After the team set up camp, Shackleton selected a small group of men to accompany him on an eight-hundred-mile journey to South Georgia Island, where they could get help. After landing there, Shackleton and two other men spent more than a day trekking across the island. Twenty-two months after the *Endurance* first set sail for Antarctica, Shackleton returned to rescue the rest of his crew. Despite the loss of his ship, an unforgiving climate, and hundreds of treacherous miles, Shackleton did not lose a single crew member.

3.   What happened right after Shackleton landed on South Georgia Island?

   A.   His ship became trapped in pack ice and sank.
   B.   His team sailed to Elephant Island in lifeboats.
   C.   He journeyed across the island to look for help.
   D.   He returned to Elephant Island to rescue his crew.

Proper treatment of minor wounds, such as cuts and scrapes, is paramount for avoiding future infections. First, rinse the wound with water to help wash away debris and cleanse the wound. Then, using tweezers sterilized with alcohol, remove any splinters or pebbles from the wound. Next, wash the wound again, this time using mild soap and fresh, clean water. When the wound is clean, gently pat it dry. Apply an antibacterial ointment to the wound to prevent infection. Finally, cover the wound with a bandage to keep out bacteria.

4.   In this paragraph, what does the word *paramount* mean?

   A.   Skilled
   B.   Extensive
   C.   Repetitive
   D.   Important

Managers at the Triangle Shirtwaist Factory, which occupied the top three floors of the Asch Building in New York City, often locked the doors to stairways and elevators to prevent employees, mainly women, from stealing and taking breaks without permission. This practice eventually led to the deaths of 146 garment workers, some as young as fourteen years old. On Saturday, March 25, 1911, a fire started in a scrap bin and quickly spread through the factory. While some workers escaped the blaze, many were trapped and died from smoke inhalation and burns. Others jumped out windows to escape the fire, falling more than a hundred feet.

5. What is the main idea of this paragraph?

   A. The Triangle Shirtwaist Factory fire led to new workplace safety laws.
   B. The Triangle Shirtwaist Factory fire was a horrible tragedy in New York's history.
   C. With proper fire training, the Triangle Shirtwaist Factory fire could have been prevented.
   D. Managers at the Triangle Shirtwaist Factory hired girls as young as fourteen to work in the factory.

Answer Explanations

1. **A.** This question asks about a detail in the paragraph—namely, the cause of a given effect. The effect is that water vapor changes from a gas to a liquid during condensation. According to the paragraph, the change results from the cooling of water vapor as it rises into the air.

2. **A.** This question asks you to make an inference. Details in the paragraph suggest that the narrator is searching for someone named Charlie. When the narrator finds Charlie, she grabs a leash from the seat of her car. Prior knowledge suggests that people often keep dogs on leashes. Therefore, by combining details in the paragraph with prior knowledge, it can be inferred that the narrator's dog had run away from home.

3. **C.** This question asks about chronological events in the paragraph—specifically, what happened *right after* Shackleton landed on South Georgia Island. The phrase "After landing there" is a clue about what Shackleton did right after he arrived on South Georgia Island. According to the paragraph, he and two other men spent more than a day trekking across the island to get help. Although Shackleton did return to Elephant Island to rescue the rest of his crew after finding help on South Georgia Island, this is not what he did *right after* landing there.

4. **D.** This question asks about an unfamiliar word in the paragraph. Context clues in the paragraph are the phrases "Proper treatment" and

REVIEW CHAPTER 4: PARAGRAPH COMPREHENSION   187

"for avoiding future infections." These clues suggest that without proper treatment, future infections could occur. Therefore, proper treatment must be *important*, which is another word for *paramount*.

5. **B**. This question asks about the main idea of the paragraph. In this paragraph, the main idea is implied, which means that the main idea is not stated directly in the paragraph. The main idea is, "The Triangle Shirtwaist Factory fire was a horrible tragedy in New York's history." All of the details in the paragraph support this statement.

Review Chapter 5:
Auto and Shop Information

The Auto and Shop Information (AS) section of the ASVAB will test your general knowledge of automobile parts and systems and the common tools and general practices used in a shop. Depending on which version of the ASVAB you take, you will have to answer either 25 questions or 22 questions about Auto and Shop.

Auto Information

You don't need to be a mechanic to pass the AS section of the test. However, you should have a good understanding of the systems and parts that make up modern automobiles. You should also understand how the systems work together and why they are important.

Modern automobiles have a number of systems that make them work. These systems include the following.

- Engine
- Ignition System
- Fuel Supply System
- Transmission System
- Lubrication System
- Brake System

- Suspension System
- Cooling System
- Exhaust and Emission Control Systems
- Electrical and Computer Systems

In the following sections, you will learn about which parts are included in these systems, how the systems work, and how they keep the vehicle moving.

Engine

One of the most important systems in the automobile is the engine. Most modern automobiles have internal combustion engines, which (as the name suggests) use combustion to create energy. The goal of an automobile engine is simple: give the vehicle energy to move.

Internal combustion engines need air, fuel, and an ignition source to run. Without all three ingredients, the engine cannot propel the vehicle. Most internal combustion engines convert petroleum fuels, like gasoline, into energy using four-stroke combustion. Four-stroke combustion engines generally have more than one cylinder. Each cylinder looks something like this.

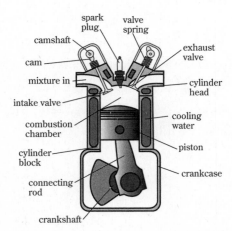

The four-stroke engine gets its name because it takes four strokes of the piston to complete its process. A piston stroke is defined as the movement of a piston from the top dead center (TDC) of the cylinder to the bottom dead center (BDC) of the cylinder, or from the BDC to the TDC.

1.   **Intake stroke**: The piston is located at the TDC of the cylinder. The intake valve is beginning to open. The piston begins to move down and creates a low-pressure system, almost like a vacuum, at the top of the cylinder. This low pressure pulls air into the cylinder through the intake valve. The air that is traveling into the cylinder is filled with fuel because it has traveled through the intake system. Therefore, during the intake stroke, the cylinder is filled with an air-fuel mixture. At the end of the intake stroke, the piston comes to the BDC of cylinder, and the intake valve nearly closes.

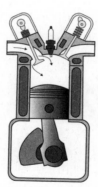

INTAKE

2.   **Compression stroke**: As the piston begins an upward stroke in the cylinder, the compression stroke beings. During the compression stroke, the piston forces the air-fuel mixture into a smaller and smaller space. As the particles in the air-fuel mixture get closer together, they become easier to ignite. Just as the piston gets close to the TDC, the spark plug ignites and combusts the air-fuel mixture.

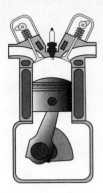

COMPRESSION

3.   **Combustion stroke** (or **power stroke**): When the air-fuel mix-
     ture is ignited, the gases heat up and expand. This expansion
     continues to move the piston passed the TDC point again. This
     next movement, or stroke, is the combustion or power stroke.
     This stroke is where the engine gets its power. The combustion
     stroke forces the piston down to the BDC.

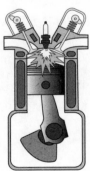

COMBUSTION

4.   **Exhaust stroke**: As the piston reaches the BDC, the exhaust valve
     begins to open. As the exhaust valve opens, the cylinder releases
     the stored gases into the exhaust system. After the exhaust valve
     opens and releases the gas, the piston continues to move and the
     entire four-stroke process begins again with the intake stroke.

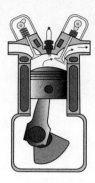

EXHAUST

Engines in modern vehicles usually have more than one cylinder, so this same process is happening in a number of cylinders at one time. Usually, vehicles have four, six, or eight cylinders. These cylinders can be arranged vertically or horizontally. The cylinders can also fire in a number of different orders. The cylinders' firing order affects the performance of the engine.

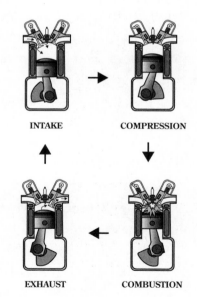

INTAKE   COMPRESSION

EXHAUST   COMBUSTION

Although the four-stroke combustion engine discussed in this chapter is an example of a gasoline engine, some vehicles run on diesel. Diesel engines are similar to engines that run on gasoline, but some important differences do exist. It's important to know about these differences when you take the ASVAB.

Ignition System

The **ignition system** of a vehicle is responsible for starting the engine and having it run continually. The main parts of the ignition system are the battery, the coil, the distributor, and the spark plugs. These parts work together to start the vehicle and keep it running.

When a vehicle first turns on, it needs power to start the engine. By starting a vehicle, the driver sends an electrical signal from the car's battery to the coil, which is also called an ignition coil. Inside the **coil**, the charge runs through different pieces of wire. The coil's **primary winding** increases the power in the charge from the battery. The charge from the twelve-volt battery increases to thousands of volts. The coil's **secondary winding** sends the increased charge, or spark, to the distributor.

The **distributor** is the part of the ignition system that sends the spark to the spark plug. It is important to have the spark reach the cylinder at the right moment so that the engine runs as efficiently as possible. Therefore, the distributor has to send each spark at exactly the right time. Once the spark reaches the spark plug, the spark plug sends it into the cylinder. The spark ignites the air-fuel mixture inside the cylinder, creating power in the engine.

Fuel Supply System

As you already know, a combustion engine needs air, fuel, and a spark to work. The automobile's **fuel supply system** moves the fuel from the tank to the engine so that the engine can run.

As you know, the ignition system supplies the spark needed for combustion. The fuel supply system supplies the air and the fuel. When a driver presses the gas pedal in a vehicle, the vehicle moves or speeds up. This increase in speed happens because pressing on the pedal opens the **throttle valve**, which allows more air in the engine. Also, pressing the pedal causes the **engine control unit** (ECU)—which is an electrical component of the car—to signal the fuel injector to add more fuel to the engine.

A **fuel injector** is an electrical component of the car that pumps a precise amount fuel into the engine. If the air-fuel ratio that enters the cylinder has too little fuel, it is called a lean mixture. A **lean air-fuel ratio** is not good for engines because this type of mixture burns at a high temperature and can damage parts of the engine. A **rich air-fuel ratio** is a mixture that has too much fuel and too little air. Rich mixtures can produce black exhaust smoke and create deposits on spark plugs. Although rich mixtures can cause problems for engines, they are not as problematic as lean mixtures.

Transmission System

The **transmission system** of a car is the system that takes the energy created by the engine and transfers it to the vehicle's wheels. If the engine was directly connected to the wheels of the car, the vehicle would move whenever the engine was running. Therefore, the transmission is the system that tells the car when the wheels should use the engine's power to move.

The **transmission** is basically a collection of gears that allows the car to move efficiently and effectively. This collection of gears is contained in a case, and the gears and case together are called the **gearbox**. The gearbox helps transform the energy from the engine into torque, which helps the tires move. Vehicles usually have one of two main types of transmissions.

- **Manual transmissions**, or **standard transmissions**, allow drivers to control when the transmission should switch gears and change the engine's energy into torque.

- **Automatic transmissions** also switch gears to change the energy from the engine into torque, but they automatically change gears so that the driver does not have to.

The gears used by the transmission depend on a number of different variables. When a vehicle starts to move from a dead stop, it should use a low gear so that it can provide enough torque to move the car. However, the low gear cannot propel the car very quickly, so as the car begins to move faster, it should be shifted from the low into a higher gear. In the same way, when a vehicle beings to slow, it should shift from a high gear to a lower gear.

Vehicles' transmissions also differ because they can control different wheels on the car. Many vehicles have **front-wheel drive**, which means the transmission is connected to the front wheels, and the back wheels follow the natural movement of the front of the vehicle. However, some vehicles also have rear-wheel drive, all-wheel drive, or four-wheel drive.

Lubrication System

The **lubrication system** in an automobile is important because without lubrication, the parts of the engine would stop because of friction. Lubrication also allows the engine parts to run smoothly.

Motor oil is the lubricant that makes the lubrication system work. Different grades and types of motor oils are used in different types of automobiles. Using a good-quality motor oil can help improve an automobile's performance and increase its lifespan. The following is a list of other important parts of the lubrication system.

- The **oil pan** is a reservoir that holds the motor oil.
- The **oil pump** is the part of the system that moves the oil through the oil galleries.
- The **pressure regulator** prevents too much pressure from building up in the system.
- The **oil filter** is the part of the system that removes impurities and debris from the lubricating oil.
- The **oil galleries** are the passageways that send oil throughout the vehicle.

When an automobile's engine runs, the oil pump draws oil from the oil pan. The oil then moves from the pump to the oil filter. After the oil has been cleaned by the filter, it moves to the oil galleries. Then, the oil galleries send the oil to the parts of the engine that need lubricating, such as the cam shaft and main bearings. After the oil passes through the automobile's system, it returns to the oil pan so it can be used again. Regularly changing an automobile's motor oil keeps the lubrication system and the entire engine running smoothly.

Brake System

Once a vehicle begins to move, it has to have a way to slow down and eventually stop. The brake system is the system that allows drivers to slow down and stop their vehicles. The main parts of an automobile's braking system are the four brakes that are each attached to a different wheel. These brakes apply pressure to the vehicle's wheels, causing it to slow down or stop.

The braking system includes a few major parts:

- The **brake pedal** is the structure in the cabin of the vehicle that the driver presses to make the brakes work. The brake pedal is attached to the master cylinder.

- The **master cylinder**, which is attached the brake pedal, puts pressure on the brake fluid when the brake pedal is pressed.

- The **fluid reservoir** provides fluid to different parts of the braking system.

- The **brake lines** are metal lines that run from the master cylinder to the brake assemblies. The brake fluid runs through the lines, and if the lines are broken, the brake fluid will leak, causing the brakes to fail.

- The **brake assemblies** have pistons inside that help operate the brakes. The brake fluid enters the brake assemblies and the pistons after it runs through the brake lines. There are two main types of brake assemblies.

  ○ **Drum brakes** contain pads called brake shoes that press on a rotating drum. This friction slows down the vehicle.

  ○ **Disk brakes** have two disks (commonly called **rotors**) that squeeze together and cause friction that slows the vehicle.

Many modern vehicles are also equipped with **antilock brakes**, which are connected to electronic and computer systems of the vehicle. These brakes react to rapid deceleration by pulsing, which allows the driver to move the wheels while the car is braking and prevents the wheels from locking so that the driver has more control.

Suspension Systems

The **suspension system** of an automobile is important because it helps maintain the right amount of friction between the tires and the road surface. Also, the suspension makes the vehicle have a smoother, more comfortable ride.

When a car drives over a bump or pothole in the road, the car's tires have to move up or down to compensate for the change. The suspension system is what allows the tires to move up and down somewhat independently from the rest of the vehicle. The suspension system is part of the vehicle's chassis, and systems vary among different types of vehicles. Most suspension systems include the following.

- **Springs** help the vehicle's wheels move up and down when the vehicle travels over uneven surfaces. Suspension systems use a number of different types of springs, including coil springs, air springs, and leaf springs.

- **Shock absorbers** are devices that absorb the energy from the springs before it can be transferred to the vehicle's body. The shock absorbers help give the vehicle a smoother, more enjoyable ride for the vehicle's occupants.

- **Struts** also help absorb energy from the springs. Furthermore, they give structural support to the suspension system.

- **Anti-sway bars** are bars that hold the two sides of the suspension system together and transfer energy from one wheel to another to provide a smoother ride. They also give the vehicle stability when it goes around curves.

Exhaust and Emissions Systems

When automobiles run, they produce waste gases that need to be released from the vehicle. Since these gases are formed when petroleum products are burned, they can contain harmful chemicals. The **exhaust and emissions systems** of an automobile are responsible for getting rid of these gases and making them less dangerous before they are released in the atmosphere.

Hydrocarbons, carbon monoxide, and nitrogen oxides are three dangerous emissions caused by vehicles. The emissions control system of the automobile reduces the amount of these toxins that enter the atmosphere.

One of the most important pieces of a vehicle's emissions control system is the catalytic converter. The **catalytic converter** is a system that converts dangerous emissions into less harmful waste products. Hot gases travel from the engine to the catalytic converter through the exhaust system. Inside the converter, chemical reactions change the carbon monoxide and hydrocarbons into water vapor and carbon dioxide. The catalytic converter also changes the nitrogen oxides into nitrogen and water.

From the catalytic converter, the waste products leave the vehicle through the exhaust system. They travel from the catalytic converter to the **muffler**, which muffles the noise of the exhaust system. From the muffler, the waste products travel to the tailpipe and into the atmosphere.

Electrical and Computer Systems

Although modern automobiles include many moving parts, they also contain intricate electrical and computer systems.

A vehicle's engine uses fuel to create energy, but other parts of the car—including the spark plugs—require electrical energy. This is why modern cars have batteries and other electrical components. Some of the most important parts of the electrical system include the following.

- The **battery** is the source of electrical energy in the vehicle. The coil in the ignition system uses energy from the battery to run the engine.

- The **charging system** helps keep the battery charged. As the vehicle runs, the alternator recharges the vehicle's battery. Even though the battery recharges while it runs, all batteries run out of energy eventually.
- The **lighting system** in the vehicle includes headlights, tail lights, brake lights, and in-cabin lights.
- The vehicle's **accessories** include items like the instrument panel, display screens, windshield wipers, defoggers, and stereos.

The engine control unit (ECU) is an electrical component of an automobile that monitors the following sensors.

- Mass airflow sensor
- Oxygen sensor
- Throttle position sensor
- Coolant temperature sensor
- Voltage sensor
- Manifold absolute pressure sensor
- Engine speed sensor

The computer systems of modern automobiles track these same sensors. When a problem is indicated with any of the sensors, the computer detects the problems. Mechanics can even use a vehicle's computer to help them diagnose and fix mechanical problems.

Cooling System

Since most of the energy created by an internal combustion engine turns into heat, the **cooling system** is necessary to keep the engine from overheating. Although keeping the engine from overheating is important, it is also important to keep the engine at a constant temperature so it can run efficiently.

The two main types of cooling systems are air cooling and water cooling. Both types of cooling systems use a coolant, which is often a mixture of ethylene glycol and water. This coolant mixture is ideal because it freezes at extremely low temperatures (–34° F). Since having pipes freeze inside a vehicle could cause major damage, a low freezing temperature is an important trait of the cooling liquid.

Air-cooling systems transfer heat away from the engine using air. Engines with air-cooling systems have metal fins on them that are designed to transfer heat away from the engine. A huge fan blows air over the fins. The air transfers the heat away from the fins and the engine. Air-cooling systems are much less common in modern vehicles than water-cooling systems.

Water-cooling systems operate by sending liquid through pipes that run around the engine. The liquid in the pipes absorbs heat from the engine. The liquid then travels to the radiator. The radiator removes the heat from the liquid and passes it into the air.

Properly maintaining a car's cooling system is vital to keeping an automobile in proper working order.

Shop Information

Just as military personnel should know general information about automobiles, they should also have a clear understanding of basic tools used in shops. The Auto and Shop Information section of the ASVAB will test you on your knowledge of basic tools and the ways they are commonly used.

Cutting and Shaping Tools

Cutting and shaping tools are very common tools seen in shops. They are also commonly asked about on the ASVAB.

SOME COMMON CUTTING AND SHAPING TOOLS

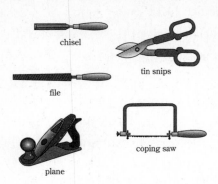

chisel

tin snips

file

coping saw

plane

- **Saws** are cutting tools that are used for many different materials and in many different situations.
  - **Hacksaws** generally have fine teeth and sit in a frame. These saws are used primarily to cut metal and plastic pipes and other small items.
  - **Table saws** are round cutting blades driven by electronic motors that sit inside a small table. Table saws are used mostly for cutting wood.
  - **Coping saws** are handsaws that are most often used to make intricate cuts and circular cuts in wood. A coping saw has a fine blade that stretches between the ends of a square frame.
  - **Ripsaws** are handsaws that are generally used to cut wood along its grain.
  - **Crosscut saws** are handsaws that are generally used to cut wood across its grain.
- **Scissors**, **shears**, and **snips** are used to cut and shape metal and other materials.
- **Files** are metal hand tools with rough edges that are used to shape wood and metal.
- **Chisels** are tools with a sharp metal blade at one and a blunt, rounded handle at the other end. The blunt end of the handle is struck with a hammer or a mallet. Chisels are generally used to chip and shape wood, but **cold chisels** are used to shape metal.

- **Planes** are woodworking tools that use a metal blade to shave off and shape wood.

Fastening Tools and Fasteners

Fastening tools and fasteners hold objects in place. They are some of the most common tools in a shop.

SOME COMMON FASTENING TOOLS AND FASTENERS

claw hammer   Phillips head screwdriver   box wrench   needle-nose pliers

wood screw   rivet   wood nail   flat washer   wing nut

FASTENING TOOLS

- **Wrenches** are tools that use torque to turn objects, including fasteners like bolts, nuts, and screws.

  ○ **Socket wrenches** are wrenches that have removable sockets that come in different sizes. The different sizes of sockets tighten and remove different sizes of nuts and bolts. Socket wrenches are also called **ratchet wrenches**.

  ○ **Allen wrenches**, which are also called **hex keys**, have hexagonal heads and are used to tighten bolts and screws.

  ○ **Open end wrenches** are wrenches with U-shaped openings that fit around and tighten fasteners.

  ○ **Box wrenches** are wrenches with closed ends that fit around nuts or bolt heads.

  ○ **Combination wrenches** have an open end wrench on one side and box wrench on the other side.

  ○ **Adjustable wrenches** have an opening on the end that gets larger and smaller to fit around different sizes of fasteners.

- **Screwdrivers** are fastening tools that use torque to turn screws.
  - **Flathead**, or **slot-head**, screwdrivers have flat blades at the tip. These screwdrivers are used to tighten and loosen flathead screws.
  - **Phillips head** screwdrivers have X-shaped tips. These screwdrivers are used to tighten and loosen Phillips head screws.
- **Pliers** are hand tools that are used to grip, bend, cut, and hold objects.
  - **Needle-nose pliers** are pliers with long, tapered jaws. These pliers are usually used to bend and cut wire.
  - **Diagonal pliers** are pliers with sharp jaws that are meant to cut wire. These pliers can also be called **wire cutters** or **diagonal cutting pliers**.
  - **Round-nose pliers** have short, rounded jaws. These pliers are used to shape wire, but they are not generally used for precision work.
  - **Channel lock pliers** are pliers with a wide, notched jaw. These pliers can be used for gripping, pulling, and pinching.
  - **Vice grips** are pliers that can be locked into place. Since they can be locked, these pliers are usually used to hold objects together.
- **Hammers** are tools that are meant to impact objects. One of the most common uses for hammers is to drive metal nails into surfaces.
  - **Straight claw hammers** and **curved claw hammers** have metal heads that are used to drive nails into wood. The claw on the back of the hammer head can be used to take nails out of wood.
  - **Ball-peen hammers** have ball-shaped heads and can be used to shape metal. These tools are also used to strike chisels.
  - **Mallets** have large heads that are usually made of rubber or wood. Mallets are use to strike chisels or other tools. They can also be used to strike metal and wood pieces into place.

FASTENERS

- **Screws** are fasteners with threads that help them stay firmly in place. Screws are used in wood, metal, plastic, and other materials. They are fastened into place with screwdrivers.

- **Nails** are metal fasteners that are pounded into place. Nails are most often pounded into place with hammers, and they are commonly used in wood. They come in many different sizes and gauges.

- **Rivets** are permanent metal fasteners that are inserted into pre-drilled holes. Rivets have a head on one side. To keep the rivet in place, the other side of the rivet is deformed so that the rivet essentially has a head on both sides.

- **Washers** are usually thin discs of metal with a hole in the middle. They are used with nuts and screws to help distribute pressure and minimize damage to a surface. Additionally, they provide a smooth surface that a nut can grip in order to stay tightly fastened.

- **Bolts** are threaded metal fasteners that go into predrilled holes. They are usually secured with **nuts**, which twist onto the threads of nuts.

Measuring Tools

Measuring tools are important in the shop because they help workers have accuracy and precision. Without measuring tools, the work done in shops could be flimsy and even dangerous.

SOME COMMON MEASURING TOOLS

measuring tape   level   plumb bob

carpenter's square   caliper

- **Tape measures** are one of the most common measuring tools in a shop. They are generally metal tapes with ruler marks that are wound and kept inside a small case.

- **Squares** are metal rulers that are used to make sure an object is square, which means it has a right angle. Squares are commonly used in framing and other types of building.

- **Calipers** are precise measuring tools use to measure the distance between two objects. Since calipers can accurately measure up to one thousandth of an inch, they are often used in machining, metal work, and jobs that need precision.

- **Levels** are measuring tools that are used to make sure objects are level when they are being put together or installed. Levels are usually long objects that look like rulers. They have glass tubes with air pockets that indicate whether an object is level.

- **Plumb bobs** are tools that hang from string and help builders ensure an object is plumb.

Drilling and Boring Tools

Drilling and boring tools allow workers to make accurate, perfectly round holes.

SOME COMMON DRILLING AND BORING TOOLS

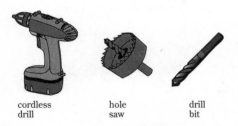

cordless   hole   drill
drill   saw   bit

- **Drill bits** are used to drill holes. Drill bits vary in size, and they can be used in wood, metal, and other materials.

- Drill bits are usually attached to an **electric drill** that uses electricity to create power and torque. To change a bit on an electric drill, you have to loosen the **chuck**, which is the part that holds the bit into place. **Cordless drills**, which are very similar to electric drills, are becoming more common. These drills have rechargeable battery packs that give them power.

- **Augers** are also capable of boring and drilling with drill bits. Augers can be handheld or machine powered.

- For creating larger holes in thin materials, **hole saws** can be attached to electric drills for cutting.

Practice Questions

Directions: Read each of the following questions. Then, select the choice that best answers each.

1. Why is antifreeze usually made up of ethylene glycol and water?

    A. Because it boils at a low temperature
    B. Because it boils at a high temperature
    C. Because it freezes at low temperature
    D. Because it freezes at a high temperature

2. In which part of the braking system does the brake fluid move in the pistons to engage the brakes?

    A. Brake pedal
    B. Fluid reservoir
    C. Master cylinder
    D. Brake assemblies

3.　What can happen in an engine when an air-fuel mixture is lean?

　　A.　The engine parts can overheat.
　　B.　The exhaust smoke can turn black.
　　C.　Spark plugs can get covered in deposits.
　　D.　The piston can move at the wrong time.

4.　What are two waste products that come out of a catalytic converter?

　　A.　Carbon dioxide and water
　　B.　Carbon monoxide and water
　　C.　Carbon dioxide and nitrogen oxides
　　D.　Carbon monoxide and nitrogen oxides

5.　During which of the four strokes that take place in a four-stroke combustion engine does the air-fuel mixture enter the cylinder?

　　A.　Power
　　B.　Intake
　　C.　Exhaust
　　D.　Compression

6.　Which of the following tools would you most likely use to hit a chisel?

　　A.　Vice grip
　　B.　Allen wrench
　　C.　Ball-peen hammer
　　D.　None of the above

7. Which of the following is a permanent metal fastener?

    A. Nut
    B. Nail
    C. Bolt
    D. Rivet

8. Which of these tools is used to make sure an object has a right angle?

    A. Level
    B. Square
    C. Plumb bob
    D. Both A and B

9. Which of the following objects would you most likely use to shape a piece of wood?

    A. Chisel
    B. Hammer
    C. Plumb bob
    D. Allen wrench

10. Why might a worker choose to use a cordless drill instead of an electric drill?

    A. Because electric drills can be used only with wood
    B. Because cordless drills are powered by battery packs
    C. Because drill bits do not fit in the chucks of electric drills
    D. Because hole saws can only be used with cordless drills

Answer Explanations

1. **C.** Antifreeze is usually made from ethylene glycol and water because the ethylene glycol stops the liquid from freezing until it reaches about −34° F. Since having the coolant freeze inside the vehicle would cause damage, it is important that it does not freeze.

2. **D.** The brake fluid flows from the brake lines into the brake assemblies where it moves the pistons that operate the brakes. The faster the fluid moves into the brake assemblies, the faster the brakes engage.

3. **A.** When an air-fuel mixture is lean, which means there is too much air and too little fuel, the parts of the engine can overheat. Lean air-fuel mixtures burn at a higher temperature than rich mixtures, and this increased heat can cause engine problems.

4. **A.** The catalytic converter is part of the emissions control system of a vehicle, and it turns harmful chemicals into less harmful waste products. The engine produces carbon monoxide and nitrogen oxides. The catalytic converter changes these into carbon dioxide and water.

5. **B.** During the intake stroke, the piston moves down from the TDC of the cylinder. As the piston moves down, it creates low pressure in the cylinder. The low pressure then pulls in the air-fuel mixture that was created by the fuel injector. At the end of the intake stroke, the piston comes close to the BDC of the cylinder.

6. **C.** Ball-peen hammers and mallets are acceptable tools for hitting chisels. Ball-peen hammers can also be used for bending and shaping metal.

7. **D.** Rivets are permanent metal fasteners. They have a cylindrical metal shaft on one side and heads on the other side. When a rivet is put into place, the cylindrical part is misshapen to create another head, making it permanent.

8. **B.** A square is a measuring tool that is used to make sure an object is square, which means it has a right angle. These tools are usually used in framing and other building projects.

9. **A**. Chisels have sharp tips that cut and shape wood. A mallet or another tool is used to hit the end of the chisel to give it enough force to cut.

10. **B**. Cordless drills are powered by battery packs. Since the drill is not plugged into an electrical outlet, it can be used in more places.

Review Chapter 6:
Mathematics Knowledge

Algebra

Essential Terms and Concepts

Algebra requires you to manipulate terms and expressions in an equation to solve for a variable. If this statement seems confusing, review the following vocabulary.

- **Variable:** An unknown quantity represented by a letter such as x, n, or a.

- **Constant:** A number. It can be a coefficient if it occurs in front of and multiplies a variable, such as the 3 in $3n$. It can also be an exponent, such as the 2 in x^2.

- **Term:** A combination of constants and/or variables, such as $3n$ or x^2.

- **Operation:** Addition, subtraction, multiplication, division, raising to a power, or taking a root.

- **Expression:** A combination of constants, variables, and operations (such as + and –) that make up part of an equation.

- **Equation:** A relationship among two or more expressions. An equation always has an equal sign (or an inequality symbol), while an expression does not.

- **Inequality:** An equation with less than or greater than symbols (<, ≤, >, ≥) in place of an equal (=) sign.

Algebra is about solving equations. Given a set of terms arranged in an equation, the goal is to find the value of a variable by isolating it on one side of the equal sign. To do this, you must add, subtract, multiply, and divide the expressions on BOTH sides of the equal sign until the variable is isolated. Think of the equation as a pan balance with the equal sign as its pivot. Whatever you do to one pan, you must do to the other to keep the pans balanced.

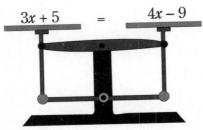

Rules for Working with Numbers
ORDER OF OPERATIONS

When an expression includes two or more operations, the order in which they are performed matters. For the expression $2 \times 7 - 1$, the result differs depending on whether you first subtract 1 from 7 ($2 \times 6 = 12$) or you multiply 2 and 7 before subtracting ($14 - 1 = 13$). To avoid ambiguity, we perform the operations in an agreed upon order:

1. Powers, Exponents, and Roots
2. Multiplication and Division
3. Addition and Subtraction

Therefore, the second answer to the equation above, 13, is correct.

ROOTS AND EXPONENTS

When a number is multiplied by itself, the result is its square. For example, the number 4 multiplied by itself (4×4) equals 16. The square can be expressed as the number raised to the **power** of 2: 4^2. The **exponent** in this case is 2 because 4 was multiplied twice. Multiplying 4^2 by 4 again raises it to the power of 3, which can be expressed as 4^3.

Examples:

$$4^1 = 4$$

$$4^2 = 4 \times 4 = 16$$

$$4^3 = 4 \times 4 \times 4 = 64$$

Exponents may also be negative numbers. A negative exponent is the equivalent of dividing by the number. It may also be thought of as the reciprocal fraction of the number.

Examples:

$$4^{-1} = \frac{1}{4}$$

$$4^{-2} = \frac{1}{4} \times \frac{1}{4} = \frac{1}{16}$$

$$4^{-3} = \frac{1}{4} \times \frac{1}{4} \times \frac{1}{4} = \frac{1}{64}$$

Taking the root of a number is the opposite of raising it to a power. The most familiar root is the **square root**, or the division of a number into two equal factors. The square root of 16 ($\sqrt{16}$) is 4. A root can also be expressed as $16^{\frac{1}{2}}$, in which the exponent $\frac{1}{2}$ is a fraction.

To multiply the same **base** raised to powers, simply add the exponents:

$$4^2 \times 4^3 = 4^{(2+3)} = 4^5$$

To divide, simply subtract the exponents:

$$4^2 \div 4^3 = 4^{(2-3)} = 4^{-1}$$

COMBINING LIKE TERMS

An algebraic equation can be simplified by combining **like terms**, or terms containing the same variable. Combine like terms by:

Adding or subtracting the coefficients:

$$3x - 5x = -2x$$

Multiplying or dividing the coefficients:

$$(4x) \cdot (8x) = 32x^2$$

FACTORING AND MULTIPLYING EXPRESSIONS

To simplify an expression such as $8x^2 - 2x$, **factor out** the common factors in both terms. The term $8x^2$ is a multiple of $2 \cdot 2 \cdot 2 \cdot x \cdot x$, and so can be divided by any of these factors. Some of these same terms are found in $2x$. Place the expression $8x^2 - 2x$ in parentheses and move the common factors outside the parentheses.

- Expression:　　$(8x^2 - 2x)$
- Factor out 2:　$2(4x^2 - x)$
- Factor out x:　$2x(4x - 1)$

Note that factoring out a term equal to itself results in the number 1.

Sometimes, you will need to multiply two expressions together, such as $(3x + 7)(2x - 3)$. Take each term in one set of parentheses and multiply it with each term in the other. You may use the FOIL technique to help you organize the process, but you do not need to. FOIL stands for first, inner, outer, last, and specifies the order of multiplication. An example of FOIL for the expression $(3x + 7)(2x - 3)$ is shown:

- **First:**　　$(3x + 7)(2x - 3) = 6x^2$
- **Inner:**　　$(3x + 7)(2x - 3) = 6x^2 + 14x$
- **Outer:**　　$(3x + 7)(2x - 3) = 6x^2 + 14x - 9x$
- **Last:**　　$(3x + 7)(2x - 3) = 6x^2 + 14x - 9x - 21$

The final step is combining like terms in the expression $6x^2 + 14x - 9x - 21$ to get $6x^2 + 5x - 21$.

Other times, you will need to do the opposite. For example, you may need to find the roots of a **polynomial** equation (an equation with one or more variables raised to an exponent greater than 1, e.g., x^2). Example:

What two expressions, multiplied together, result in the expression $4x^2 + 2x - 5$? Ask:

- What two constants, multiplied together, result in the constant? (There may be several possibilities here. List them all.) These are possible candidates for the **last** terms in the original form.
- What two coefficients, multiplied together, result in the coefficient of the x^2 term? These are possible candidates for the **first** terms in the original form.
- Finally, narrow down the choices by trial and error and elimination.

Solving Equations and Inequalities
SOLVING EQUATIONS

Use the rules for working with numbers to solve equations. Usually, this means determining the value of a variable. Do this by isolating the variable on one side of the equal sign and moving the constants to the other side of the equal sign. Remember that the two sides in an equation are like the two pans of a balance: they must always be equal. Therefore, whatever operation is performed on one side of the equation must be performed on the other. If you subtract a term from one side, you must subtract it from the other side also. Example: Solve for x in $3x + 5 = 4x - 9$.

- Start with:
  $$3x + 5 = 4x - 9$$
- Subtract 5 from both sides:
  $$-5 = -5$$
  $$3x = 4x - 14$$
- Subtract $4x$ from both sides:
  $$-4x = -4x$$
  $$-x = -14$$
- Divide both sides by -1:
  $$(-1) = (-1)$$
- Solve for x:
  $$x = 14$$

SOLVING INEQUALITIES

Just as the term implies, an inequality is a relationship in which expressions are unequal. One expression may be greater than (>), greater than or equal to (≥), less than (<), or less than or equal to (≤) the other.

An inequality is essentially asking, what value for this variable makes this unequal relationship true? For the inequality $x ≥ 18$, all values for x greater than and including 18 satisfy the inequality.

Solve inequalities just as you would solve an equation. However, if an inequality is multiplied by a negative number, the less than/greater than sign must be reversed. Why? Consider the inequality $x > -3$. The values of x that satisfy this inequality include $-2, -1, 0, 1, 2$, etc. If both sides are multiplied by -1, it becomes $-x > 3$. Do the same values satisfy this statement? No; substituting 2 for x, $-2 > 3$ is incorrect. Therefore, the sign must be flipped to give $-x < 3$.

Solving Simultaneous Equations

Some questions may present two equations with two different variables and ask you to solve for one or both. The simplest way to solve simultaneous equations is the **substitution method**, in which you express one variable in terms of the other and substitute it into one of the original equations. This results in an equation with only one variable, which can then be solved. Example:

$$Eq1:\quad 4x = 8 - y$$

$$Eq2:\quad 5x + 2y = 13$$

- Rearrange Equation 1 to isolate one of the variables:
- Eq1: $\qquad\qquad\qquad 4x = 8 - y$
- Add y: $\qquad\qquad\qquad y + 4x = 8$
- Subtract $4x$: $\qquad\qquad\qquad y = 8 - 4x$
- Substitute the expression equal to y into Equation 2:
- Eq2: $\qquad\qquad\qquad 5x + 2y = 13$
- Substitute y: $\qquad\qquad 5x + 2(8 - 4x) = 13$

- Then, solve for the remaining variable in the equation:
- Distribute: $5x + 2(8 - 4x) = 13$

  $5x + 16 - 8x = 13$

- Combine: $5x + 16 - 8x = 13$

  $-3x + 16 = 13$

- Solve: $-3x = 13 - 16$

  $-3x = -3$

  $x = 1$

Interest Rates

Problems involving interest rates can be solved using the equation $I = prt$. The terms stand for the following:

- I is interest, the amount a sum of money increases.
- p is the principal, or the original amount of money invested.
- r is the rate of interest (specifically the annual rate).
- t is the length of time that the money was invested, usually given in years.

Example: If $500 is invested at a rate of 4.5 percent for 2 and a half years, the interest earned on the principal is $I = prt = \$500 \times 0.045 \times 2 = \$45$.

A question may also ask for principal, rate, or time given the interest. Rearrange the equation $I = prt$ to solve for whichever variable is asked for. Example: If a principal of $1000 is invested for 5 years and earns $850 in interest, find the interest rate. Divide both sides of the equation $I = prt$ by p and t to isolate r.

$$r = \frac{I}{pt}$$

$$r = \frac{\$850}{\$1000 \times 5}$$

$$r = 0.17 = 17\%$$

Geometry

The Coordinate Plane

Equations may be considered lines on a **coordinate plane**, a two-dimensional surface marked off by a horizontal x-axis and a vertical y-axis. Each axis is a number line, and the two axes meet at a right angle at the **origin** (0, 0). Each **point** on the plane can be specified by a pair of **coordinates**, values for x and y which are expressed in parentheses as (x, y). Any line on the plane can be specified by two points.

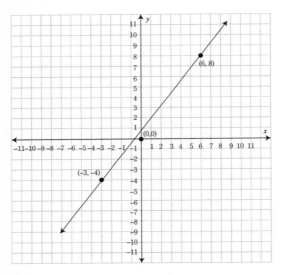

Lines on a coordinate plane have a **slope**, which is the ratio of the vertical increase to the horizontal increase. It can also be thought of as the ratio of the change in the y value to the change in the x value. The slope of a line can be:

- positive if the line tilts upward from left to right.
- negative if the line tilts down from left to right.
- zero if the line is exactly horizontal.
- "no slope" if the line is exactly vertical.
- equal to 1 if the line increases along the y-axis at the same rate it increases along the x-axis.
- less than 1 if the line rises at a slower rate (a flatter line).

- greater than 1 if the line rises at a faster rate (a steeper line).

Given two coordinates, the slope of a line can be calculated as $m = \dfrac{y_2 - y_1}{x_2 - x_1}$ (where x_1 is the lesser x-coordinate and x_2 is the greater x-coordinate).

The point at which the line crosses the y-axis is called the y-**intercept**. When an equation is given in the form $y = mx + b$, the variable m stands for the slope and the variable b stands for the y-intercept.

Lines, Planes, and Angles

Much of geometry and algebra involves a single plane. A **plane** is any flat, two-dimensional space, such as this sheet of paper. **Lines** have only one dimension and extend infinitely in either direction. Therefore, geometry often involves **line segments** with definite lengths and endpoints. A **point** is a location on a line or plane.

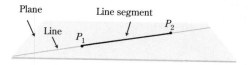

Lines and planes are infinitely long. A line segment is defined by two points on a plane and has a definite length.

Parallel lines continue in the same direction without ever intersecting. Non-parallel lines intersect to form **angles**. Lines that intersect at 90 degrees are **perpendicular**.

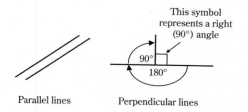

Because a straight line is considered a 180-degree angle, the angles that form along an intersected line must add up to 180. For example, perpendicular lines form 90-degree angles. When two lines intersect, the angles opposite each other (the **vertical angles**) are equal. Note the results when two parallel lines are intersected by a third line: The same set of angles forms on each line.

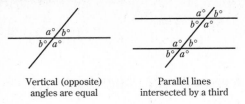

Vertical (opposite)
angles are equal

Parallel lines
intersected by a third

Perimeter, Area, Volume

Two-dimensional shapes have a **perimeter**, the total length of all lines, and **area**, the size of the plane they cover. When discussing the area of a three-dimensional shape, the term **surface area** is used. Think of the surface area as the wrapping paper needed to completely cover a package. Three-dimensional shapes also have **volume**, the amount of space they fill up. The perimeter of a **polygon** (a shape made up of sides and angles) can be found by adding the lengths of all the sides. (The circumference of a circle is discussed later.)

Triangles

Triangles are polygons made up of three sides and three angles. The three angles must add up to 180 degrees. Therefore, knowing two of the angles is enough to find the third. Triangles are classified as **right**, **equilateral**, **isosceles**, or **scalene**.

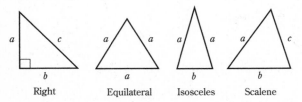

Right   Equilateral   Isosceles   Scalene

- **Right triangle:** A triangle with one 90-degree (right) angle. May also be equilateral.
- **Equilateral:** A triangle with three equal sides and three equal angles.
- **Isosceles:** A triangle with exactly two equal sides and two equal angles.
- **Scalene:** A triangle with unequal sides and angles.

Right triangles allow you to determine the length of one side if you know the other two. The longest side of a right triangle, opposite the right angle, is called the **hypotenuse**. The other two, shorter sides are called the **legs**. The legs and hypotenuse are related according to the **Pythagorean Theorem**, which states that if you take the lengths of the legs, square them, and add them together, the sum is the square of the hypotenuse.

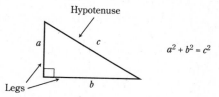

Parts of a Right Triangle and the Pythagorean Theorem

Pythagorean theorem:

- $c^2 = a^2 + b^2$
- $c = \sqrt{a^2 + b^2}$ (rearranged to solve for c)

Example: For a right triangle with legs $a = 6$ and $b = 8$, determine the hypotenuse, c.

- $c^2 = a^2 + b^2$
- $c^2 = 6^2 + 8^2$
- $c^2 = 36 + 64$
- $c^2 = 100$
- $c = \sqrt{100} = 10$

The lengths 6, 8, and 10 are multiples of 3, 4, and 5, a **Pythagorean triple**. Recognizing multiples of these triples helps to solve problems such as these more quickly. For example, 9, 12, and 15 are multiples of 3 and the triple 3, 4, 5. Triples include:

- 3, 4, 5
- 5, 12, 13
- 7, 24, 25

- 8, 15, 17
- 9, 40, 41

AREA OF A TRIANGLE

A right triangle can be thought of as a rectangle divided in half diagonally. Therefore, its area is one half the product of the two side lengths. In triangles, these lengths are called the **base** and the **height**. The height of a triangle is the line extending from one angle perpendicular to the opposite side. The formula for the area of any triangle is $\frac{1}{2}bh$.

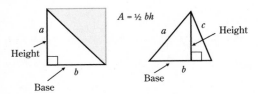

Area of a Triangle

Squares, Rectangles, and Prisms

A square has four sides and four angles. All the angles in a square are right angles (90 degrees) and all the sides are equal. The perimeter of a square is simply four times the side length ($4s$), and the area is the square of the side (s^2).

The three-dimensional shape formed by six squares, the **cube**, has a volume of s^3. Its surface area is the sum of the areas of each **face**.

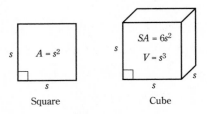

Square   Cube

Similar to a square, a rectangle consists of four right angles. Its opposite sides are parallel and equal. The area of a rectangle can be found by multiplying its length by its width.

The three-dimensional shape formed by rectangles, the **prism**, has a volume of $l \times w \times h$. Its surface area is the sum of the areas of each face.

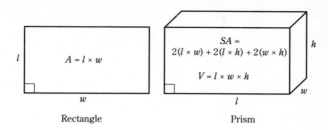

Rectangle   Prism

Squares and rectangles are actually specific types of a larger class of shapes called **quadrilaterals**, which consist of four sides and four angles. If both the opposite sides of a quadrilateral are parallel, it is called a **parallelogram**. If only one pair of sides is parallel, it is a **trapezoid**.

To find the area of a parallelogram, multiply the base (the length of one side) by the height (the perpendicular line drawn from the base to the opposite side): $A = b \times h$. This is similar to the method for finding the area of a triangle, as the figure below demonstrates.

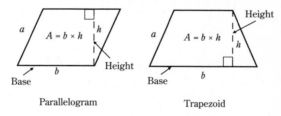

Parallelogram   Trapezoid

Circles and Spheres

A circle does not consist of discrete sides and angles like a polygon. Instead, it can be thought of as a series of points, all an equal distance away from a central point. This distance is the **radius**, and allows you to calculate all the other aspects of a circle or its three-dimensional counterpart, the **sphere**.

- The **diameter**, the longest line that can be drawn within a circle, is twice the radius ($d = 2r$).

- The **circumference**, the length of the outside of the circle, is twice the radius multiplied by the irrational number π (pi), which is equal to approximately 3.14 ($c = 2\pi r$).

- The **area** of a circle is πr^2.
- The **surface area** of a sphere is $4\pi r^2$.
- The **volume** of a sphere is $\frac{4}{3}\pi r^3$.

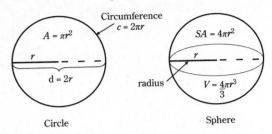

Circle   Sphere

Practice Questions

1. $(3x + 5)(2x - 4) =$

    A. $5x^2 + 2x - 1$
    B. $6x^2 + 7x + 1$
    C. $5x^2 - 6x + 20$
    D. $6x^2 - 2x - 20$

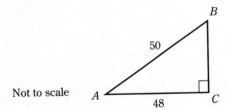

2. In the triangle ABC, what is the length of line segment BC?

    A. 14
    B. 50
    C. 69
    D. 196

3. A square has an area of 324 square centimeters. What is the length of its perimeter?

    A.   18 cm
    B.   72 cm
    C.   81 cm
    D.   162 cm

4. $3 \cdot 5^2 - 2 + 4 =$

    A.   69
    B.   77
    C.   219
    D.   227

5. A line goes through the points (1, 2) and (3, 8). What is the slope of the line?

    A.   2
    B.   3
    C.   4
    D.   5

6. A principal of $8,000 is invested at a rate of 6.6 percent. How long must the principal be invested in order to return $1,000 in interest?

    A.   6 months
    B.   19 months
    C.   23 months
    D.   121 months

7.　If $2j + k = 13$ and $j + 3k = 19$, find k.

　　A.　1
　　B.　3
　　C.　5
　　D.　7

$$-2x + 15 \geq -2 - x$$

8.　Which of the following satisfies the above inequality?

　　A.　$x \leq 13$
　　B.　$x \geq 13$
　　C.　$x \leq 17$
　　D.　$x \geq 17$

9.　A sphere has a diameter of 16 units. What is its surface area?

　　A.　64π
　　B.　256π
　　C.　384π
　　D.　683π

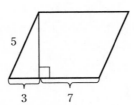

10.　What is the area of the quadrilateral?

　　A.　25
　　B.　40
　　C.　43
　　D.　50

Answer Explanations

1. **D.** Multiply the two terms using the distributive property of multiplication. Using FOIL, the results are:

- First: $3x \cdot 2x = 6x^2$
- Outer: $3x \cdot -4 = -12x$
- Inner: $5 \cdot 2x = 10x$
- Last: $5 \cdot -4 = -20$

Combining like terms, $-12x + 10x = -2x$. Adding the terms together results in the expression $6x^2 - 2x - 20$.

2. **A.** Use the Pythagorean theorem to determine the length of line segment BC, which is a leg of the right triangle. Segment AB is the hypotenuse and segment AC is the remaining leg. Rearrange the equation for the Pythagorean theorem to isolate BC. Then substitute known values and solve.

$$AC^2 + BC^2 = AB^2$$

$$BC^2 = AB^2 - AC^2$$

$$BC^2 = 50^2 - 48^2$$

$$BC = \sqrt{50^2 - 48^2}$$

$$BC = \sqrt{2500 - 2304} = \sqrt{196} = 14$$

3. **B.** The area of a square is the square of the length of one side (s^2). Take the square root of the area to find the side length: $\sqrt{324} = 18$. The perimeter of a square is the sum of the lengths of all its sides. There are 4 sides, so $18 \times 4 = 72$.

4. **B.** Use the correct orders of operations to evaluate the expression. First, take the square of 5^2, which is 25. The expression becomes $3 \cdot 25 - 2 + 4$. Next, multiply the terms 3 and 25: $75 - 2 + 4$. Finally, carry out addition and subtraction. Note that there are no parentheses

around (2 + 4), so the two terms should be subtracted and added separately. The result is 77.

5.   **B**. The slope of a line is the ratio of the change along the vertical (y) axis to the change along the horizontal (x) axis. From the coordinates given, the change along the y-axis is $8 - 2 = 6$. The change along the x-axis is $3 - 1 = 2$. The ratio 6 to 2 is 3.

6.   **C**. Divide both sides of the equation $I = prt$ by p and r to isolate and solve for t.

$$t = \frac{I}{pr}$$

$$t = \frac{\$1000}{\$8000 \times 0.066}$$

$$t = 1.9 \text{ years} \approx 23 \text{ months}$$

7.   **C**. Solve the set of simultaneous equations for k. First, express j in terms of k:

$$j + 3k = 19$$

$$j = 19 - 3k$$

Next, substitute this expression for j in one of the original equations and solve for k:

$$2j + k = 13$$

$$2(19 - 3k) + k = 13$$

$$2(19 - 3k) + k = 13$$

$$38 - 6k + k = 13$$

$$38 - 5k = 13$$

$$-5k = 13 - 38 = -25$$

$$k = 5$$

8. **C.** Solve the inequality for x by isolating x on one side. Remember to reverse the inequality symbol when multiplying the equation by a negative number.

$$-2x + 15 \geq -2 - x$$

$$-x \geq -17$$

$$x \leq 17$$

9. **B.** The formula for the surface area of a sphere is $SA = 4\pi r^2$. Because the diameter is twice the radius, the radius is one half of 16, or 8. Substituting this value into the equation yields $SA = 4\pi 8^2 = 4 \times \pi \times 64 = 256\pi$.

10. **B.** First, find the height (dashed line) by determining the side of the right triangle. The hypotenuse is 5 and one leg is 3; therefore, the remaining leg (the height) must be 4. (Recall that 3, 4, 5 is a Pythagorean triple.) Next, find the base by adding the two lengths given: $3 + 7 = 10$. Lastly, multiply the base by the height to find the area: $A = bh = 10 \times 4 = 40$.

Review Chapter 7:
Mechanical Comprehension

Understanding Machines

The Mechanical Comprehension subtest of the ASVAB tests your understanding of simple machines and some of the basic principles of physics. **Physics** is the study of matter and energy and their interactions, and it influences many aspects of everyday life, such as how much you weigh or how much force you need to apply to a refrigerator to push it up a ramp.

The Mechanical Comprehension subtest includes 25 questions to be answered in 19 minutes. Some questions may assess your basic understanding of simple machines, while others may require you to recall formulas that explain how different physical quantities relate to each other or use formulas to determine a particular quantity.

Important Terms and Symbols

The following table includes a list of common terms or concepts with which you should be familiar when taking the ASVAB's Mechanical Comprehension subtest. The table provides a simple explanation for each term or concept and the symbol often used to represent this concept in formulas.

TERM/CONCEPT	EXPLANATION	SYMBOL
acceleration	the rate of change of velocity with time	a
acceleration due to gravity	the acceleration of a body in free fall under the influence of Earth's gravity, which is equal to about 9.8 meters per second squared (m/s²)	g
displacement	the difference between an object's final and initial positions	d
distance	a measure of how far an object has traveled	d
force	a push or pull equal to the product of an object's mass and its acceleration	F
friction	a force that opposes movement	—
gravitational potential energy	the stored energy of an object, which depends upon its position in a gravitational field	$PE_{gravitational}$
height	the distance an object is raised	h
inertia	an object's resistance to a change in its state of motion or rest	—
kinetic energy	the energy of an object in motion	KE
mass	a quantity that describes the amount of matter in an object	m

TERM/CONCEPT	EXPLANATION	SYMBOL
mechanical advantage	the ratio of resistance to effort, or the ratio of the force applied to an object by a machine to the force applied to the machine by a human	MA
mechanical energy	the sum of the potential energy and the kinetic energy of an object in a closed system	ME
power	the rate at which work is done	P
pressure	a measure of force per unit area	P
scalar quantity	a quantity with magnitude but no direction	—
time	a measurement of the duration of a particular action	t
torque	a force that rotates an object around an axis	T
vector quantity	a quantity with both magnitude and direction	—
velocity	a measurement of the rate and direction of change of an object	v
weight	the force gravity exerts on an object's mass	W
work	the product of a force applied to an object and the object's displacement as a result of the applied force	W

Newton's Laws of Motion

To understand mechanics, one must understand how objects move in response to the forces applied to them. In 1687, English physicist Sir Isaac Newton developed three laws of motion. These three laws serve as the base upon which the study of mechanics is built:

- **Newton's first law ("law of inertia")**: The velocity of an object in motion remains constant unless the object is acted upon by an external net force. If an object is at rest, it will remain at rest unless acted upon by an external net force.

- **Newton's second law**: The acceleration of an object is directly proportional to and in the same direction as the net force applied to the object and has a magnitude that is inversely proportional to the mass. This law is represented by the formula $F = ma$, where F is the net force in newtons (N), m is the mass in kilograms (kg), and a is the acceleration in meters per second squared (m/s^2).

- **Newton's third law**: When one object exerts a force on a second object, the second object exerts an equal but opposite force on the first object. In other words, for every action, there is an equal but opposite reaction.

What Is Force?

The simple definition of **force**, as explained in the table, is a push or a pull. It's important to understand, however, that force is a vector quantity, which means that it has both magnitude (a measure of the force that is applied) and direction (the direction in which the force is applied).

Forces exist all around you, even if you're not aware of them. When you set an apple on a table, the apple's **weight** (the force gravity exerts on an object's mass) exerts a force in the downward direction on the table. Meanwhile, the table also exerts an upward force (also known as the **normal force**) on the apple. In this case, the apple has no **net force** (the sum of all the forces acting on an object, also known as the resultant force) acting on it, because the forces acting on it are equal and opposite in direction—in other words, the downward pull of gravity and the upward push of the table are equal. (Remember Newton's third law of motion: For every action, there is an equal but opposite reaction.) If one of these forces was stronger than the other, the net force on the apple would be greater in one direction than in the other, and the apple would move in the direction of the stronger force.

Another example of force is friction. Friction is a force that opposes movement. Both objects at rest and objects in motion experience friction. Friction occurs between the surfaces of two objects that touch, such as a chest of drawers and a hardwood floor. For example, a chest of drawers at rest on a hardwood floor experiences a **static frictional force** that opposes its movement. To push the chest of drawers across the floor—that is, to make the chest of drawers start to move—you would have to apply enough force to overcome the static frictional force between the chest of drawers and the floor.

An object in motion, such as a Frisbee sliding across a paved driveway, experiences a **sliding frictional force** in the opposite direction of its movement. The sliding frictional force opposes the movement of the Frisbee across the driveway and eventually causes the Frisbee to stop sliding. As the Frisbee slides in one direction, the frictional force between the Frisbee and the pavement acts in the opposite direction.

In addition, it's important to note that heavy objects experience more friction than light objects. This occurs because the normal force—that is, the upward force applied to an object in reaction to the downward force of the object's weight—for heavy objects is greater than the normal force for light objects.

Making Mechanical Calculations

On the Mechanical Comprehension subtest of the ASVAB, knowing and understanding the formulas used to calculate different quantities will give you an excellent advantage. The following table provides common formulas used for mechanical calculations along with a brief explanation:

TO CALCULATE...	USE THE FORMULA...	EXPLANATION
acceleration	$a = \dfrac{\Delta v}{\Delta t}$	Acceleration (in meters per second squared) is equal to the change in velocity (in meters per second) divided by the change in time (in seconds).
force	$F = ma$	The net force (in newtons) acting on an object is equal to the product of the object's mass (in kilograms) and the acceleration that results from the force (in meters per second squared).
gravitational potential energy	$PE_{gravitational} = mgh$	The gravitational potential energy of an object (in Joules) is equal to the product of the object's mass (in kilograms), the acceleration due to gravity (9.8 m/s²), and the height of the object (in meters).
kinetic energy	$KE = \dfrac{1}{2}mv^2$	The kinetic energy of an object (in Joules) is equal to the product of half of the object's mass (in kilograms) and the square of the velocity of the object (in meters per second).

TO CALCULATE...	USE THE FORMULA...	EXPLANATION
mechanical advantage	$MA = \dfrac{F_{resistance}}{F_{effort}}$	Mechanical advantage is equal to resistance, the force applied by a machine to an object (in newtons), divided by effort, the force applied to the machine by a human (in newtons).
mechanical energy	$ME = PE + KE$	Mechanical energy is equal to the sum of the potential energy and the kinetic energy of an object in a closed system.
power	$P = \dfrac{W}{t}$	Power (in Joules per second or watts) is equal to work (in Joules) divided by time (in seconds).
pressure	$P = \dfrac{F}{A}$	Pressure (in Pascals or newtons per meter squared) is equal to force (in newtons) divided by area (in meters squared). NOTE: Pressure may also be measured in pounds per square inch (psi), where the force (in pounds) is divided by the area (in square inches).
velocity	$v = \dfrac{d}{t}$	Velocity (in meters per second) is equal to distance (in meters) divided by time (in seconds).

TO CALCULATE...	USE THE FORMULA...	EXPLANATION
weight	$W = mg$	The weight of an object (in newtons) is equal to the product of the object's mass (in kilograms) and the acceleration due to gravity (9.8 m/s²).
work	$W = Fd$	Work (in Joules) is equal to the product of a force applied to an object (in newtons) and the displacement (in meters) of the object.

Simple Machines

Simple machines make work easier by giving you a **mechanical advantage**. In other words, they reduce the amount of force required to do work. All simple machines rely on the basic principles of mechanics outlined earlier in this chapter. Simple machines fall into six categories including levers, inclined planes, pulleys, screws, wedges, and wheels and axles.

Levers

Levers fall into three categories. First-class levers are perhaps the most well-known category of levers. A **first-class lever** is basically a bar (a metal rod, a wooden board, a sturdy stick) positioned on a fixed pivot point, or fulcrum. The lever is placed under a load and over a fulcrum. A downward force is applied to the end of the lever opposite the load. This downward force causes the lever to lift the load. The closer the fulcrum is to the load you want to lift, the less force you need to apply to the lever to lift the load. A lever provides a mechanical advantage by reducing the amount of force required to lift a load.

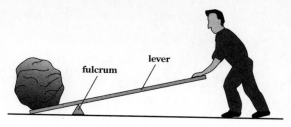

When working with levers, use the following formula to determine unknown variables:

$$W \times d_1 = F \times d_2$$

In this formula, W is the weight of the load in newtons (N), d_1 is the distance from the load to the fulcrum, F is the applied force in newtons (N), and d_2 is the distance from the fulcrum to the person applying the force to the lever. Consider the following:

A man uses a lever to lift a boulder weighing 200 N. The lever is positioned on a fulcrum 2 meters from the boulder. The man stands at the opposite end of the lever, a distance of 3 meters from the fulcrum, and applies a downward force. How much force must he apply to lift the boulder?

To answer the question, plug the given information into the formula and solve:

$$W \times d_1 = F \times d_2$$
$$200 \text{ N} \times 2 \text{ m} = F \times 3 \text{ m}$$
$$400 \text{ N-m} = F \times 3 \text{ m}$$
$$400 \text{ N-m} \div 3 \text{ m} = F$$
$$F \approx 133 \text{ N}$$

Therefore, the man must apply a force of about 133 N to move a boulder that weighs 200 N.

Unlike a first-class lever, where the fulcrum is positioned between the load and the applied force, a **second-class lever** places the load between the fulcrum and the applied force. A wheelbarrow is an example of a second-class lever. The fulcrum is the wheel, located at one end, and the force is applied to the handles at the other. The heavy load (for example, a load of gravel) is located between the fulcrum and the applied force.

With **third-class levers**, the force is applied between the fulcrum and the load. For example, a pair of grilling tongs is composed of two third-class levers. The fulcrum is the point where the two arms of the tongs meet. The pinching end of the tongs, where food is held, is the load. To hold the load, force is applied to each arm of the tongs somewhere between the fulcrum and the load.

Inclined Planes

An **inclined plane** is, in simpler terms, a ramp. An inclined plane does not decrease the amount of work that must be done to move an object to a particular height. It does, however, decrease the amount of force required to do work by increasing the distance over which the force is applied.

When it comes to inclined planes, it helps to compare the formulas for force and weight:

$$Force = mass \times acceleration \text{ or } F = ma$$

$$Weight = mass \times acceleration \text{ due to gravity } \text{ or } W = mg$$

On its face, the formula for weight looks different from the formula for force, but if you break it down into its parts, you can see that the formulas include the same information. Recall that acceleration due to gravity is a type of acceleration, which means that $g = a$. Therefore, $ma = mg$, which means that $F = W$ or $F = mg$.

Now compare the formulas for gravitational potential energy and work:

$$PE_{gravitational} = mass \times acceleration \text{ due to gravity} \times height$$

$$\text{or } PE_{gravitational} = mgh$$

$$Work = Force \times distance \text{ or } W = Fd$$

Again, the formula for work looks different from the formula for gravitational potential energy, but if you break it down into its parts, you can see that the formulas include the same information. Recall from the previous example that $F = mg$. If you substitute mg for F in the formula for work, you see that $W = mgd$. Also, note that height (h), the distance an object is raised, in the formula $PE_{gravitational} = mgh$, is the displacement of an object, or the difference between its initial height and its final height. In the formula $W = Fd$, d is the displacement of an object, or the difference between its initial and final positions, which means that $h = d$. Therefore, $W = mgh$. Since $PE_{gravitational} = mgh$, you can see that $W = PE_{gravitational}$.

The comparison of these formulas proves that the amount of work done to slide an object up an inclined plane is equal to the final gravitational potential energy of the object when it's lifted straight up.

Work Required with an Inclined Plane

$W = Fd$

$W = (mg)d$

$W = (68 \text{ kg} \times 9.8 \text{ m/s}^2)(1 \text{ m})$

$W = (666.4 \text{ N})(1 \text{ m})$

$W = 666.4 \text{ N-m or } 666.4 \text{ J}$

Work Required without an Inclined Plane

$PE_{gravitational} = mgh$

$PE_{gravitational} = (68 \text{ kg})(9.8 \text{ m/s}^2)(1 \text{ m})$

$PE_{gravitational} = (666.4 \text{ N})(1 \text{ m})$

$PE_{gravitational} = 666.4 \text{ N-m or } 666.4 \text{ J}$

$$W = PE_{gravitational}$$

To determine the mechanical advantage of using an inclined plane, use the following formula:

$$\frac{\text{Length of ramp}}{\text{Height of ramp}} = \frac{\text{Object's weight}}{\text{Force required to move object}} \quad \text{or} \quad \frac{1}{h} = \frac{W}{F}$$

Then, plug in the numbers and solve (remember that an object's weight is equivalent to its mass multiplied by the acceleration due to gravity, or mg).

Force Required with an Inclined Plane

$$\frac{l}{h} = \frac{W}{F}$$

$$\frac{2\ m}{1\ m} = \frac{(68\ kg)\,(9.8\ m/s^2)}{F}$$

$$F(2m) = (666.4\ N)\,(1\ m)$$

$$F = \frac{666.4\ N\text{-}m}{2\ m}$$

$$F = 333.2\ N$$

Force Required without an Inclined Plane

$$F = ma$$

$$F = (68\ kg)\,(9.8\ m/s^2)$$

$$F = 666.4\ N$$

By using an inclined plane, and barring friction, a force of 333.2 N is needed to move an object weighing 666.4 N.

The comparison of these formulas proves that the amount of force required to slide an object up an inclined plane is less than the amount of force required to lift the object straight up.

Pulleys

Pulleys are another type of simple machine. A **fixed pulley** is composed of a single grooved wheel that holds a belt, rope, or chain. A fixed pulley changes the direction of an applied force, but it does not change the magnitude of the applied force required to lift an object. For example, when using a pulley to lift a heavy object, you would pull down on the belt, rope, or chain to lift up the object.

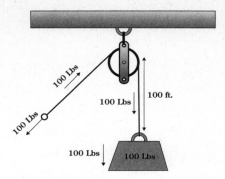

A **block and tackle**, however, is a series of pulleys that provides a mechanical advantage by decreasing the force required to lift an object while increasing distance. In other words, you apply a smaller force to the rope or belt but pull the rope or belt farther to lift the object.

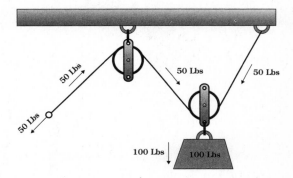

Pulleys can also transmit rotational motion. **Belt-drive pulleys** consist of two or more wheels connected by a belt. As one wheel rotates, the belt rotates, which causes the other wheel to rotate. In a belt-drive pulley system, all the wheels rotate in the same direction, unless the belt between two wheels is crossed. Then, those two wheels rotate in opposite directions.

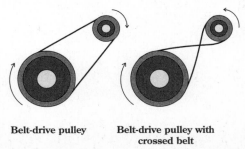

Belt-drive pulley   Belt-drive pulley with crossed belt

Screws

A **screw** is an inclined plane wrapped in a continuous spiral around a cylinder. The ridges on the screw are known as the **thread**, and the distance between the ridges is known as the **pitch** of the thread. The closer the threads of a screw are—that is, the smaller the pitch—the easier it is to turn the screw. Generally, when you turn a screw clockwise (to the right), it tightens into place, and when you turn it counterclockwise, it loosens. This is where the saying "Righty, tighty, lefty, loosey" comes from. To insert a screw into a wall, a board, or some other material, you must rotate it. As the screw rotates, its threads cut into the material, thereby securing the screw in place.

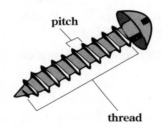

Wedges

A simple machine used to split materials is a **wedge**. A wedge is actually a type of inclined plane, but unlike an inclined plane, which remains stationary while in use, a wedge moves. A wedge typically has a sharp edge. An example of a wedge is a chisel. The sharp edge of a chisel can be placed between two objects (such as boards or bricks). When the wedge is driven between the objects, it splits them apart. Wedges can also be used to lift heavy objects by driving the wedge between the object and the surface upon which it rests. In addition, wedges can hold objects in place (such as a doorstop).

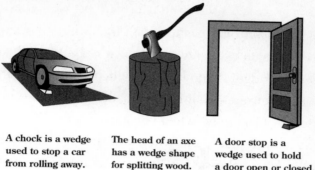

A chock is a wedge
used to stop a car
from rolling away.

The head of an axe
has a wedge shape
for splitting wood.

A door stop is a
wedge used to hold
a door open or closed.

To determine the mechanical advantage of using a wedge, use the following formula:

$$Mechanical\ Advantage = \frac{Slope}{Width} \text{ or } MA = \frac{l}{w}$$

In this formula, l is the length of the slope of the wedge and w is the width of the wide end of the wedge. Consider the following:

A wedge is 4 centimeters wide and has a slope that is 8 centimeters long. What is the mechanical advantage of the wedge?

$$MA = \frac{l}{w}$$

$$MA = \frac{8 \text{ cm}}{4 \text{ cm}}$$

$$MA = \frac{2}{1}$$

Therefore, this wedge has a mechanical advantage of 2 to 1 or 2:1.

Wheels and Axles

The **wheel and axle** is a simple machine that consists of a wheel attached to a shaft (the axle) in such a way that when one or the other is rotated, both the wheel and the axle move. The wheel and axle can be used to increase force or increase distance. Examples of both uses of the wheel and axle can be found on a car. For example, the steering wheel increases force. The steering wheel has a large radius (the measure of a circle from its center to its outer edge). It is attached to an axle with a much smaller radius. To rotate the axle without the wheel would require a great amount of force. However, the radius of the wheel is so much larger than the radius of the axle that when you apply a small force to rotate the wheel, the force on the axle is multiplied. Therefore, the wheel increases the force on the axle.

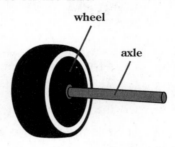

The wheel and axle can also be used to increase distance. For example, the tires on a car are attached to an axle. When the axle rotates, the tires rotate. Because the axle has a much smaller radius than the tires, however, the tires rotate through a much greater distance than the axle in the same amount of time. For example, the length of the radius of the wheels of a lawn mower is 5 times greater than the length of the radius of the axle. If the axle rotates 4 inches per second, then the wheels rotate at a speed 5 times greater than that of the axle: 4 inches per second × 5 = 20 inches per second. Therefore, each rotation of 4 inches by the axle results in a rotation of 20 inches by the wheels.

To determine the mechanical advantage of a wheel and axle, use the following formula:

$$Mechanical\ Advantage = \frac{radius\ of\ wheel}{radius\ of\ axle} \text{ or } MA = \frac{r_{wheel}}{r_{axle}}$$

Gears

Gears are not actually simple machines, but it's important to understand how they work because they are used in many mechanical devices. **Gears** are rotating wheels with teeth that fit together with other gears. Like pulleys, gears can transmit motion. When gears touch—that is, when their teeth interlock—they always rotate in opposite directions.

gears

A gear with a smaller radius rotates faster and makes more revolutions per minute than a gear with a larger radius. The ratio between the numbers of teeth on two interlocking gears determines the speed at which the gears rotate. For example, if two gears are the same size and have the same number of teeth, they will rotate at the same speed. However, if one gear has 5 teeth and the other has 10 teeth, the gears will rotate at different speeds. In this situation, the ratio of the number of teeth is 5:10, which can be further reduced to a gear ratio of 1:2. This means that for each revolution of the gear with 5 teeth, the gear with 10 teeth makes half a revolution. Or, for each revolution of the gear with 10 teeth, the gear with 5 teeth makes two revolutions.

Sprockets, like gears, are wheels with teeth, but unlike gears, sprockets never interlock. Instead, sprockets mesh with a chain or some other material. Two sprockets that are joined by a chain rotate in the same direction. A sprocket with a smaller radius rotates faster and makes more revolutions per minute than a sprocket with a larger radius.

sprockets

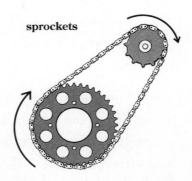

Practice Questions

Directions: Read each question, and then choose the correct answer.

1. How does a block and tackle decrease the magnitude of the force required to lift an object?

    A. By decreasing the mass of the object to be lifted
    B. By changing the direction of the rotation of the pulleys
    C. By increasing the distance the rope or belt must be pulled
    D. By placing the object between a fulcrum and the applied force

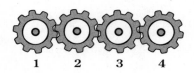

2. Which two gears in the image shown above rotate in the same direction?

    A. 1 and 2
    B. 1 and 3
    C. 2 and 3
    D. 3 and 4

3. What is the formula for finding the weight of an object?

    A. $P = \dfrac{W}{t}$

    B. $P = \dfrac{F}{A}$

    C. $W = mg$

    D. $W = Fd$

4. What is kinetic energy?

    A. The energy of motion
    B. The stored energy of an object
    C. The total energy in a closed system
    D. The energy that opposes movement

5. The nutcracker above is an example of a(n)

    A. wedge.
    B. fixed pulley.
    C. inclined plane.
    D. second-class lever.

6. The distance between each ridge on a screw is known as the
    _____ of the screw.

    A. pitch
    B. angle
    C. radius
    D. thread

7. A worker is using a first-class lever to lift a load of 150 N. The lever is 5 meters long and the fulcrum is 1 meter from the load. How much downward force does the worker have to apply to the lever to lift the load?

   A. 30.0 N
   B. 37.5 N
   C. 50.0 N
   D. 75.5 N

8. An inclined plane provides a mechanical advantage by

   A. decreasing work and increasing distance.
   B. decreasing force and increasing distance.
   C. decreasing work and decreasing distance.
   D. decreasing force and decreasing distance.

9. What is the mechanical advantage of a wheel with radius 15 inches attached to an axle with radius 3 inches?

   A. 5:1
   B. 3:1
   C. 5:3
   D. 15:1

10. What is net force?

   A. The force that opposes movement
   B. The sum of all forces acting on an object
   C. The force caused by the downward pull of gravity
   D. The upward force that reacts to the weight of an object

Answer Explanations

1. **C.** A block and tackle is a series of pulleys that decreases the force required to lift a load by increasing distance. The pulleys bear some of the weight of the load, thereby decreasing the amount of force needed to pull the rope to lift the object. However, the result is that more of the rope (increased distanced) must be pulled to lift the object.

2. **B.** Gears with interlocking teeth rotate in opposite directions. Because gear 1 and gear 2 have interlocking teeth, they rotate in opposite directions. This means that gear 2 and gear 3 also rotate in opposite directions. Therefore, gear 1 and gear 3 have to rotate in the same direction.

3. **C.** The weight (W) of an object can be determined by multiplying the object's mass (m) by the acceleration due to gravity (g). Therefore, the correct formula is $W = mg$.

4. **A.** Kinetic energy is the energy of motion. The total energy in a closed system (that is, kinetic energy plus potential energy) is known as mechanical energy, while stored energy is known as potential energy.

5. **D.** The nutcracker is an example of a second-class lever, because it places the load (in this case, the nut) between the fulcrum (the point where the two handles of the nutcracker meet) and the applied force (the force is applied to the handles).

6. **A.** A screw is an inclined plane wrapped in a continuous spiral around a cylinder. The ridges on the screw are known as the thread, and the distance between each ridge is known as the pitch of the thread.

7. **B.** To solve, use the formula $W \times d_1 = F \times d_2$, where W is the weight of the load in newtons, d_1 is the distance from the load to the fulcrum in meters, F is the force required to lift the load in newtons, and d_2 is the distance from the fulcrum to the worker in meters:

$$W \times d_1 = F \times d_2$$
$$150 \text{ N} \times 1 \text{ m} = F \times 4 \text{ m}$$
$$150 \text{ N-m} = F \times 4 \text{ m}$$
$$150 \text{ N-m} \div 4 \text{ m} = F$$
$$F = 37.5 \text{ N}$$

8. **B.** An inclined plane provides a mechanical advantage by decreasing force and increasing distance. An inclined plane spreads work over a greater distance, thereby lessening the amount of force required to do the work. The amount of work is the same, regardless of whether an inclined plane is used.

9. **A.** To solve, use the formula $MA = \dfrac{r_{wheel}}{r_{axle}}$, where MA is the mechanical advantage, r_{wheel} is the radius of the wheel in inches, and r_{axle} is the radius of the axle in inches:

$$MA = \frac{r_{wheel}}{r_{axle}}$$
$$MA = \frac{15 \text{ in}}{3 \text{ in}}$$
$$MA = \frac{5}{1}$$

Therefore, the mechanical advantage is 5:1.

10. **B.** Net force is the sum of all the forces acting on an object. Net force is also known as the resultant force.

Review Chapter 8:
Electronics Information

Understanding Electronics

The Electronics Information subtest of the ASVAB tests your understanding of the basics of electricity. *Electricity* is the term used to describe many phenomena that result from the movement and interaction of electrons, which are one of three types of subatomic particles that make up atoms. Electricity occurs in nature, and it can also be produced.

The Electronics Information subtest includes 20 questions to be answered in 9 minutes. Some questions may assess your understanding of electrical concepts, while others may require you to identify parts of circuits or use formulas to calculate current, voltage, or resistance. It's important to note that only some military careers require a top score on this subtest.

Important Terms and Symbols

The following table includes a list of common terms or concepts with which you should be familiar when taking the ASVAB's Electronics Information subtest. The table provides a simple explanation for each term or concept and the symbol often used to represent this concept in formulas.

TERM/CONCEPT	EXPLANATION	SYMBOL (ITALICIZED) / ABBREVIATION
alternating current (AC)	an electric current that moves back and forth along a conductor at regular intervals	—
ammeter	a device used to measure current	—
amperage	the strength of a current of electricity (in amperes)	—
ampere (amp)	the unit of measurement for electric current that is equal to one coulomb per second	A
atom	a basic unit of matter composed of a dense nucleus packed with protons and neutrons and surrounded by a cloud of electrons	—
conductor	a material that allows for easy flow of electric current	—
coulomb	the unit of measurement for the amount of electricity transferred by a current of one ampere in one second	C
current	the rate of flow of an electric charge caused by the movement of electrons between two points	I
direct current (DC)	an electric current that moves in only one direction in a conductor	—
electromotive force	(*see* voltage)	—

TERM/CONCEPT	EXPLANATION	SYMBOL (ITALICIZED) / ABBREVIATION
electron	a negatively charged particle that orbits the nucleus of an atom	—
insulator	a material that does not allow for easy flow of electric current	—
intensity	(*see* current)	—
kilowatt	1,000 watts	kW
kilowatt-hour	the amount of energy used by one kilowatt in one hour, equivalent to 3.6 million Joules	kWh
milliamp	$\dfrac{1}{1,000}$	mA
neutron	an uncharged particle found in the nucleus of an atom	—
ohm	the unit of measurement for resistance, represented by the Greek letter omega (Ω); one ohm is equal to the amount of resistance in a circuit that allows one volt of electrical pressure to produce a current of one ampere	Ω
ohmmeter	a device used to measure resistance	—

TERM/CONCEPT	EXPLANATION	SYMBOL (ITALICIZED) / ABBREVIATION
Ohm's law	a law, developed by Georg Simon Ohm, which states that current is directly proportional to voltage and inversely proportional to resistance and expressed by the following formula: Current $(I) =$ $\dfrac{\text{Voltage } (E)}{\text{Resistance } (R)}$	$I = \dfrac{E}{R}$
power	the rate at which energy is transferred or converted	P
proton	a positively charged particle found in the nucleus of an atom	—
resistance	opposition to the flow of an electric current	R
semiconductor	a material that is neither a good conductor nor a good insulator	—
shell	any of the various orbits around the nucleus of an atom that are occupied by electrons	—
valence shell	the outermost shell of an atom	—
volt	the unit of measurement for voltage	V

TERM/CONCEPT	EXPLANATION	SYMBOL (ITALICIZED) / ABBREVIATION
voltage	the difference in electric potential energy per unit charge between two points; also known as electrical pressure, electrical potential, or electromotive force	E (or V)
voltmeter	a device used to measure voltage	—
watt	the unit of power equal to the power produced by one ampere across a potential difference of one volt	W

Electrons and Electron Movement

To understand the basics of electricity and electronics, you must understand what electrons are and how they move. **Electrons** are negatively charged particles that orbit the nucleus of **atom**, which is the basic unit of matter. The atom's nucleus is composed of positively charged particles called **protons** and uncharged particles called **neutrons**. Electrons may occupy a number of different orbits around the nucleus of the atom known as **shells**. The outermost shell is called the **valence shell**, and electrons in this shell are called valence electrons. The valence shell of an atom can hold a maximum of eight electrons.

Atoms with just one or two valence electrons are unstable and will give up their valence electrons. For example, Electron A is the valence electron orbiting one atom, and Electron B is the valence electron orbiting another atom. Suddenly, Electron A collides with Electron B, which spins Electron B out of orbit. Most of the energy from Electron A is passed to Electron B during the collision, so Electron A takes over Electron B's former orbit. Meanwhile, Electron B, which has absorbed most of Electron A's energy, moves on to collide with Electron C, and the process continues. This chain reaction creates a flow of electrons known as an electrical **current**, which is the rate of flow of an electric charge caused by the movement of electrons between two points.

Materials composed of atoms that have just one or two valence electrons allow for the easy flow of electrons and, in turn, the flow of electricity. These materials are known as **conductors**. Copper, silver, gold, and aluminum are all examples of good conductors. Water is also a good conductor.

Materials composed of atoms with full valence shells do not allow for the easy flow of electrons and, in turn, resist the flow of electricity. These materials are called **insulators**. Glass, porcelain, and rubber are examples of good insulators.

Materials composed of atoms with valence shells that are about half full are neither good conductors nor good insulators. These materials are known as **semiconductors** and are often used to build parts used in electronic devices. Silicon is one of the most well known semiconductors.

Making Electrical Calculations

On the Electronics Information subtest of the ASVAB, knowing and understanding the formulas used to calculate different quantities will give you an excellent advantage. The following table provides common formulas used for electrical calculations along with a brief explanation:

TO CALCULATE...	USE THE FORMULA...	EXPLANATION
current	$I = \dfrac{E}{R}$	Current (in amperes) is equal to voltage (in volts) divided by resistance (in ohms).

TO CALCULATE...	USE THE FORMULA...	EXPLANATION
power	$P = IE$	Power (in watts) is equal to the product of current (in amperes) and voltage (in volts).
resistance	$R = \dfrac{E}{I}$	Resistance (in ohms) is equal to voltage (in volts) divided by current (in amperes).
voltage	$E = IR$	Voltage (in volts) is equal to the product of current (in amperes) and resistance (in ohms).

Current, Voltage, and Resistance

An electrical current, as explained previously, is the rate of flow of an electric charge caused by the movement of electrons between two points. The **intensity**, or strength, of this rate of flow is measured in **amperes** (A) with a device called an **ammeter**. One ampere is equal to one coulomb per second. A **coulomb** (C) is the amount of electricity transferred by a current of one ampere in one second. An electrical current that moves in only one direction along a conductor is known as a **direct current** (DC). An electrical current that moves back and forth along a conductor at regular intervals is known as an **alternating current** (AC). But what causes the flow of electrons from one point to another? The answer is pressure, or voltage.

Voltage (also known as electrical pressure, electrical potential, or **electromotive force**) is the difference in electric potential between two points. In other words, voltage is the total amount of energy necessary to send an electric charge along a path between two points on a conductor. Voltage is measured in **volts** (V) using a device called a **voltmeter**.

It's important to note, however, that electrical currents typically encounter obstacles on their way from one end of a conductor to the other. These obstacles create **resistance**, which is opposition to the flow of an electric current. Many circuits (which are discussed later) include resistors to control the flow of electricity, which prevents the circuits from overheating. Resistance is measured in units called **ohms** (Ω) on a device called an **ohmmeter**.

Ohm's Law

The relationship between current, voltage, and resistance is described by Ohm's law, which is named for the German physicist who first discovered it, Georg Simon Ohm. In 1827, Ohm published a book, which in English translates to The Galvanic Circuit Investigated Mathematically. In this work, Ohm stated that current is directly proportional to voltage and inversely proportional to resistance. This idea is represented by the following formula:

$$\text{Current} = \frac{\text{Voltage}}{\text{Resistance}} \quad \text{or} \quad I = \frac{E}{R}$$

In other words, the voltage at any point along a circuit is a product of the intensity of the current and the resistance at that point of the circuit:

$$E = IR$$

Now consider the following example:

A wall outlet is supplying power to a hair dryer with a resistance of 8 ohms. The current flowing through the hair dryer is 15 amperes. What is the voltage of the outlet?

To answer this question, plug the given information into the formula and solve. You need to find the voltage, so use the formula $E = IR$:

$$E = IR$$
$$E = (15 \text{ A})(8 \ \Omega)$$
$$E = 120 \text{ V}$$

Therefore, the wall outlet is supplying the hair dryer with 120 volts of electricity.

Electric Power and Basic Circuits

The rate at which electric energy moves through an electrical circuit is called **electric power**. The SI unit for measuring electric power is **watts**. The formula used to find electrical power is $P = I \times E$. So, to find electrical power, you should multiply the voltage by the current.

Electric power must flow through a **circuit**. A circuit is made up of at least three things: a power source, a load, and conductors that connect the load to the power source. The current running through a circuit runs from the negative terminal of the power source toward the positive terminal. A **closed circuit** is a circuit in which all three of these components are connected, allowing the current to flow. An **incomplete circuit** is not completely connected, and it will not allow electrical power to run through it.

As the electrical power flows through the circuit, it must pass through the conductors. The **conductors** are parts of the circuit that allow the energy to flow. Generally, the conductors are wires. In a closed circuit, the electrical power passes from the power source through the conductors to the load. A **load** is the part of the circuit that changes the electrical energy into a different type of energy. For example, a heater is a type of a load. A heater resists the electric power and changes it from electric energy into heat energy.

The three main parts of a circuit can be configured in different ways to create different types of circuits.

- A **series circuit** is configured so that the electric power can travel through only one path. So, if any part of a series circuit is broken, the entire circuit will not work. In a series circuit, the current is the same at all points in the circuit.

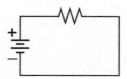

- A **parallel circuit** is configured so that the electric power can run through different paths. In a parallel circuit, the pieces are arranged on different branches in the circuit. If one part of a parallel circuit is broken, the energy can use one of the other branches to move. In a parallel circuit, power is shared among different components.

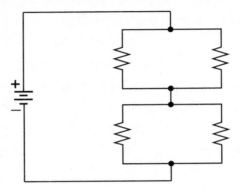

- A **combination circuit**, which is also called a **series-parallel circuit**, is a circuit that includes at least one series connection between two parts of the circuit and at least one parallel connection between two parts of the circuit.

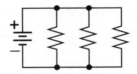

Although circuits need to have only three parts (a voltage source, a load, and conductors that connect the load to the voltage source), they can and usually do include a number of other components. Output components such as a buzzer and lamps are powered by the circuit. Other devices such as resistors and transformers change and manipulate the electric power running through the circuit. It is important to know the many different components that can make up simple circuits before you take the ASVAB.

To make understanding and drawing circuits easier, professionals use symbols to represent the many possible components of circuits. The following table explains the components that can make up circuits. The table also shows the common symbols that are used to represent the components in diagrams and other drawings.

NAME	DEFINITION	SYMBOL
POWER SOURCES		
Cell	A **cell** supplies chemical energy that can be turned into electrical energy.	—∣⊢—
Battery	A **battery** is a power source with multiple cells. Batteries have both positive (+) and negative (−) ends.	—∣∣⊢—
AC power source	An **AC power source** uses alternating current to power a circuit.	—o∿o—
DC power source	A **DC power source** uses direct current to power a circuit.	—o⁺ o⁻—
Fuse	A **fuse** is a connector that will melt and break the connection in the circuit if too much current runs through it. Fuses are used for safety.	—▭—

NAME	DEFINITION	SYMBOL
WIRES AND CONNECTORS		
Wire	**Wires** are usually metal, and they connect the components of circuits.	
Jointed wires	When wires are connected at places in a circuit, they are called **jointed wires**. When jointed wires are pictured in diagram, it is important to show they are connected so that the audience does not think they are separate wires.	
Unjointed wires	**Unjointed wires** in circuit diagrams are wires that run over or under each other, but do not connect. It is important to indicate that unjointed wires do not connect so the audience is not confused.	
Ground	A **ground** is a connection that does not have voltage.	

NAME	DEFINITION	SYMBOL
OUTPUT DEVICES		
Lamp	A **lamp** is an output device that produces light from electrical power.	
Motor	A **motor** is an output device that produces movement from electrical power.	
Heater	A **heater** is an output device that produces heat from electrical power.	
Bell	A **bell** is an output device that produces sound from electrical power.	
Buzzer	A **buzzer** is an output device that produces sound from electrical power.	

NAME	DEFINITION	SYMBOL
AUDIO AND RADIO DEVICES		
Microphone	A **microphone** is an audio component that converts sound into electrical energy.	
Earphone	**Earphones** are audio components that convert electrical energy into sound.	
Speaker	A **speaker** is an audio component that converts electrical energy into sound.	
Amplifier	An **amplifier** is different from other audio and radio devices because it is itself another circuit. Amplifiers can increase current and voltage.	
SWITCHES		
On/Off switch	When the **on/off switch** is in the *on* position, energy can pass through it. When the switch in the *off* position, energy cannot pass through it.	

NAME	DEFINITION	SYMBOL
Push Switch	A **push switch** is a switch that connects or breaks a connection in a circuit only when the push button is being held down.	
Relay Switch	A **relay switch** is controlled by a second electric circuit. The second circuit is completely separate from the first.	
DIODES		
Diode	A **diode** is an electrical device with two terminals, which allow energy to flow in only one direction through it. Diodes are like valves that allow energy out but do not allow it to come back in through the same direction.	
Light-Emitting Diode (LED)	A **light-emitting diode (LED)** is a diode that emits visible light when electric power runs through it.	

NAME	DEFINITION	SYMBOL
Photodiode	A **photodiode** is a diode that can turn light into electrical power.	
OTHER COMPONENTS		
Resistor	A **resistor** is a passive connector in a circuit that resists the flow of electricity. Resistors are used to regulate the amount of electric power running through a circuit to maintain safety. Resisters can be output devices such as lamps and heaters.	OR
Variable resistor	**Variable resistors** can be modified to change the amount of resistance they have. A rheostat is a variable resistor that is used when the current flowing through a circuit is high. A potentiometer is a variable resistor that is commonly used for audio devices.	OR

NAME	DEFINITION	SYMBOL
Inductor	An **inductor** is a coil that stores energy in a magnetic field.	
Capacitors	**Capacitors**, which are also known as **condensers**, store electrical energy. AC current passes through capacitors, but DC current is stored in capacitors. When power is supplied to a capacitor, the capacitor charges, and when the current is stopped, the capacitor releases its energy slowly. Therefore, capacitors can take in variable current and send out a smoother current.	
Polarized Capacitor	A **polarized capacitor** has a positive (+) side and negative (−) side. These capacitors must be installed in the correct order because they have different poles.	

NAME	DEFINITION	SYMBOL
Transistor	A **transistor** is an electrical component that can amplify, reduce, or otherwise control electrical power. Transistors have three terminals.	
Transformer	A **transformer** is a component that transfers energy from one circuit to another.	

Practice Questions

Directions: Read each question, and then choose the correct answer.

1. What is the outermost orbit around the nucleus of an atom?

    A. Neutron
    B. Valence shell
    C. Semiconductor
    D. Alternating current

2. The rate of flow of an electric current is measured in units called

    A. volts (V).
    B. ohms (Ω).
    C. amperes (A).
    D. coulombs (C).

3.   Which of the following is a circuit that connects to another circuit?

    A.   Motor
    B.   Heater
    C.   Resister
    D.   Amplifier

4.   An alarm clock powered by a 9-volt battery has a resistance of 9,000 ohms. What is the current of the alarm clock?

    A. $\dfrac{1}{1,000}$ A

    B. $\dfrac{1}{100}$ A

    C.   1 A

    D.   10 A

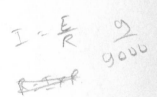

5.   If a single break in a circuit causes the entire circuit to stop running, it is a

    A.   series circuit.
    B.   parallel circuit.
    C.   combination circuit.
    D.   series-parallel circuit.

6.   Which of the following is pictured here?

    A.   Fuse
    B.   Ground
    C.   Battery
    D.   Amplifier

7. Which of the following formulas is used to express Ohm's law?

   A. $I = ER$

   B. $E = \dfrac{R}{I}$

   C. $R = IE$

   D. $I = \dfrac{E}{R}$

8. A switch that allows current to run through it when it is closed is a called a(n)

   A. push switch.
   B. relay switch.
   C. on-off switch.
   D. None of the above

9. The atoms of a particular material have one valence electron. This material is most likely a(n)

   A. ammeter.
   B. insulator.
   C. conductor.
   D. semiconductor.

10. Which of the following images is the symbol for a variable resistor?

A.

B.

C.

D.   Y

Answer Explanations

1. **B.** The various orbits around the nucleus of an atom, which are oc-cupied by electrons, are known as shells. The outermost shell is called the valence shell. A neutron is an uncharged particle in the nucleus of an atom. A semiconductor is a material that is neither a good conductor nor a good insulator. An alternating current is an electric current that moves back and forth along a conductor at regular intervals.

2. **C.** The rate of flow, or strength, of an electric current is measured in units called amperes (A). Resistance, or opposition to the flow of an electric current, is measured in units called ohms (Ω). Voltage is mea-sured in units called volts (V). A coulomb (C) is a unit of measurement for the amount of electricity transferred by a current of one ampere in one second.

3. **D.** The amplifier is a component that is actually a circuit that con-nects to other circuits. Amplifiers can increase, or amplify, voltage and current.

4. **A.** An alarm clock powered by a 9-volt battery and with a resistance of 9,000 ohms has a current of $\frac{1}{1,000}$ amperes (A), which is also known as 1 milliamp (mA):

$$I = \frac{E}{R}$$

$$I = \frac{9 \text{ V}}{9{,}000 \ \Omega}$$

$$I = \frac{1}{1{,}000} \text{ A or 1 mA}$$

5. **A.** A series circuit is configured so that electrical energy can only flow through one path. If that path is broken in any way, the entire circuit stops working. Parallel circuits and combination circuits (also called series-parallel circuits) can sometimes continue to function with a break because the electric power has another path it can follow.

6. **B.** The symbol pictured represents a ground. A ground is a connection that does not have voltage.

7. **D.** Ohm's law states that current is directly proportional to voltage and inversely proportional to resistance and is represented by the following formulas:

1. $I = \dfrac{E}{R}$

2. $E = IR$

3. $R = \dfrac{E}{I}$

8. **C.** An on-off switch can be in two positions: open and closed. In the open position (which is also the *off* position), the switch breaks the connection in the circuit. In the closed position (which is also the *on* position), the switch completes the connection in the circuit.

9. **C.** Conductors are materials composed of atoms that have just one or two valence electrons that allow for the easy flow of electrons and, in turn, the easy flow of electricity. Examples of good conductors include copper, silver, gold, aluminum, and water.

10. **A.** The image in choice A is the symbol for the variable resistor. Variable resistors can be modified to change the amount of resistance they use in a particular circuit.

THE BIG PICTURE: HOW TO PREPARE YEAR-ROUND

No matter how far in the future you plan to take the ASVAB examination, the time to start preparing is *now*. And this part of the book is here to help. In the **Strategies for Long-Term Preparation** chapter (page 279), you will learn how to register for the test, how to make the most of your preparation time both in the classroom and outside of it, and how to manage the stress a test of this magnitude may bring. This section also includes two full-length **practice exams** (pages 287 and 383), including in-depth answer explanations for each question. As you get closer to your test date, make sure you are using all of the materials provided in this book. That way, when the day of the exam arrives, you'll be ready to earn your top score!

Strategies for Long-Term Preparation

Step 1: Get Registered

Your reason for wanting to take the ASVAB drives where you'll actually sit for the test. If you're taking the exam as part of the Career Exploration Program or because you think you might be interested in the military after you graduate, you'll take this test at your school. Your school probably offers the ASVAB to all juniors/seniors. However, in the event that your school does not regularly conduct ASVAB testing, contact your guidance counselor. This person should be able to assist you in getting registered for the exam.

If you're taking this test because you're definitely joining the military, it's very important that you do well, particularly if you're trying to qualify for one of the better jobs/careers. The ASVAB is offered at Military Entrance Processing Stations (MEPS) year-round as well as in a variety of mobile locations. If you're still in school, your guidance counselor can make arrangements for you. Or, make an appointment with the local recruiter for the branch of the service in which you're interested in enrolling. Your recruiter will handle the administrative work for you and set up a time/location for your test.

Here are some important points to keep in mind as you get started.

- *Do you know what you need to know?* We can't emphasize enough how important it is to make sure you have accurate information about this test. This is particularly true if you're planning on joining the military and wish to maximize your career opportunities. For more information on ASVAB and the military, visit the Department of Defense's site on the web (www.defense.gov), the military's official site of the ASVAB (todaysmilitary.com/before-serving-in-the-military/asvab-test), or the Career Exploration Program site (www.asvabprogram.com). These sites include information about testing, special accommodations for disabilities, and so on. These sites also show you how your score is derived and used.

- Taking the ASVAB does *not* mean you have to join the military. You don't become automatically enrolled or obligated to the service because you've taken the test. Many people take the ASVAB just to get a read on where their career potential lies.

- Your personal information and test results will not be used in any nefarious way. This is important. The U.S. government doesn't use identifying information or test results except as indicated, which means your information and scores are provided to the various branches of the service. Recruiters may then contact you, if they feel you're a good fit for their service. Results are kept on file for up to two years.

Step 2: Become an Expert Student

To do well on the exam, you must retain a ton of information both in and out of the classroom. You will have to work hard and study. Did you know that studying is a discipline in and of itself that many people just don't know how to do well? It's true. Even the smartest people need to learn *how* to study in order to maximize their ability to learn.

One of the most critical study skills involves notes. More specifically, it involves taking effective notes rather than just writing down everything your teacher says. Don't underestimate how important good note-taking is both during class AND while you're studying alone or with a partner. Good note-taking serves several purposes. First (and most obviously), note-taking is important for making sure you have recorded the key points being made by your instructor (or your study partner). Since this person is very familiar with the material and the test, he or she knows where you should focus your time, so you should glean as much knowledge from him or her as possible. Second, effective note-taking is important because the process of working on notes can actually help you in your retention of the material. For example, the deceptively simple act of writing and rewriting your notes reinforces your memory just from doing the activity. Additionally, writing in conjunction with listening or reading forces your brain to fire additional cognition skills, making it a lot more likely that you'll remember what you're recording.

Here are some tips for taking great notes.

- *Listen actively*. The first key to taking good notes is to practice *active listening*—that is, listening in a structured way to understand and evaluate what's being said. Active listeners are not distracted, thinking about other things, nor considering what they will say next (in the classroom, this means opening up your mind rather than thinking about some question you might ask your teacher). Active listening also does not involve writing down every single thing the teacher says. Rather, it means listening in a structured way so that you hear the main ideas, pay attention to cues that impart meaning, and keep your eyes on the speaker (not on your notebook).

  ○ Listen for main ideas. Before you even begin the note-taking process, consider the topic under discussion and be ready to organize your notes around that topic. Is it a person, place, movement? Is it a particular era or concept? Do some pre-thinking about the topic and work from that angle. Also listen for transitions into new topics as the teacher works his or her way through the material.

  ○ Pay attention to cues. If you're taking notes in class, certain words and phrases tend to reflect the way the discussion is organized.

For example, the teacher usually starts with an introduction, and this introduction generally provides the framework around how the topic will be treated. For example, "Today we will trace the origins of the industrial revolution. We will follow it from Britain to the rest of the world." Listen for transition words such as "next," "the following," and numbered/bulleted lists.

- Don't just stare at your notebook. Information is conveyed by speakers in a number of ways, many of them non-verbal. Keep an eye on the instructor's body language and expressions. These are the type of non-verbal cues that will help you determine what's important and what's not.

- *What do good notes look like?* Good notes are not just a jumbled mass of everything. It's unrealistic and ineffective to try to write down everything there is to say about a topic. Instead, you should learn to focus on key words and main ideas. Here are some tips on how to proceed.

  - Start with a clean sheet. Indicate today's date and the main/primary topic. This will jog your memory later on when you study these notes.

  - If the instructor is using slides, don't just copy word-for-word what's on the slide. Instead, jot down the title of the slide and the key idea, concept, or overall topic under discussion (this should be apparent from either the title of the slide deck, the title of the slide itself, or the instructor's introduction).

  - Listen actively to your instructor's treatment of the material and his or her points of emphasis. Try to *really listen* to what is being said. Then, as your teacher makes important points, write them down in bullet-point/summarized fashion. Don't worry too much about organization in the moment. Just do your best to capture the discussion in a way that makes sense to you.

  - If you're confused about something, ask for clarification. Many students make the mistake of not asking for help when the teacher makes a statement that is confusing or unclear. Sometimes even the best teachers go too fast or fail to transition you through the material plainly. It's much better to ask for help than to write down a bunch of information that makes no sense to you later.

○ This is an important and often-overlooked point: once class is over, REWRITE or RETYPE your notes, using the opportunity to also fold in information from your textbook or other resources. This is your opportunity to bring real organization, clarity, and understanding to the material. You should rewrite or retype your notes regularly (preferably daily, but if that's not possible, at least weekly). You'll be amazed at how much more sense the material makes if you take the time to look at it critically and rework it in a way that makes sense to you on a regular basis.

○ Take notes from your books and other resources as well as your class notes—see the section below on "reading to understand." This test covers *a lot* of material. Paying attention to what gets attention in resources can help you focus.

○ Review your notes before class every day. Doing so serves as a reminder of where you are chronologically, and also helps you to transition from concept to concept and era to era. Work mindfully to make connections among the material that you're learning. Those connections will serve you well later.

• *How do you read to understand?* Material such as this book and your class textbook can make the difference between a passing and failing grade, or between a so-so and an excellent score. However, you need to understand what you're reading so that you can supplement your class notes.

○ Do a complete read through. Start with the objectives of the chapter. Review the questions at the end.

○ Map out the main ideas. Once you've read through the material and have an overall understanding, write down the main ideas and leave space to fill in details. Wherever possible, find your own words. Avoid copying text exactly from the book. Paraphrasing the material in your own words helps you engage with the material and facilitates your learning.

○ Re-read the material. Once you have the main ideas mapped out, you should re-read the material with an eye toward filling in details under each of the main ideas.

○ Fill in the details. Now that you've re-read, write details under each main idea—again, do not copy the words exactly from the book, but use your own words so that you retain the information. Use details from the book or other resource AND from your class notes.

○ Put the book aside, and read through your notes. Do you understand what you've written? Have you accurately represented the main ideas? Did you fill in the appropriate level of detail?

○ Review, review, review. Read them over and over again. That's how you get the information to stick.

Step 3: Create a Realistic Study Plan

If you're like many students with challenging classes, extracurricular activities, and other priorities, you may have only a limited amount of time to review for this exam. This section will help you get the most out of your limited test preparation time and make it really count. You need a plan specifically for you—one that addresses *your* needs and considers the time you have available. No two people will have exactly the same plan or use this book in exactly the same way. To develop a personalized test prep plan, you'll need to identify your weak points and then allocate time to address them efficiently and effectively.

Here are the three basic steps to creating a personalized test prep plan.

1. Identify your weak points. Start by taking the diagnostic test in this book. This will show you what you're up against. It will also help you get a feel for the exam and identify the subject areas

where you need to focus. Based on your performance, you can prioritize the subjects to review, starting with the areas in which you are weakest. If your time is limited or if you feel you're not ready to take a complete practice test, focus your review by skimming the diagnostic test and identifying those areas where you have the most difficulty with understanding.

2. Develop a review plan and a schedule. Figure out how much time you can devote each week to test preparation and reserve specific blocks of time for this purpose. Create a written schedule that includes specific time slots and activities or content areas for review. This will help you pace yourself to get through all of the material you want to review. You'll likely find there are content areas or question types you want to focus on more than others. Also make sure your plan includes time to master test-taking strategies and actually take the practice tests.

3. Marshal your self-discipline. The hard part about a plan for test prep is making yourself stick to it. Schedule your test prep time actively in your calendar. Don't let it get pushed aside by more seemingly urgent activities. You've come a long way; don't blow the test by failing to prepare for it. Develop a plan for your needs in the time you have available and then stick with it.

For some people, it helps to have a study partner. A partner may make it easier to hold to the schedule and it may also help you to study more effectively. You and your partner can quiz each other, share information, and exchange ideas. However, for other people, having a study partner makes it harder to stay on topic and focus on studying. Try to figure out, based on past experience, how you can best enforce your study plan and most effectively use your time.

Step 4: Use All the Resources at Your Disposal

This book is an excellent way to prepare for this test. It includes not only the diagnostic test but two FULL practice tests. Each test has unique questions so you get the opportunity to address all different areas of the content in all different ways.

Additionally, another practice exam is available to you free of charge at www.mymaxscore.com. Detailed answers and explanations are provided for every question.

Check out one of the websites for the ASVAB program:

- Career Exploration Program—www.asvabprogram.com
- The Military's Official ASVAB site—todaysmilitary.com/before -serving-in-the-military/asvab-test

You'll also find lots of other test resources in your library, at the local bookstore, or online. Look around to see what's available and figure out ways to work that material into your study time if you can.

Good luck! Happy studying!

This book contains two practice exams. Visit mymaxscore.com to download your free third practice test with answers and explanations.

ASVAB Practice Exam 1

ASVAB
Part 1
General Science
Time—11 minutes
25 questions

Directions: This test assesses your knowledge of general science principles usually covered in high school classes. Choose the best answer for each question and then mark the space on your answer sheet that corresponds to the question number.

1.   Which of the following is an example of homeostasis?

   A.   Growing
   B.   Digesting
   C.   Sweating
   D.   Reproducing

2. The SI unit for power is a

    A. watt.
    B. joule.
    C. newton.
    D. newton-meter.

3. Dinosaurs were dominant during the

    A. Cenozoic Era.
    B. Paleozoic Era.
    C. Mesozoic Era.
    D. Precambrian Era.

4. Compared to an ocean, a cup of hot tea has

    A. less thermal energy and a lower temperature.
    B. less thermal energy and a higher temperature.
    C. more thermal energy and a lower temperature.
    D. more thermal energy and a higher temperature.

5. Which of the following is NOT true of all living things?

    A. They reproduce.
    B. They grow and develop.
    C. They have cells with nuclei.
    D. They respond to their environment.

6. A fixed pulley changes the _____ of a force.

    A. size
    B. speed
    C. power
    D. direction

7. Which era of the geologic time scale is the longest?

   A. Cenozoic Era
   B. Paleozoic Era
   C. Mesozoic Era
   D. Precambrian Era

8. The basic unit of structure of all living things is the

   A. cell.
   B. organ.
   C. tissue.
   D. organ system.

9. A force of 100 newtons is used to move a box 4 meters. How much work is done?

   A. 25 N
   B. 25 N-m
   C. 200 J
   D. 400 J

10. Earth's land masses were once joined together to form a giant super-continent called

    A. Gaia.
    B. Laurasia.
    C. Pangaea.
    D. Gondwana.

11. Which of the following is an example of a chemical change?

     A. Iron rusts.
     B. Wax melts.
     C. Water freezes.
     D. Sugar stirred in water disappears.

12. The control center of the cell is the

     A. nucleus.
     B. ribosome.
     C. cytoplasm.
     D. mitochondria.

13. The product of mass and velocity is

     A. work.
     B. force.
     C. power.
     D. momentum.

14. At mid-ocean ridges, tectonic plates

     A. diverge.
     B. converge.
     C. remain stationary.
     D. slide past one another.

15. Which of the following indicates a physical change?

     A. A precipitate forms.
     B. Bubbles of gas form.
     C. Light and heat are given off.
     D. A substance changes from a liquid to a solid.

16. Both plant and animal cells have

    A.   cell walls.
    B.   vacuoles.
    C.   chloroplasts.
    D.   fixed rectangular shapes.

17. A wedge and a screw are types of

    A.   levers.
    B.   pulleys.
    C.   inclined planes.
    D.   wheels and axles.

18. Tectonic plates slide past each other at

    A.   transform faults.
    B.   mid-ocean ridges.
    C.   divergent plate boundaries.
    D.   convergent plate boundaries.

19. Which type of energy is in natural gas?

    A.   Heat
    B.   Light
    C.   Chemical
    D.   Mechanical

20. A cell undergoing mitosis has 48 chromosomes. How many chromosomes does each daughter cell have?

    A. 6
    B. 12
    C. 24
    D. 48

21. An airplane travels 1,260 km from Chicago to San Francisco in 3 hours. Its velocity is

    A. 420 km/hr.
    B. 420 km/hr westward.
    C. 1,260 km/hr.
    D. 1,260 km/hr westward.

22. Most geologists believe the movement of tectonic plates is caused by

    A. volcanoes.
    B. earthquakes.
    C. conduction of heat in Earth's mantle.
    D. convection currents in Earth's mantle.

23. The scientific name of an organism consists of its

    A. class name and order name.
    B. phylum name and class name.
    C. genus name and species name.
    D. kingdom name and phylum name.

24. A rock that enters Earth's atmosphere and hits the ground is called a(n)

   A. comet.
   B. meteor.
   C. asteroid.
   D. meteorite.

25. Which of the following is a property of a fluid?

   A. It is easily compressed.
   B. It has a crystalline structure.
   C. It expands to fill its container.
   D. Its particles are not rigidly attached to one another.

END OF PART 1

ASVAB

Part 2

Arithmetic Reasoning

Time—36 minutes

30 questions

Directions: This test assesses your skills in arithmetic. Choose the correct answer and then mark the space on your answer sheet. Use scratch paper for any figuring you need to do.

1. On Thursday, the high temperature measured by a weather station was –13.2°C. On Friday, the temperature measured at the same station was –22.9°C. How many degrees did the temperature change?

    A. –36.1°
    B. –9.7°
    C. 9.7°
    D. 36.1°

2. Analeigh divides a pizza into 7 equal slices and eats 2 of the slices. She divides a second pizza into 8 equal slices and eats 2 slices from this second pizza. What fraction of the 2 pizzas combined did Analeigh eat?

    A. $\dfrac{15}{56}$

    B. $\dfrac{15}{28}$

    C. $\dfrac{2}{15}$

    D. $\dfrac{4}{56}$

3. The temperature increases from −3°C to 17°C over the course of a day. How many degrees did the temperature increase?

   A. 3
   B. 14
   C. 17
   D. 20

4. Noel buys a jacket for $50.37, including sales tax. The price of the jacket prior to sales tax was $46.00. What is the sales tax on the jacket?

   A. 8.5 percent
   B. 9.0 percent
   C. 9.5 percent
   D. 10.0 percent

5. A car uses 1 gallon of gasoline for every 26 miles it travels. If the car travels 50 miles per day, how many gallons of gasoline will it use over 20 days?

   A. 10.4
   B. 38.5
   C. 65
   D. 520

6. The monthly cost of childcare is 20 percent of Kevin's monthly salary. He pays $600 per month for childcare. What is his monthly salary?

   A. $2,600
   B. $2,800
   C. $3,000
   D. $3,200

7. Miroslav has accrued 2,378 rollover minutes with his cell phone plan. If he plans to use an equal amount of rollover minutes per month for the next 5 months, how many rollover minutes will he have left at the beginning of the sixth month?

    A. 2 minutes
    B. 3 minutes
    C. 4 minutes
    D. 5 minutes

8. A contractor received the following number of checks per month from clients over the past six months: 4, 2, 6, 4, 2, and 1. What is the median number of checks the contractor received per month?

    A. 2
    B. 3
    C. 4
    D. 5

9. Ann runs 1 mile in 86 percent of the time it takes Kim to run 1 mile. It takes Kim exactly 12 minutes to run 1 mile. How many minutes does it take Ann to run a mile?

    A. 10.08 minutes
    B. 10.32 minutes
    C. 10.40 minutes
    D. 10.68 minutes

10. Aubrey receives the following grades on five math tests: 86, 92, 80, 99, and 88. What is her average grade for the five tests?

    A. 88
    B. 89
    C. 90
    D. 91

11. Jillian decreases the monthly fee for her health insurance plan by raising her deductible. She previously paid $396.00 per month for her plan. She now pays $257.40 per month. What was the percent decrease of her monthly health insurance fee?

    A. 32 percent
    B. 33 percent
    C. 34 percent
    D. 35 percent

12. Sam has a drawer filled with tube socks in equal numbers of three different colors: pink, orange, and gray. The 30 total socks are arranged randomly in the drawer. If Sam reaches into the drawer without looking and pulls out an orange sock, what will be the probability that the next sock she pulls out in the same way will also be orange?

    A. $\dfrac{1}{3}$

    B. $\dfrac{9}{29}$

    C. $\dfrac{2}{30}$

    D. $\dfrac{9}{60}$

13. During the first 3 days of a trip, Carl drove 240 miles per day. During the last 4 days of the trip, he drove 380 miles per day. What is the average number of miles he drove per day over the course of 7 days?

    A. 280 miles
    B. 300 miles
    C. 320 miles
    D. 340 miles

14. Jacob pulls two numbers out of a bag. The first number is 3 less than 2 times the second number. The second number is 18. What is the first number?

   A. 31
   B. 33
   C. 36
   D. 38

15. Elaine spins a spinner with eight equally spaced sections labeled 1 through 8. What is the probability the spinner will land on a 2 or a number greater than 5?

   A. $\dfrac{1}{2}$

   B. $\dfrac{3}{8}$

   C. $\dfrac{1}{16}$

   D. $\dfrac{3}{64}$

16. Four pencils and three erasers cost $3.17. If eight pencils and five erasers cost $6.07, how much does one eraser cost?

   A. $0.27
   B. $0.35
   C. $0.56
   D. $0.59

17. Amanda moves into a new, more expensive apartment. In her new apartment, Amanda pays $1,509 per month, which is approximately 228 percent of the rent she paid previously. Which of the following is the best estimate for her rent in her previous apartment?

    A. $642.86
    B. $648.92
    C. $661.84
    D. $668.86

18. An attorney in Flagstaff charges $200 per hour for services. This rate is 80 percent of the hourly rate charged by an attorney in Tempe. What is the hourly rate charged by the attorney in Tempe?

    A. $245
    B. $250
    C. $265
    D. $280

19. Bob cuts a 15-ft roll of wrapping paper into equal sections, each $\frac{3}{2}$-ft long. How many sections of wrapping paper does he have?

    A. 2.5
    B. 10
    C. 18
    D. 22.5

20. Andrew drives 391 miles in 5 hours and 45 minutes. What is his average speed?

    A. 65 miles per hour
    B. 66 miles per hour
    C. 68 miles per hour
    D. 70 miles per hour

21. Bruce receives a raise during his third year of employment. His new annual salary is $54,000. If his original annual salary was $50,000, what was the percent increase of his raise?

    A.   6 percent
    B.   8 percent
    C.   10 percent
    D.   12 percent

22. Ashley and Benjamin work together to finish a job. Ashley can plant 8 trees per hour. Benjamin can plant 6 trees per hour. If they work together to plant 35 trees, how long will it take them to finish the job?

    A.   2.5 hours
    B.   3 hours
    C.   3.5 hours
    D.   4 hours

23. To use an LCD projector at a business conference, Keisha must pay a $135 registration fee plus $16 for each session she uses the projector. What is the total cost of using the projector for 3 sessions?

    A. $192
    B. $183
    C. $167
    D. $154

24. Monique is thinking of a number that is 14 less than 3 times Ana's number. If Monique's number is 181, what is Ana's number?

    A.   58
    B.   60
    C.   63
    D.   65

25. Eric rolls a regular, six-sided die. What is the probability that he will roll either a 3 or a prime number?

A. $\dfrac{1}{3}$

B. $\dfrac{1}{2}$

C. $\dfrac{2}{3}$

D. $\dfrac{3}{4}$

26. What is the next multiple of 8 in the sequence 48, 52, 56, 60, 64...?

A. 66
B. 68
C. 70
D. 72

27. Ms. Garcia buys a box of pencils and hands out three pencils to each of her students. She then has two pencils left over. How many pencils may have been in the original, unopened box?

A. 100
B. 101
C. 102
D. 103

28. A raffle sells 500 raffle tickets to a total of 80 people. What is the average number of raffle tickets purchased per person?

    A. $\dfrac{25}{4}$

    B. $\dfrac{8}{50}$

    C. $\dfrac{16}{100}$

    D. $\dfrac{6}{25}$

29. Abria spends the same amount of money per month on ink cartridges. If the total cost of ink cartridges for 8 months is $1,151.36, what will be the total cost of ink cartridges for 24 months?

    A. $2,098.10
    B. $2,822.14
    C. $3,294.16
    D. $3,454.08

30. Trisha ran $3\dfrac{3}{8}$ miles on Friday and $4\dfrac{5}{6}$ miles on Saturday. How many total miles did she run?

    A. $8\dfrac{1}{6}$ miles

    B. $8\dfrac{5}{24}$ miles

    C. $8\dfrac{1}{12}$ miles

    D. $8\dfrac{5}{48}$ miles

END OF PART 2

ASVAB
Part 3
Word Knowledge
Time—11 minutes
35 questions

Directions: This test is about the meanings of words. Each question has an underlined word. You must decide which word in the answer choice has nearly the same meaning as the underlined word. Then mark this space on your answer sheet.

1. The teacher <u>admonished</u> the student for his rude behavior on the bus.

   A. Scolded
   B. Censored
   C. Damaged
   D. Compensated

2. <u>Anarchy</u> most nearly means

   A. stability.
   B. rebellion.
   C. monarchy.
   D. contagion.

3. The <u>brevity</u> of his abbreviated speech startled the crowd.

   A. Clarity
   B. Briefness
   C. Insincerity
   D. Tediousness

4. Brandish most nearly means

    A. wield.
    B. tarnish.
    C. finesse.
    D. conceal.

5. We were grateful for the cessation of the blaring alarm bell.

    A. Inhibition
    B. Termination
    C. Containment
    D. Commencement

6. Copious most nearly means

    A. scant.
    B. abundant.
    C. restricted.
    D. resplendent.

7. The X-ray showed an abnormal curvature in the shape of the patient's spine.

    A. Arch
    B. Tumor
    C. Stretch
    D. Temperature

8. Corroborate most nearly means

    A. deny.
    B. verify.
    C. finance.
    D. compliment.

9. Critics did not hesitate to <u>denounce</u> the research results.

   A. Betray
   B. Resolve
   C. Condemn
   D. Interrogate

10. The <u>dissonant</u> chords of the song made the music instructor wince.

   A. Melodious
   B. Congruous
   C. Harmonious
   D. Cacophonous

11. <u>Eccentric</u> most nearly means

   A. uneasy.
   B. unkempt.
   C. unattractive.
   D. unconventional.

12. When called on unexpectedly to do an <u>extemporaneous</u> speech, the student's hands began to shake.

   A. Oratorical
   B. Persuasive
   C. Clandestine
   D. Unrehearsed

13. <u>Erroneous</u> most nearly means

   A. incorrect.
   B. irrational.
   C. unconscious.
   D. unreasonable.

14. <u>Furtive</u> most nearly means

   A.   secretive.
   B.   energetic.
   C.   temporary.
   D.   exhaustive.

15. The instructor's wild <u>gesticulations</u> distracted the class from the information he was presenting.

   A.   Theories
   B.   Formulas
   C.   Conjectures
   D.   Movements

16. The <u>heirloom</u> had been in the family for generations and was worth a great deal of money.

   A.   Flagon
   B.   Bauble
   C.   Valuable
   D.   Photograph

17. The television show went on <u>hiatus</u> for three months, which disappointed many of its viewers.

   A.   Tour
   B.   Break
   C.   Strike
   D.   Commercial

18. <u>Inadvertently</u> most nearly means

   A. unhappily.
   B. unconsciously.
   C. unintentionally.
   D. unsatisfactorily.

19. Learning a new job often begins with learning the <u>jargon</u> used between employees about the equipment.

   A. Manners
   B. Language
   C. Nonsense
   D. Terminology

20. <u>Labyrinth</u> most nearly means

   A. knoll.
   B. maze.
   C. massacre.
   D. investment.

21. The classes are <u>mandatory</u>, so it is essential you attend if you want to earn your certification.

   A. Required
   B. Impartial
   C. Optional
   D. Traditional

22. <u>Nebulous</u> most nearly means

    A.   tenuous.

    B.   mystical.

    C.   meticulous.

    D.   comprehensible.

23. The doctor made a <u>notation</u> in his records that the patient was using a new prescription.

    A.   File

    B.   Code

    C.   Comment

    D.   Document

24. The young child's <u>petulant</u> attitude was a clear sign that the outing to the zoo had been unsuccessful.

    A.   Sulky

    B.   Affable

    C.   Gregarious

    D.   Noteworthy

25. Her cynical attitude made it clear that she was simply <u>patronizing</u> me.

    A.   Belittling

    B.   Tolerating

    C.   Compromising

    D.   Complimenting

26. <u>Proximity</u> most nearly means

   A.   novice.
   B.   vicinity.
   C.   remedy.
   D.   prototype.

27. The two siblings <u>quibbled</u> over everything from who was the strongest to who was the tallest.

   A.   Agreed
   B.   Decided
   C.   Bickered
   D.   Conversed

28. <u>Reconcile</u> most nearly means

   A.   reject.
   B.   revise.
   C.   reunite.
   D.   resume.

29. The troop's actions had been <u>sanctioned</u> by the government and the military.

   A.   Ordered
   B.   Repelled
   C.   Prohibited
   D.   Authorized

30. <u>Sparse</u> most nearly means

   A. scant.
   B. sodden.
   C. solemn.
   D. skeptical.

31. The hungry dog was <u>tenacious</u> about getting fed.

   A. Flippant
   B. Indecisive
   C. Ambivalent
   D. Determined

32. <u>Transparent</u> most nearly means

   A. solid.
   B. clear.
   C. blatant.
   D. transplant.

33. The <u>vintage</u> clothing store only sold items that were at least forty years old.

   A. Antique
   B. Whimsical
   C. Innovative
   D. Contemporary

34. <u>Zealot</u> most nearly means

   A.   patriot.
   B.   fanatic.
   C.   spectator.
   D.   theologian.

35. <u>Vulnerable</u> most nearly means

   A.   receptive.
   B.   invincible.
   C.   impervious.
   D.   susceptible.

END OF PART 3

ASVAB

Part 4

Paragraph Comprehension

Time—13 minutes

15 questions

Directions: This test assesses your ability to understand what you read. This section includes reading passages followed by questions or incomplete statements. Read the paragraph and select the choice that best completes the statement or answers the question. Mark your choice on your answer sheet.

Core samples taken below the floor of the Arctic Ocean have surprised researchers, who had assumed that the peak carbon-dioxide levels reached some 55 million years ago would have heated up the entire planet except for the Polar Regions. However, researchers discovered that the average temperature at the North Pole was in the seventies during that era. It was a balmy, Florida-like land of giant alligators and massive palm trees. Over the next million years, as green things grew, the poles cooled down and eventually became the ice-covered lands we know today.

1.   It can be inferred from the passage that the cooling trend at the North Pole was caused by the

   A.   loss of heat from the sun's rays.
   B.   gradual buildup of ice and snow.
   C.   movement of tectonic plates beneath the surface.
   D.   absorption of carbon dioxide by the growth of greenery.

All U.S. presidents need a private retreat when their presidency ends, and Thomas Jefferson was no exception. Jefferson designed and built Poplar Forest, an unusual octagonal-shaped home, which was about ninety miles from Monticello, his official residence. There, he could meet friends and family and follow his many interests in studying, writing, and gardening. Today that unique building is being restored using the same tools and materials as in Jefferson's time.

2. According to the passage, Thomas Jefferson used Poplar Forest for all of the following EXCEPT

   A. reading books.
   B. tending a garden.
   C. holding staff meetings.
   D. gathering with relatives.

Four crews of the U.S. Army Air Services took off from Seattle in 1924 in an attempt to become the first to fly around the world. Utilizing four Douglas World Cruiser biplanes, they planned to cross over Japan, India, the Middle East, Europe, and England on their way. One plane crashed in Alaska, but the remaining three did not give up. After 175 days, landings in 61 cities, and some 27,500 miles, the crews returned safely to Seattle. They had been the first; others were to follow.

3. Which best restates the main idea of the passage?

   A. U.S. pilots' round-the-world flight was the first of many.
   B. Many nations collaborated to aid the round-the-world flight.
   C. U.S. pilots conquered the challenge of a round-the-world flight.
   D. A round-the-world air flight was considered impossible in 1924.

Perhaps the most famous theater in history, London's Globe began its life as the scene of many of William Shakespeare's major works. The Globe's stage was ideally suited to the swiftly moving action of Elizabethan drama. The forestage was used for general action and could become whatever the players said it was. Behind it a curtained area could serve as a bedroom, as in *Othello*, or a cave, as in *The Tempest*. Above that, a gallery was ideal for *Romeo and Juliet*'s balcony scene. Permanent doors on either side allowed for entrances and exits, and trap doors provided for sudden appearances or disappearances.

4. What is the author's primary purpose in this passage?

   A. To explain how Shakespearean scenes were performed
   B. To speculate about how Shakespeare's plays were interpreted
   C. To describe the stage of a theater used during the Shakespearean era
   D. To create the illusion of an actual visit to a Shakespearean playhouse

Animals that live in and around mangrove swamps have developed some unusual and surprising techniques to survive. The four-eyed fish floats along, using its dual vision to search for prey both above and below the water's surface—at the same time. The fiddler crab seems to be playing a tune but is actually using its large claw to discourage potential predators. The mudskipper's strong tail allows it to leap out of the water in pursuit of a meal or to avoid an enemy.

5. According to the passage, why does the fiddler crab wave its large claw?

   A. To locate prey
   B. To defend itself
   C. To attract a mate
   D. To protect its young

Recent studies have explored some remarkable theories about reading ability in children. Using second graders, researchers compared the verbal scores of groups that had received earlier musical training and those that had not. Students who had studied piano for two years showed higher scores in vocabulary and reading over a year than those who had no musical background. Other analysts have pointed out that the two groups scored the same when the study began. Why didn't the piano students top the non-musical group from the start? The consistently higher scores seem to indicate that early musical training improves a child's facility in school.

6. What is the main idea of the passage?

    A. Children who do not take piano lessons will fall behind musically trained students.
    B. Children who receive early musical training have an advantage when learning to read.
    C. Children who take music lessons will score the same on initial verbal tests as those with no musical background.
    D. Children who have musical training will do better in school than those who have never learned to play a musical instrument.

In the early years of American football, before pads and helmets, the game was a slow, agonizing, and very dangerous struggle. On a rain-soaked field, the competitors resembled little more than a writhing, groaning pile of mud. The object of the game was to pull and push the player with the ball through the other team, and some athletes sewed suitcase handles onto their uniforms to facilitate this tactic. Injuries mounted until a group of powerful coaches decided to make a change. In 1906, sports history was recorded when a player from St. Louis University threw the first legal forward pass.

7. The passage supports which of the following conclusions?

    A. Players tended to resist the forward pass when first introduced.
    B. Allowing the forward pass helped to make football a safer game.
    C. There were no rules about throwing the ball forward in football prior to 1906.
    D. Early football players considered wearing pads and helmets a sign of weakness.

In this age of instant messaging, the older traditions of newspapering seem almost quaint. In the 1920s world of "Front Page" journalism, reporters roamed city "beats" to dig up facts for a possible "scoop." They phoned the information in to "rewrite," where a harried writer pounded out the story on a manual typewriter. When finished, a "copy boy" rushed the story to the "rim," or "slot," where gimlet-eyed editors checked and polished it. Approved by the "City Editor," the copy went down to the pressroom, where machine operators molded hot lead into lines of type for the latest edition.

8. According to the passage, in old-style journalism, a news story was usually written by the

    A. reporter.
    B. City Editor.
    C. copy editor.
    D. rewrite person.

The divers stood on the bluff overlooking the hidden cove. Would this be the place where they would find their dreamed-of treasure? Descending to the beach, they faced what seemed like mountains of enormous waves. They entered the surge, swam for deeper water, dove, and found the bottom at twenty feet. Thrashing kelp ponds slowed them, and the lime-colored sunlight that filtered down made it almost impossible to find the rich green that they sought. Then one diver turned over a smooth rock and realized that this was it—jade—a raw jewel worth hundreds in the surface world.

9. Which word best characterizes the mood of the story?

A. Terror
B. Suspense
C. Certainty
D. Tranquility

Adding electric current to a Spanish-style guitar allowed players to become soloists in the Big Band era of the 1930s and 1940s. But there was a problem: The guitar was hollow beneath the strings. When electric current was added, the sound reverberated in that empty space and the result was distortion. A solid body guitar would solve the problem, but the instrument introduced in 1935 was constructed of plastic and was heavy and difficult to play. A lighter version was developed by musician Les Paul in 1941 and caught on immediately, leading to the mass-produced Leo Fender instrument in the early 1950s.

10. According to the passage, changing to a solid-body electric guitar was an advantage because it

A. substituted plastic for wood.
B. improved the instrument's tone.
C. allowed guitars to be mass-produced.
D. made playing the instrument much easier.

Theodore Roosevelt, that hardy leader of the "Rough Riders," was considered a tenderfoot when he visited his western ranch as a young New York Assemblyman. Cowboys of the Dakota

Badlands scoffed at this eastern dude and figured he'd give up after one hard winter. But Teddy surprised the doubters. He rode with them through blinding blizzards. He impressed them with his dead-shot skill on a game hunt. He teamed with leather-tough trail hands on a lengthy search for thieves. During his 1901–09 terms as president, he founded the U.S. Forest Service, created more than fifty wildlife refuges, and approved five new national parks.

11. The passage suggests that Theodore Roosevelt's western ranching experience

    A.   changed him into a more competitive person.

    B.   convinced him to exchange ranching for politics.

    C.   gained him voting majorities among working people.

    D.   prepared him for his role as an environmental activist.

The manager of Dinah's Luncheonette surveyed her customers' preferences and discovered that the fishwich was not as popular as the chickwich, people requested the sesame-seed bun less often than the wheat type, and mayonnaise was preferred over mustard on most sandwiches.

12. Based on information in the paragraph, which sandwich is the most popular at Dinah's?

    A.   Chickwich on wheat bun with mustard

    B.   Chickwich on wheat bun with mayonnaise

    C.   Fishwich on sesame seed bun with mustard

    D.   Fishwich on sesame seed bun with mayonnaise

In 1773, a book of her original poems was published in London. At the time, Phillis Wheatley was a twenty-year-old African American who had been captured by slave traders at the age of eight and sold to a family in Boston, the Wheatleys. The family's eighteen-year-old daughter, Mary, taught the young girl to read and write English. Phillis was very adept, and by the age of twelve, she was reading both English and Latin. At thirteen, she began writing poetry, inspired by British authors Alexander Pope and Thomas Gray. Her book, *Poems on Various Subjects: Religious and Moral*, brought her fame and praise from people such as George Washington.

13. It can be inferred from the passage that Phillis Wheatley

    A. attended university in the United States.
    B. moved to London following publication of her book.
    C. became the first African American writer to achieve publication.
    D. helped to originate the African American genre in English literature.

Elizabeth strolled through the orchard, inhaling deeply of the rich aromas coming from the sugar house. Spring had arrived early this year, allowing the trees to give up their treasure. Elizabeth knew that it would require boiling down some forty gallons of sap to create one gallon of the golden fluid. She smiled as she pictured the faces of the kids when she prepared their favorite breakfast—flapjacks with pure, sweet maple syrup.

14. Which term best characterizes the mood of the story?

    A. Joy
    B. Sadness
    C. Comfort
    D. Disappointment

In the late eighteenth century, a young textile worker in England named Ned Ludd smashed his machine in protest over a reprimand by his boss. In 1811, factory workers who were plagued by unemployment and poverty named Ludd as a symbolic leader of their rebellion when they used sledgehammers to smash the machines that were replacing them. The movement spread across northern England and soon generated violence that claimed lives. Coming at the beginnings of the Industrial Revolution, these "Luddite" protests resonated with people who saw their gentle way of life being transformed by a race of "mechanical men."

15. Based on information in the paragraph, a "Luddite" in today's world would be a person who

    A.   refuses to purchase or use a cell phone.

    B.   wants to return to a pre-technological way of life.

    C.   hacks into wi-fi networks to steal personal information.

    D.   creates a disturbance to disrupt electronic communication.

END OF PART 4

ASVAB

Part 5
Mathematics Knowledge
Time—24 minutes

25 questions

Directions: This test assesses your ability to solve general mathematical problems. Select the correct answer from the choices given. Mark the corresponding space on your answer sheet. Use scratch paper as needed to solve each problem.

1. The product of $(3x - 9)$ and $(-12x + 4)$ is

     A. $-36x^2 - 96x - 36.$
     B. $84x - 36.$
     C. $-36x^2 + 120x - 36.$
     D. $-36x^2 + 96x - 36.$

2. A square has a perimeter of 108 inches. What is the square's area?

     A. 729 in^2
     B. 972 in^2
     C. $1,296 \text{ in}^2$
     D. $2,916 \text{ in}^2$

3. A rectangle has a width of $4x + 2$ and a length of $2x - 1$. What is the area of the rectangle?

     A. $8x^2 - 2$
     B. $8x^2 - 8x - 2$
     C. $8x^2 + 8x - 2$
     D. $8x^2 - 16x - 2$

4. What is the 18th square number?

    A. 256
    B. 289
    C. 311
    D. 324

5. Which of the following statements is true?

    A. All rhombi are squares.
    B. All squares are rectangles.
    C. All parallelograms are trapezoids.
    D. All trapezoids are parallelograms.

6. What is the solution to the inequality $-3x - 6 \geq 108$?

    A. $x \geq -38$
    B. $x \geq -34$
    C. $x \leq -38$
    D. $x \leq -34$

7. Jessica ran $3\frac{3}{4}$ miles on Friday, $3\frac{1}{5}$ miles on Saturday, and $2\frac{1}{2}$ miles on Sunday. What is the average number of miles she ran during the three days?

    A. $3\frac{3}{5}$ miles

    B. $3\frac{3}{20}$ miles

    C. $3\frac{6}{20}$ miles

    D. $3\frac{1}{4}$ miles

8. What is the product of $3^{\frac{1}{2}}$ and $3^{\frac{1}{6}}$?

    A. $\sqrt[3]{3^4}$
    B. $\sqrt{3^6}$
    C. $\sqrt[4]{3^6}$
    D. $\sqrt[6]{3^4}$

9. A triangle has a base of $3x$ and a height of $2x + 2$. Which expression represents the area of the triangle?

    A. $6x$
    B. $3x(x + 1)$
    C. $3x(x + 2)$
    D. $6x(x + 1)$

10. The length of a rectangle increases by 4 units while the width remains the same. Which expression can be used to determine the area of the enlarged rectangle, where l and w represent the length and width of the original rectangle, respectively?

    A. $lw + 2w$
    B. $lw + 8w$
    C. $lw + 4w$
    D. $lw + 6w$

11. What are the zeros of $6x^2 + 42x - 180$?

    A. -10 only
    B. -3 and -10
    C. 3 and -10
    D. 3 only

12. The hypotenuse of a triangle is $\sqrt{157}$ inches. The measurement of the hypotenuse is between

    A. 10 and 11 inches.
    B. 11 and 12 inches.
    C. 12 and 13 inches.
    D. 13 and 14 inches.

13. Angles A and B are vertical angles. Angles A and C are supplementary. If $m\angle C = 114°$, what is $m\angle B$?

    A. 24°
    B. 66°
    C. 57°
    D. 33°

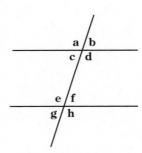

14. Which angles are congruent in the figure above?

    A. b and e
    B. f and h
    C. a and h
    D. c and g

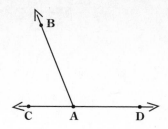

15. In the figure above, $m\angle DAB = 107°$. What is $m\angle BAC$?

    A. 69°
    B. 71°
    C. 73°
    D. 74°

16. What is the sum of the interior angles in a regular octagon?

    A. 900°
    B. 1,080°
    C. 1,260°
    D. 1,440°

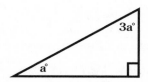

17. What is the measure of the angle opposite the base of the triangle shown above?

    A. 15°
    B. 22.5°
    C. 45°
    D. 67.5°

18. How many diagonals are found inside a regular hexagon?

    A. 5
    B. 6
    C. 8
    D. 9

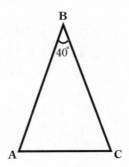

19. What is $m\angle C$ in the isosceles triangle above?

    A. 65°
    B. 70°
    C. 40°
    D. 140°

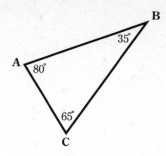

20. Which of the following statements is true about the triangle shown above?

    A. $AC > AB > BC$
    B. $BC < AB < AC$
    C. $BC > AB > AC$
    D. $AC < BC < AB$

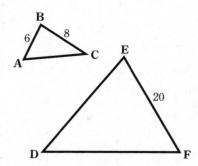

21. The triangles shown above are similar. What is the length of *DE*?

    A. 12
    B. 14
    C. 15
    D. 16

22. The point (3, 4) lies on a circle with a center at (0, 0). What is the area of the circle?

    A.   31.4 units²

    B.   50.2 units²

    C.   78.5 units²

    D.   82.7 units²

23. A cylinder has a volume of 7,385.28 cubic centimeters and a height of 12 centimeters. What is the radius of the cylinder?

    A.   13 cm

    B.   14 cm

    C.   15 cm

    D.   16 cm

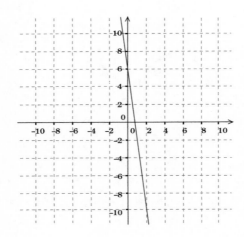

24. What is the slope of the line shown here?

    A.   −8

    B.   −4

    C.   4

    D.   8

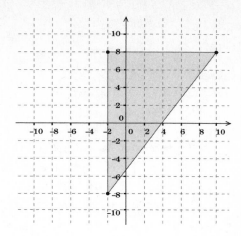

25. What is the length of the hypotenuse of the triangle graphed here?

    A. 16 units
    B. 18 units
    C. 20 units
    D. 22 units

END OF PART 5

ASVAB
Part 6
Electronics Information
Time—9 minutes
20 questions

Directions: This section assesses your knowledge of electrical, radio, and electronics information. Choose the correct answer and mark the corresponding space on your answer sheet.

1. All elements of matter fit into which of these categories?

    A.　Conductors, electrons, and insulators
    B.　Electrons, neutrons, and semiconductors
    C.　Conductors, semiconductors, and electrons
    D.　Conductors, semiconductors, and insulators

2. A conductor has how many valence electrons?

    A.　More than six
    B.　More than five
    C.　Fewer than four
    D.　Fewer than three

3. Charged bodies either attract or repel each other with a force that is _____ to the product of their individual charges and _____ to the square of the distance between them.

    A.　electrically charged; directly proportional
    B.　electrically charged; inversely proportional
    C.　directly proportional; inversely proportional
    D.　inversely proportional; directly proportional

4. The four main parts of a transformer are the

    A. core, primary winding, enclosure, and distributor rotor.

    B. core, secondary winding, enclosure, and ignition switch.

    C. core, primary winding, secondary winding, and enclosure.

    D. primary winding, secondary winding, enclosure, and spark plug.

5. All of the following statements about transformers are true EXCEPT

    A. transformer cores are laminated to prevent current loss.

    B. the maximum voltage a winding can handle is determined by the type of wire used.

    C. the maximum current a transformer winding can carry is determined by the diameter of its wire.

    D. the power-handling capability of a transformer can be increased if heat can be efficiently and safely removed.

6. Atom shells are given _____ designations, and the outermost shell of an atom is called the _____ shell.

    A. letter; valence

    B. valence; name

    C. number; valence

    D. None of the above

7. Electric current can best be described as the movement of

    A. ions through a conductor in the same direction.

    B. ions through a conductor in opposite directions.

    C. electrons through a conductor in the same direction.

    D. electrons through a conductor in opposite directions.

8. Which are examples of good insulators?

    A. Copper, glass, silicon, and plastic
    B. Rubber, glass, dry wood, and plastic
    C. Rubber, copper, dry wood, and plastic
    D. Aluminum, dry wood, glass, and plastic

9. A material that quickly loses magnetism when its magnetizing force
    is removed is called a _____ and is considered a _____ material.

    A. temporary magnet; low-reluctance
    B. temporary magnet; high-reluctance
    C. permanent magnet; low-reluctance
    D. permanent magnet; high-reluctance

10. A bar-shaped magnet dipped in iron filings will gather most of
    the filings

    A. in the center because of the law of magnetic poles.
    B. in the center because magnets contain electrically charged
        particles.
    C. at the ends because magnetic force is concentrated on the
        outer edges.
    D. on the ends because most bar-shaped magnets are temporary
        magnets.

11. Which of the following statements about electrons are true?

    A. A body with an excess of electrons is negative.
    B. A body with a deficiency of electrons is positive.
    C. Both A and B
    D. Neither A nor B

12. What are the six methods for producing voltage?

    A.   Friction, pressure, heat, light, chemical action, and wind

    B.   Friction, pressure, heat, light, chemical action, and electricity

    C.   Friction, pressure, heat, light, chemical action, and magnetism

    D.   Friction, heat, electricity, magnetism, wind, and chemical action

13. Which of the following is the symbol for a fixed carbon resistor?

    A. 

    B. 

    C. 

    D. 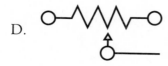

14. The ability of a resistor to dissipate heat is measured in

    A.   ohms.

    B.   watts.

    C.   hours.

    D.   coulombs.

15. What is the correct notation of a 20,000-ohm resistor?

    A.   2 kΩ

    B.   200 kΩ

    C.   20 kΩ

    D.   None of the above

16. Resistors generally contain color-coded bands to provide important information to working technicians. What are the first four bands in order of importance?

    A. Black, brown, red, and orange
    B. Red, brown, orange, and black
    C. Black, red, brown, and orange
    D. Brown, black, red, and orange

17. If there is no fourth band on a resistor, the resistor has __ percent tolerance.

    A. 5
    B. 10
    C. 15
    D. 20

18. All of the following are considered a load EXCEPT

    A. a light bulb.
    B. a television set.
    C. a stereo speaker.
    D. an electric motor.

19. When a switch on a circuit is closed, which of the following is true?

    A. The circuit is complete.
    B. Current continues to flow until the switch is opened.
    C. Current flows from the power source, through the circuit, and back to its power source.
    D. All of the above

20. What is the correct expression of Ohm's law?

A. $I = \dfrac{E}{R}$, where I = current in amperes, E = voltage in volts, and R = resistance in ohms

B. $I = \dfrac{R}{E}$, where I = current in amperes, E = voltage in volts, and R = resistance in ohms

C. $I = RE$, where I = current in amperes, E = voltage in volts, and R = resistance in ohms

D. $I = RE^2$, where I = current in amperes, E = voltage in volts, and R = resistance in ohms

END OF PART 6

ASVAB
Part 7
Auto and Shop Information
Time—11 minutes

25 questions

Directions: This test assesses your knowledge of automobiles, shop practices, and tools. Choose the correct answer to each question and then mark the corresponding space on your answer sheet.

1. Which has an air-to-fuel ratio of 14.7:1?

   A. A steam engine
   B. A reciprocating engine
   C. A rotary and piston engine
   D. An internal combustion engine

2. In an engine, what transfers thermal energy between two mediums for cooling and heating?

   A. Radiator
   B. Spark plugs
   C. Transfer case
   D. Catalytic converter

3. In an internal combustion engine, heat is removed by

   A. spark plugs.
   B. copper pipes.
   C. galvanic pockets.
   D. antifreeze and water.

4. What type of hammer is best for metalworking?

    A. Gavel
    B. Ball peen
    C. Claw hammer
    D. Splitting maul

5. All of these are types of screwdrivers EXCEPT

    A. hex.
    B. square.
    C. Phillips.
    D. splitting maul.

6. A suspension design that uses two arms, each with two points affixed to a chassis and a joint at the knuckle is called a

    A. leaf spring.
    B. damper arm.
    C. Fournier mount.
    D. double wishbone.

7. A miter box is used to

    A. cut wood.
    B. tighten bolts.
    C. gap spark plugs.
    D. store shop tools.

8. The act of bending the ground electrode on a spark plug is known as

    A. gapping.
    B. recharging.
    C. resurfacing.
    D. discharging.

9. Who would most likely make window casings and ornamental woodwork?

   A. A framer
   B. A cabinetmaker
   C. A trim carpenter
   D. A formwork carpenter

10. A wrench with interchangeable heads is called a(n)

    A. socket wrench.
    B. open-end wrench.
    C. moveable wrench.
    D. combination wrench.

11. What type of handsaw is typically used for cutting curves in wood?

    A. Rip saw
    B. Coping saw
    C. Crosscut saw
    D. Compass saw

12. If a screw needs to be countersunk, which type should be used?

    A. Flathead screw
    B. Oval-head screw
    C. Fillister-head screw
    D. All of the above

13. What does a camshaft do?

   A. Turns the linear motion of the piston into a circular motion
   B. Supplies the spark that ignites the air-fuel mixture and causes combustion
   C. Opens and closes the valves that release the air-fuel mixture into an engine
   D. Prevents the air-fuel mixture from leaking during compression and combustion

14. The part of a car that restricts the amount of pollution it produces is the

   A. radiator.
   B. crankshaft.
   C. transmission.
   D. catalytic converter.

15. In woodworking, a plane is used to

   A. remove paint.
   B. smooth wood.
   C. remove thin layers of wood.
   D. secure wood to another object.

16. Which of the following is LEAST likely to use an internal combustion engine?

   A. A motorcycle
   B. A speedboat
   C. A lawn mower
   D. A steam-powered locomotive

17. A washer is used to

    A.   reduce vibration.

    B.   prevent galvanic corrosion.

    C.   distribute the load of a screw.

    D.   All of the above

18. All of the following are types of pliers EXCEPT

    A.   diagonal.

    B.   cross-peen.

    C.   needle-nose.

    D.   tongue and groove.

19. In an internal combustion engine, oil level is measured with a(n)

    A.   dipstick.

    B.   drain pool.

    C.   oil indicator gauge.

    D.   None of the above

20. What is the main function of a serpentine belt?

    A.   To run the windshield wipers

    B.   To transmit power to auxiliary devices

    C.   To cause the transmission to change gears

    D.   To ensure the cylinders actuate in proper sequence

21. Which of the following is an example of a major automotive system?

    A.   Fuel system

    B.   Brake system

    C.   Ignition system

    D.   All of the above

22. What part of an engine houses the combustion chamber, the intake and exhaust valves, and the intake and exhaust ports?

    A.   Camshaft
    B.   Engine block
    C.   Cylinder head
    D.   Connecting rod

23. What is the best way to tighten a wing nut?

    A.   By hand
    B.   With a cotter pin
    C.   With lineman pliers
    D.   With a flat-tipped screwdriver

24. All of the following are part of the suspension and steering system EXCEPT

    A.   springs.
    B.   drive shaft.
    C.   control arms.
    D.   shock absorbers.

25. An object in an engine that moves up and down in the engine's cylinders is called a

    A.   pin.
    B.   ring.
    C.   piston.
    D.   crankshaft.

END OF PART 7

ASVAB
Part 8
Mechanical Comprehension
Time—19 minutes

25 questions

Directions: This test assesses your knowledge of mechanics. Choose the correct answer to each question and then mark the corresponding space on your answer sheet.

1. A load distributing system splits a load between ___ anchors, and to be safely effective, its angle must be less than ____ degrees.

    A. 2; 120
    B. 2; 180
    C. 3; 120
    D. 3; 180

2. Which of these is a simple machine?

    A. Scissors
    B. Tweezers
    C. Bottle opener
    D. All of the above

3. What is mechanical advantage?

    A. A way to increase force needed to move a load
    B. The use of technology that only humans can use
    C. A way to reduce the force needed to move a load
    D. The use of electrically powered motors to do work

4. An example of a 1:1 mechanical advantage ratio is

    A. a knot attached to a load.
    B. nothing attached to a load.
    C. a pulley attached to a load.
    D. None of the above

5. When stacking two simple mechanical load systems, one with a ratio of 2:1 and one with a ratio of 3:1, your mechanical advantage becomes

    A. 3:1.
    B. 4:1.
    C. 6:1.
    D. 8:1.

6. If 100 newtons of force are applied at a 30-degree angle to move a 15-kilogram object a distance of 5 meters, how much work is done?

    A. 43.3 J
    B. 86.6 J
    C. 433 J
    D. 866 J

7. What is a simple machine that you can use to gain mechanical advantage?

    A. A lever
    B. A pulley
    C. Both A and B
    D. Neither A nor B

8. What is a fulcrum?

    A. A type of pulley
    B. A first-class lever
    C. A load-bearing machine
    D. The point where a lever arm pivots

9. Force is measured by

    A. ohms.
    B. watts.
    C. inertias.
    D. newtons.

10. Using the formula for force, calculate the amount of force required to accelerate a 10-kilogram ball at 5.5 m/s².

    A. 5.5 N
    B. 55 N
    C. 550 N
    D. 5,500 N

11. When two pulleys are working together in a system, the larger pulley turns ___ than the smaller pulley.

    A. faster
    B. slower
    C. Both A and B
    D. Neither A nor B

12. A device with two gears, one 2" in diameter and the other 6" in diameter, has a ratio of

    A. 1:3.
    B. 3:1.
    C. 3:3.
    D. None of the above

13. Torque is a force that

    A. tends to rotate objects.
    B. pushes an object forward.
    C. pushes an object backward.
    D. tends to push an object sideways.

14. Newton's third law of motion states that

    A. for every action, there is an equal and opposite reaction.
    B. an object at rest stays at rest unless acted upon by another force.
    C. the change in acceleration with which an object moves is inversely proportional to the mass of the object.
    D. the change in velocity with which an object moves is directly proportional to the magnitude of force applied.

15. What is the formula for power?

    A. $W = P \Delta t$
    B. $P = Wt$
    C. $P = \dfrac{W}{t}$
    D. None of the above

16. How many tons can a chain with links 2" in diameter safely hold?

    A.   4 tons
    B.   8 tons
    C.   32 tons
    D.   50 tons

17. Friction affects machines by

    A.   making them less efficient.
    B.   causing an increase in strength.
    C.   helping them become more efficient.
    D.   causing an increase in mechanical advantage.

18. Work is the act of

    A.   exerting energy on an object that cannot move.
    B.   using force to move an object 1 meter at a time.
    C.   using force to move an object 1 meter at a time when both the force and the movement of the object are in the same direction.
    D.   using force to move an object any distance when both the force and the movement of the object are in the same direction.

19. Which of the following are simple machines?

    A.   Wheel and axle systems
    B.   Levers, screws, and pulleys
    C.   Inclined planes and wedges
    D.   All of the above

20. Which of the following statements about levers is true?

    A. There are three classes of levers.
    B. A bar on a lever can only be straight.
    C. Levers cannot change the direction of a force.
    D. None of the above

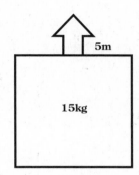

21. Using the diagram above, determine the amount of work performed when an upward force is used to lift a 15 kg box to a height of 5 m at constant speed.

    A. 7.35 J
    B. 73.5 J
    C. 735 J
    D. 7,350 J

22. The stored energy of position possessed by an object is

    A. equilibrium.
    B. elastic energy.
    C. potential energy.
    D. gravitational pull.

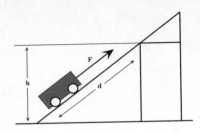

23. If a cart with a mass of 3 kg is pulled at a constant speed to the top of a 0.45 m ramp, what is the potential energy of the cart at the height of the ramp? (See figure above.)

A.   1.25 J
B.   9.8 m/s²
C.   13.2 J
D.   132 J

24. Which of the following statements describes an isolated system?

A.   Two gliders collide on a friction-free track.
B.   One vacuum cleaner is being pushed across shag carpet.
C.   Two cars collide on a dirt road that exerts large frictional forces.
D.   None of the above

25. In Newton's second law of motion, $F = ma$, the letters represent

A.   force, mass, and acceleration.
B.   force, mass, and adjusted velocity.
C.   force, magnitude, and acceleration.
D.   force, magnitude, and adjusted velocity.

END OF EXAM

Practice Exam 1 Answers and Explanations

Answer Key

PART 1: GENERAL SCIENCE

1. C
2. B
3. C
4. B
5. C
6. D
7. D
8. D
9. D
10. C
11. A
12. A
13. D
14. A
15. A
16. B
17. C
18. A
19. C
20. D
21. B
22. D
23. C

24. D
25. D

PART 2: ARITHMETIC REASONING

1. B
2. B
3. D
4. C
5. B
6. C
7. B
8. B
9. B
10. B
11. D
12. B
13. C
14. B
15. D
16. A
17. C
18. B
19. B

20. C

21. B

22. A

23. B

24. D

25. B

26. D

27. B

28. A

29. D

30. B

PART 3: WORD KNOWLEDGE

1. A

2. B

3. B

4. A

5. B

6. B

7. A

8. B

9. C

10. D

11. D

12. D

13. A

14. A

15. D

16. C

17. B

18. C

19. B

20. B

21. A

22. A

23. C

24. A

25. A

26. B

27. C

28. C

29. D

30. A

31. D

32. B

33. A

34. B

35. D

PART 4: PARAGRAPH COMPREHENSION

1. D

2. C

3. C

4.	C	13.	B
5.	B	14.	D
6.	B	15.	C
7.	B	16.	B
8.	D	17.	D
9.	B	18.	D
10.	B	19.	B
11.	D	20.	C
12.	B	21.	C
13.	D	22.	C
14.	A	23.	B
15.	D	24.	A
		25.	C

PART 5: MATHEMATICAL KNOWLEDGE

1. C
2. A
3. A
4. D
5. B
6. C
7. B
8. D
9. B
10. C
11. C
12. C

PART 6: ELECTRONICS INFORMATION

1. D
2. D
3. C
4. C
5. B
6. A
7. C
8. B
9. A
10. C
11. C

12. C
13. C
14. B
15. C
16. A
17. D
18. B
19. D
20. A

16. D
17. D
18. B
19. A
20. B
21. D
22. C
23. A
24. B
25. C

PART 7: AUTO AND SHOP INFORMATION

1. D
2. A
3. D
4. B
5. D
6. D
7. A
8. A
9. C
10. A
11. B
12. A
13. C
14. D
15. C

PART 8: MECHANICAL COMPREHENSION

1. A
2. D
3. C
4. A
5. C
6. C
7. C
8. D
9. D
10. B
11. B
12. B
13. A
14. A

15.	C	21.	C
16.	C	22.	C
17.	A	23.	C
18.	D	24.	A
19.	D	25.	A
20.	A		

Answer Explanations

PART 1: GENERAL SCIENCE

1. **C.** Homeostasis is the process by which your body tries to maintain a normal internal environment. For example, when your body overheats, your skin releases water through your pores. Water evaporating from your skin cools your body temperature, thus maintaining a normal body temperature of 98.6°F.

2. **B.** The SI unit for power is the watt. A joule is the SI unit of energy, or work. The energy needed to lift an apple one meter upward against the force of gravity is equal to about one joule. A joule is equivalent to a newton-meter. A newton is the SI unit for force. A watt is the rate of energy conversion and is equal to one joule (or one newton-meter) per second. It is roughly equal to the power used to lift the apple one meter in one second.

3. **C.** The dinosaurs were dominant during the Mesozoic Era. The Precambrian Era lasted from 4.6 billion years ago to the beginning of the Paleozoic Era 570 million years ago. The Paleozoic Era lasted from 570 million years ago until the Mesozoic Era 250 million years ago. The Mesozoic Era lasted from about 250 million years ago to 65 million years ago. The Cenozoic Era, the most recent era, has lasted from 65 million years ago to the present.

4. **B.** A cup of hot tea has less thermal energy and a higher temperature. Thermal energy, or heat, is the total energy of vibrating atoms and molecules. Temperature should not be confused with heat. Temperature

is a measure of the average heat or thermal energy of the particles in a substance. Since it is an average measurement, it does not depend on the number of particles in an object. An ocean has much more thermal energy than a cup of tea because it has many more molecules, but it has a lower average heat, or temperature.

5. **C.** All living things reproduce, grow, and develop at some stage in their lives. Also, all living things respond to their environment to survive. However, not all living things are made of cells that have nuclei. For example, bacteria are unicellular organisms that do not have nuclei.

6. **D.** A fixed pulley is a pulley that has a rope around a wheel and axle that does not move. It changes the direction of the effort force, but it does not increase the size of the effort force. Work is made easier by changing the direction of the force (pulling down instead of up).

7. **D.** The Precambrian is by far the longest era, comprising about 90 percent of the time scale.

8. **D.** The basic unit of structure of living things is the cell. Cells are organized into tissues, tissues are organized into organs, and organs are organized into organ systems.

9. **D.** Work is measured in joules (J) and is equal to force measured in newtons (N) multiplied by displacement measured in meters (m). The amount of work done is 100 N x 4 m = 400 N-m, which is 400 J.

10. **C.** The supercontinent was called Pangaea. It broke apart to form Laurasia and Gondwana, and these two supercontinents broke apart to form the continents as they exist today.

11. **A.** When iron rusts, it combines with oxygen to form a new substance, iron oxide. This is a chemical change. In chemical changes, substances are altered chemically and display different physical and chemical properties after the change. New substances are formed through a reorganization of the atoms. In a physical change, the substances are not altered chemically. A physical change can affect the size, shape, or color of a substance but does not affect its composition.

The substances may be changed to another phase, such as a gas, liquid, or solid, or separated or combined. Sugar dissolving, water freezing, and wax melting are all reversible physical changes.

12. **A.** The nucleus directs all the activities of the cell. Mitochondria provide the energy the cell needs to carry on its life functions. Ribosomes are involved in protein synthesis. The cytoplasm is the area between the nucleus and the cell membrane.

13. **D.** The momentum of an object is equal to mass × velocity. The more mass an object has, the more momentum it has. The faster it is moving, the more momentum it has. Thus, a car has more momentum than a bicycle moving at the same speed. If one car is moving faster than another car with the same mass, the first car has more momentum.

14. **A.** Tectonic plates move apart, or diverge, at mid-ocean ridges.

15. **A.** A substance that changes from a liquid to a solid is a physical change. The other examples all indicate a chemical reaction, which chemically alters a substance.

16. **B.** Both plant and animal cells have vacuoles for storing nutrients and waste products. Only plant cells have cell walls and chloroplasts for carrying on photosynthesis. Most plant cells have fixed rectangular shapes, whereas animal cells have irregular shapes.

17. **C.** A wedge and a screw are both types of inclined planes. An inclined plane is a ramp connecting a lower level with a higher level. A wedge is two inclined planes back to back. A screw is an inclined plane wrapped around a cylinder. They both have a mechanical advantage that is equal to the length of the ramp divided by its height. Less force is needed to move the screw and the wedge through a resistance, but the force is applied through a greater distance.

18. **A.** Earth's crust is made up of moving plates. These plates meet each other at one of three kinds of boundaries. At divergent plate boundaries, such as the mid-ocean ridges, the plates are moving apart. At convergent plate boundaries, like those just off the coast of the state of Washington,

the plates are moving together and one plate is moving under the other. At transform faults, such as those at the San Andreas Fault in California, the plates are sliding past one another.

19. **C.** The carbon compounds in natural gas contain chemical energy. When it is burned, this chemical energy releases light and heat energy.

20. **D.** Each daughter cell has the same number of chromosomes as the original cell, 48. On the other hand, if a cell undergoes meiosis to produce sex cells, each resulting sex cell has only 24 chromosomes.

21. **B.** Velocity is a vector quantity, meaning it has direction and speed, which equals distance divided by time in a certain direction. The velocity of the airplane = 1,260 km/3 hr westward = 420 km/hr westward.

22. **D.** Most geologists believe that convection currents in Earth's mantle cause the movement of Earth's plates. Up-currents under the ocean ridges cause the plates to spread, and down-currents under trenches cause the sea floor to be pulled under the continental plates.

23. **C.** Every organism can be classified at seven different levels: kingdom, phylum, class, order, family, genus, and species. The kingdom is the largest group and is very broad. Each successive group contains fewer organisms, but the organisms are more similar. The last two groups, genus and species, make up the scientific name of an organism.

24. **D.** A meteorite is a small mass of matter that has fallen to Earth's surface from outer space. A meteor is a small body of matter from outer space that enters Earth's atmosphere, appearing as a streak of light. It burns up in the atmosphere before reaching the ground. An asteroid is a small rocky body orbiting the sun. Large numbers of asteroids are found between the orbits of Mars and Jupiter. A comet is a celestial object consisting of a nucleus of ice and dust. When near the sun, a comet develops a "tail" of gas and dust particles pointing away from the sun.

25. **D.** Gases are easily compressed and expand to fill their containers. Solids have crystalline structures. Liquids are made up of particles that are not rigidly attached to one another, so they flow easily.

PART 2: ARITHMETIC REASONING

1. **B.** Because the temperature decreased from –13.2°C to –22.9°C, the difference can be found by subtracting the temperature on Friday from the temperature on Thursday: –22.9 – (–13.2) = –22.9 + 13.2 = –9.7. Because the temperature decreased, the answer must be a negative value.

2. **B.** Analeigh eats $\frac{2}{7}$ of the first pizza and $\frac{2}{8}$ of the second pizza. To add two fractions, their denominators must be identical. This can be achieved by multiplying the first fraction by the denominator of the second and vice versa: $\frac{2\times7}{8\times7}=\frac{14}{56}$ and $\frac{2\times8}{7\times8}=\frac{16}{56}$. The two fractions can now be added by simply adding the numerators and reducing the result: $\frac{16}{56}+\frac{14}{56}=\frac{30}{56}=\frac{15}{28}$.

3. **D.** The difference between 17 and –3 can be found by subtracting the initial temperature (–3) from the final temperature (17): 17 – (–3) = 17 + 3 = 20. Therefore, you know that the temperature increased 20 degrees.

4. **C.** The first step to solving this is problem is finding out the amount of tax Noel paid. To find the tax, find the difference between $50.37 and $46.00: $50.37 – $46.00 = $4.37. The next step is to find out what percentage of $46.00 is $4.37. Represent the unknown percent with an x: 4.37 = 46x. Then, solve for x: x = 0.095, or 9.5%. Therefore, the rate of sales tax on the jacket was 9.5 percent.

5. **B.** If the car travels 50 miles per day for each of 20 days, then the total number of miles traveled is 1000. One gallon of gasoline is required for every 26 miles. The total amount of gasoline consumed can be found by dividing the total number of miles by the miles per gallon:

$$\frac{1000\text{mi}}{1}\div\frac{26\text{mi}}{\text{gallon}}=\frac{1000\text{mi}}{1}\times\frac{\text{gallon}}{26\text{mi}}\approx38.5\text{ gallons.}$$

6. **C.** The monthly cost of day care ($600) is equal to 20% (0.20) of his monthly salary. This relationship can be translated into the

following equation: $600 = 0.2x$. Then, solve the equation for x: $\dfrac{600}{0.2} = \dfrac{0.2x}{0.2} = 3000 = x$. Thus, Kevin's monthly salary is $3,000. This amount can also be determined by multiplying $600 by 5 since 20% is $\dfrac{1}{5}$ of 100%.

7.   **B.** The total number of rollover minutes, or 2,378, should be divided by 5, giving a quotient of 475.6. Then, the whole number portion of 475 minutes should be multiplied by 5 months, giving 2,375 minutes. Then, subtract 2,375 minutes from the total number of rollover minutes (2,378 minutes): $2,378 - 2,375 = 3$ minutes. At the beginning of the sixth month, Miroslav will have 3 rollover minutes remaining.

8.   **B.** The median number can be found by writing the numbers in as-cending order and finding the average of the middle two values. Thus, the number of checks received per month can be arranged as follows: 1, 2, 2, 4, 4, 6. The middle two values are 2 and 4; the average of these two numbers is 3. Thus, the median number of checks received per month is 3.

9.   **B.** Ann finishes 1 mile in 86 percent of the time it takes Kim to finish a mile: $a = 0.86k$, where a represents the time it takes Ann to finish a mile, and k represents the time it takes Kim to finish a mile. The prob-lem gives Kim's time as 12 minutes, so this time can be substituted for the variable k in the equation: $a = 0.86(12)$, or $a = 10.32$. Thus, it takes Ann 10.32 minutes to finish running 1 mile.

10. **B.** The average can be determined by finding the sum of the five test scores and dividing by the total number of tests, or 5. Thus, the average can be written as $\dfrac{86+92+80+99+88}{5}$, or $\dfrac{445}{5}$, or 89. Thus, Aubrey's average on the five tests is 89.

11. **D.** The difference in the cost of the two premiums under the two different plans is: $396 - $257.40 = $138.60. This difference is equal to the product of some percent decrease and the original monthly cost

of \$396. This relationship can be modeled using the equation: 138.60 = 396x. Solving for x gives $x = 0.35$, or 35%. Therefore, the percent decrease in her monthly health insurance premium is 35 percent.

12. **B.** Before Sam pulls out the first orange sock, there are 30 socks in the drawer and 10 of them are orange. After Sam pulls out the first orange sock, 29 socks remain in the drawer, and 9 of them are orange. Therefore, the probability of her pulling out a second orange sock becomes $\dfrac{9}{29}$.

13. **C.** This problem represents a weighted average. Since Carl drove 240 miles per day for 3 days and 380 miles per day for 4 days for a total of a 7-day trip, the following expression can be written: $\dfrac{3(240) + 4(380)}{7}$, which equals 320. Thus, the average number of miles driven per day over the course of 7 days is 320 miles.

14. **B.** The first number can be represented by the equation $f = 2s - 3$, where f represents the first number and s represents the second number. Substituting a value of 18 for the second number gives $f = 2(18) - 3$, or $f = 33$. Thus, the first number is 33.

15. **D.** The probability of event A and event B occurring can be represented by this formula: $P(A \text{ and } B) = P(A) \times P(B)$. The probability of the spinner landing on a 2 is 1 out of 8, or $\dfrac{1}{8}$. The probability of the spinner landing on a number greater than 5 is 3 out of 8, or $\dfrac{3}{8}$. Thus, the probability of the spinner landing on a 2 and a number greater than 5 is $\dfrac{1}{8} \cdot \dfrac{3}{8}$, or $\dfrac{3}{64}$.

16. **A.** To determine the cost of one eraser, the sentences can be translated into equations and solved for the point of intersection, which is the point at which the costs are the same. The graphs intersect at the point (0.27, 0.59), where the x value represents the cost of one eraser, and the y value represents the cost of one pencil. The cost given for Choice A

may also be substituted into the two translated equations for an accuracy check. Doing so gives

$$4p + 3(0.27) = 3.17$$
$$4p + 0.81 = 3.17$$
$$4p = 2.36$$
$$p = 0.59$$

The resulting cost per pencil and cost per eraser can be substituted into the other equation to verify the accuracy of the cost. Doing so gives

$$8(0.59) + 5(0.27) = 6.07$$
$$4.72 + 1.35 = 6.07$$
$$6.07 = 6.07$$

The two costs are correct. Therefore, the cost of one eraser is $0.27.

17. C. Amanda's current rent ($1,509) equals the product of 228% (or 2.28) of some unknown amount. This relationship can be represented using this equation: $1509 = 2.28x$. Solving for x gives $x \approx 661.84$. Therefore, the best estimate for the amount of monthly rent paid at the previous residence is $661.84.

18. B. The hourly rate charged by the attorney in Flagstaff is equal to the product of 80% and some unknown rate. To find the unknown rate, replace it with x and use this equation: $200 = 0.80x$. Solving for x gives $x = 250$. The attorney in Tempe charges an hourly rate of $250.

19. B. When dividing 15 by $\frac{3}{2}$, rewrite the expression as $15 \cdot \frac{2}{3}$, which equals $\frac{30}{3}$ or 10. Thus, a 15-ft. roll of wrapping paper, when cut into equal sections of $\frac{3}{2}$ ft., can be cut into 10 sections.

20. C. Speed equals distance divided by time. The distance (391 miles) can be divided by the time (5 hours and 45 minutes, or 5.75 hours): 391 miles ÷ 5.75 = 68 miles per hour.

21. B. The amount of his raise totals $4,000. The amount of his raise equals the product of an unknown percent increase and his original

salary of \$50,000. This relationship can be shown with the equation 4,000 = 50,000x, where x equals the unknown percentage. Solving for x gives x = 0.08, which equals 8%. Thus, the percent increase of his raise was 8 percent.

22. **A.** Together, they can plant 14 trees in 1 hour, so you can write this ratio: $\dfrac{1 \text{ hour}}{14 \text{ trees}}$. Thus, the length of time it will take them to finish the job can be represented by the expression $35 \text{ trees} \times \dfrac{1 \text{ hour}}{14 \text{ trees}}$, which reduces to $\dfrac{35}{14}$ hours, or 2.5 hours.

23. **B.** The cost can be represented by the equation $y = 16x + 135$, where y represents the cost and x represents the number of sessions that require an LCD projector. Since Keisha uses an LCD projector for 3 sessions, you should replace x with 3: $y = 16(3) + 135$, or $y = 183$. The total cost of attending the conference is \$183.

24. **D.** Monique's number can be represented by the following equation: $m = 3a - 14$, where m represents Monique's number and a represents Ana's number. Since you know the value of m (181), insert that number in the equation: $181 = 3a - 14$. Solving for a gives: $181 = 3a - 14 \rightarrow 181 + 14 = 3a - 14 + 14 \rightarrow 195 = 3a \rightarrow 65 = a$. Therefore, Ana's number is 65.

25. **B.** The probability of event A or event B occurring can be represented by this formula: $P(A \text{ or } B) = P(A) + P(B) - P(A \text{ and } B)$. The probability of rolling a 3 is 1 out of 6, or $\dfrac{1}{6}$. The probability of rolling a prime number is 3 out of 6, or $\dfrac{3}{6}$. (Note that the number 1 is neither prime nor composite.) The probability of rolling a 3 and a prime number is 1 out of 6, or $\dfrac{1}{6}$, since 3 is also a prime number. Thus, the probability of rolling a 3 or a prime number can be written as $\dfrac{1}{6} + \dfrac{3}{6} - \dfrac{1}{6} = \dfrac{3}{6} \rightarrow \dfrac{1}{2}$.

26. **D.** The sequence consists of multiples of 4. The next number in the sequence is 68. However, this number is not evenly divisible by 8, and

the question asks for the next multiple of 8. The next number after 68 is 72, which is the product of 8 and 9.

27. **B.** If Ms. Garcia hands out 3 pencils to each of her students and has 2 pencils left over, then the number of pencils originally in the box must be 2 more than a multiple of 3. First, subtract 2 from each of the answer choices: $100 - 2 = 98$. Then, $101 - 2 = 99$. Next, $102 - 2 = 100$. Finally, $103 - 2 = 101$. The only answer that is a multiple of 3 is 99 ($99 \div 3 = 33$). Therefore, Ms. Garcia must have had 101 pencils in the box.

28. **A.** If a raffle sells 500 raffle tickets to a total of 80 people, the average number of tickets per person can be determined by dividing the total number of tickets by the total number of people. This number, expressed as a fraction that has been reduced, is $\frac{500}{80} = \frac{50}{8} = \frac{25}{4}$.

29. **D.** The following proportion can be used to solve the problem: $\frac{8}{1151.36} = \frac{24}{x}$. Solving for x gives $8x = 27{,}632.64$, or $x = 3{,}454.08$. Thus, the total cost of ink cartridges for 2 years is $3,454.08.

30. **B.** To determine the total number of miles run, the mixed numbers can first be converted to improper fractions. Doing so gives $\frac{27}{8} + \frac{29}{6}$. Finding the least common denominator allows you to add the fractions, giving $\frac{81}{24} + \frac{116}{24}$, or $\frac{197}{24}$. This improper sum can be converted to a mixed number by dividing 24 into 197, finding the quotient and placing the remainder over the denominator of 24. Thus, the total number of miles she ran was $8\frac{5}{24}$.

PART 3: WORD KNOWLEDGE

1. **A.** *Admonished* most nearly means *scolded*. *Damaged* means harmed or ruined, *compensated* means to pay or reward, and *censored* means to limit or restrict.

2. **B.** *Anarchy* most nearly means *rebellion*, as in "The absence of a

leader left the town in anarchy." *Stability* means reliability, *monarchy* refers to a governmental rule under a king, and *contagion* means the spread of disease.

3. **B.** *Brevity* most nearly means *briefness*. *Insincerity* means untrue or hypocritical, *tediousness* means monotonous or boring, and *clarity* means clear and obvious.

4. **A.** *Brandish* most closely means *wield*, as in "The solider said he would brandish a weapon." *Conceal* means to cover up or hide, *tarnish* means to discolor, and *finesse* means subtlety or diplomacy.

5. **B.** *Cessation* most nearly means *termination*. *Commencement* means to start or begin, *containment* means to keep in one place, and *inhibition* means to be inhibited or reserved.

6 **B.** *Copious* most nearly means *abundant*, as in "The copious amount of food my father cooked for dinner could feed an army." *Restricted* means limited, *scant* means meager, and *resplendent* means decorated *or* garnished.

7. **A.** *Curvature* most nearly means *arch*. A *tumor* is a growth, to *stretch* means to lengthen muscles, and *temperature* means fever.

8. **B.** *Corroborate* most nearly means *verify*, as in "A witness corroborated her story." *Deny* means to contradict, *compliment* means to praise, and *finance* means to pay for or sponsor.

9. **C.** *Denounce* most closely means *condemn*. *Betray* means to go against someone, *interrogate* means to thoroughly question, and *resolve* means to determine or decide.

10. **D.** *Dissonant* most closely means *cacophonous*. *Melodious* means full of melody and beauty, *harmonious* means full of harmony and song, and *congruous* means appropriate or consistent.

11. **D.** *Eccentric* most closely means *unconventional*, as in "The unconventional old woman always wore pink dresses and carried an umbrella when she was outdoors." *Unattractive* means not pretty, *uneasy* means

to be nervous or uncomfortable, and *unkempt* means messy or in need of grooming.

12. **D.** *Extemporaneous* most closely means *unrehearsed*. *Oratorical* means having to do with public speeches, *persuasive* means convincing, and *clandestine* means secretive.

13. **A.** *Erroneous* most nearly means *incorrect*, as in "The article contained erroneous information and inaccurate statistics." *Irrational* means foolish, *unconscious* means unaware, and *unreasonable* means illogical.

14. **A.** *Furtive* most closely means *secretive*, as in "The thief wanted to be furtive, so he wore a suit." *Temporary* means short-lived, *energetic* means to be full of energy and vigor, and *exhaustive* means tiring or thorough.

15. **D.** *Gesticulations* most nearly means *movements*. *Formulas* means mathematical figures, *conjectures* are possible ideas, and *theories* are ideas or hypotheses.

16. **C.** *Heirloom* most nearly means *valuable*. A *photograph* is a *picture*, a *flagon* is a flask, and a *bauble* is a trinket.

17. **B.** *Hiatus* most nearly means *break*. When workers stop working for union reasons, it is referred to as a *strike*. A *commercial* is an advertisement, and to go on a *tour* is to travel.

18. **C.** *Inadvertently* means *unintentionally*. *Unhappy* means not happy, *unsatisfactory* means not satisfactory, and *unconsciously* means not consciously.

19. **B.** *Jargon* most nearly means *terminology*. *Language* means spoken words, *nonsense* refers to something that does not make sense, and *manners* are rules of etiquette and behavior.

20. **B.** *Labyrinth* most nearly means *maze*. A *knoll* is a small hill, an *investment* is money put into a stock or business, and a *massacre* is a massive killing.

21. **A.** *Mandatory* most nearly means *required*. *Impartial* means neutral

or unbiased, *optional* means voluntary, and *traditional* means something that has been done for years.

22. **A.** *Nebulous* most nearly means *tenuous*, as in "The concept of love is sometimes nebulous." *Meticulous* means precise and careful, *comprehensible* means understandable, and *mystical* means magical or supernatural.

23. **C.** *Notation* most nearly means *comment*. A *code* is a specialized pattern, a *document* is a paper or file, and a *file* is a group of papers or documents.

24. **A.** *Petulant* most nearly means *sulky*. *Noteworthy* means unusual or notable, *affable* means friendly or social, and *gregarious* means outgoing and talkative.

25. **A.** *Patronizing* most nearly means *belittling*. *Complimenting* means praising, *tolerating* means putting up with, and *compromising* means meeting in the middle.

26. **B.** *Proximity* most nearly means *vicinity*, as in "She and I became lab partners because of our proximity; our desks were next to each other." *Remedy* means a cure for something, a *prototype* is a model of an original, and a *novice* is someone learning something new.

27. **C.** *Quibbled* most nearly means *bickered*. *Agreed* means to have the same opinion about something, *decided* means to have made a decision, and *conversed* means to have talked.

28. **C.** *Reconcile* most nearly means to reunite, as in "The girls reconciled and became friends once again." *Revise* means to change or alter, *resume* means to start again, and *reject* means to deny or push away.

29. **D.** *Sanctioned* most nearly means *authorized*. *Ordered* means demanded, *prohibited* means stopped or prevented, and *repelled* means kept away.

30. **A.** *Sparse* most nearly means *scant*. *Solemn* means serious or sad, *sodden* means extremely wet, and *skeptical* means cynical or questioning.

31. **D.** *Tenacious* most nearly means *determined*. *Indecisive* means unable

to decide, *ambivalent* means torn between two actions or emotions, and *flippant* means frivolous or dismissive.

32. **B.** *Transparent* most nearly means *clear*, as in "He saw her take the ring through the transparent window." *Solid* means dense, and *blatant* means obvious. To *transplant* something means to move it from one place to another.

33. **A.** *Vintage* most nearly means *antique*. *Innovative* means new or unusual, *whimsical* means playful or imaginative, and *contemporary* means modern.

34. **B.** *Zealot* most nearly means *fanatic*, as in "Zealots of freedom started a riot in the park." A *patriot* is a person loyal to his or her country, a *spectator* is someone who watches an event, such as a baseball game, and a *theologian* is a person who studies religion.

35. **D.** *Vulnerable* most nearly means *susceptible*, as in "Mary's allergies made her vulnerable to illnesses." *Receptive* means open and welcoming, *invincible* means impossible to harm, and *impervious* means not responsive.

PART 4: PARAGRAPH COMPREHENSION

1. **D.** You have to make an inference to answer this question. The passage says that 55 million years ago the temperature in the Polar Regions was in the seventies. It also says that over the next million years, as green things grew, the area cooled down significantly. From this information, you can infer that the correct answer is that the cooling trend at the North Pole was caused by the absorption of carbon dioxide by the growth of greenery.

2. **C.** This question asks you to recall a detail from the passage. The passage says that Thomas Jefferson used Poplar Forest to study, write, and garden. It does not say that he held staff meetings there, so this is the correct answer.

3. **C.** This passage asks you to identify the main idea of the passage. The main idea is that the U.S. pilots accomplished an amazing feat; they flew

around the world. Therefore, the best answer is Choice C: U.S. pilots conquered the challenge of a round-the-world flight.

4.   **C.** The author's main purpose in writing this passage is to tell you about the versatility of the Globe, a stage used during the Shakespearean era. Therefore, the best answer is Choice C: to describe the stage of a theater used during the Shakespearean era.

5.   **B.** The passage says that the fiddler crab seems to be playing a tune but is actually using its large claw to discourage potential predators. Therefore, the best answer choice is B: the fiddler crab waves its large claw to defend itself.

6.   **B.** This question asks you to choose the main idea, or what the entire passage is about. Some of the answer options give details in the passage, but Choice B gives the main idea: Children who receive early musical training have an advantage when learning to read.

7.   **B.** The passage does not indicate that players intended to resist the forward pass when it was first introduced (Choice A), and it does not say that there weren't any rules in the game before 1906 (Choice C). While early football players may have considered wearing pads and helmets a sign of weakness, there isn't any evidence in the passage to support this conclusion. The passage does say that injuries mounted until a group of powerful coaches decided to make a change—and this change was the forward pass. Therefore, Choice B is the best answer.

8.   **D.** This question asks you to recall a detail from the passage. The passage says that reporters called in the facts and information they discovered, and a rewrite person pounded out the story on a manual typewriter. Therefore, the best answer is Choice D.

9.   **B.** This question asks you to choose a word that best describes the mood of the story. The divers are not certain they can get the jade—they face obstacles such as kelp ponds and lime-colored sunlight. Therefore, the best answer is Choice B, suspense.

10. **B.** This is a cause-and-effect question. If you look back at the passage,

you'll see that the details support that idea that a solid-body guitar would improve the sound of the instrument. Therefore, the best answer choice is B: Changing to a solid-body electric guitar was an advantage because it improved the instrument's tone.

11. **D.** According to the passage, Roosevelt did not give up during his western ranching years and instead likely learned a great deal about the outdoors. After this, he became an environmental activist. Therefore, the best answer is that his western ranching experience prepared him for his role as an environmental activist.

12. **B.** To answer this question, you have to combine the details in the passage. The passage says that the chickwich is the more popular sandwich and that people prefer the wheat-type bun and mayonnaise. Therefore, the most popular sandwich is the chickwich on a wheat bun with mayonnaise.

13. **D.** This passage asks you to make an inference based on the information provided in the passage. The passage says that Wheatley was an African American and that she published a famous book of poems. Therefore, the best conclusion is that she helped to originate the African American genre in English literature.

14. **A.** This question asks you to choose a word describing the mood of the story. Elizabeth is happy in the passage, so you can eliminate choices B and D. Of the remaining choices, *joy* more closely describes the mood of the passage than *comfort*.

15. **D.** To correctly answer this question, you need to be aware that the Luddites wanted to stop the machinery; they were not necessarily criminal otherwise. Therefore, the best answer is Choice D: creates a disturbance to disrupt electronic communication.

PART 5: MATHEMATICAL KNOWLEDGE

1. **C.** The product of the binomials can be written as $-36x^2 + 12x + 108x - 36$, which simplifies to $-36x^2 + 120x - 36$.

2.   **A.** The perimeter can be written as $4s = 108$, which can be simplified to $s = 27$. The length of each side of the square is 27 inches. The area of a square can be determined using the formula, $A = s^2$. Thus, the area of the square is 27^2, or 729, square inches.

3.   **A.** The area of the rectangle is equal to the product of the length and width. Thus, the area can be written as $(2x - 1)(4x + 2)$, or $8x^2 - 4x + 4x - 2$, which simplifies to $8x^2 - 2$.

4.   **D.** The square numbers can be written as the sequence 1, 3, 9, 16, 25, ... The term numbers of the sequence can be written as 1, 2, 3, 4, 5, ... Thus, each square number is the square of the term it represents, written n^2. The value of the 18th square number is equal to 18^2 or 324.

5.   **B.** All squares are rectangles because squares are quadrilaterals with sides forming four right angles. Parallelograms are not trapezoids, and trapezoids are not parallelograms. Only some rhombi are squares, whereas all squares are rhombi.

6.   **C.** The inequality can be solved as follows:

$$-3x - 6 \geq 108$$
$$-3x \geq 114$$
$$x \leq -38$$

7.   **B.** The average number of miles run over the course of the three days can be determined by finding the total number of miles run and dividing by the number of days. A common denominator allows the mixed numbers to be added: $3\frac{15}{20} + 3\frac{4}{20} + 2\frac{10}{20} \rightarrow 9\frac{9}{20}$. This sum can be written as the improper fraction: $\frac{189}{20}$. Division of this sum by 3 can be written as $\frac{189}{20} \cdot \frac{1}{3}$, which reduces to $\frac{63}{20}$, or $3\frac{3}{20}$. Thus, the average number of miles run was $3\frac{3}{20}$ miles.

8.   **D.** The expressions can be multiplied by writing the base of 3 raised

to the power of the sum of the given exponents. Thus, the product can be written as $3^{\frac{1}{2}+\frac{1}{6}}$ or $3^{\frac{4}{6}}$, which can also be written as $\sqrt[6]{3^4}$.

9. **B.** The area of the triangle can be represented as $A = \frac{1}{2}(3x)(2x+2)$, or $A = \frac{1}{2}(6x^2 + 6x)$, which reduces to $A = 3x^2 + 3x$. Factoring out a $3x$ gives the expression $3x(x+1)$.

10. **C.** The enlarged rectangle has dimensions of w and $l + 4$. The product of these dimensions gives $lw + 4w$. Thus, the expression $lw + 4w$ can be used to determine the area of the enlarged rectangle. For example, when adding 4 units to the length of a rectangle with a length of 2 units and a width of 2 units, the new area will be equal to $(2)(2) + (4)(2)$, or 12 square units.

11. **C.** The zeros can be determined in several ways: by factoring, setting each factor equal to zero, and solving; by using the quadratic formula; by graphing; or by using the table feature of a graphing calculator. The zeros of the function are the values of x that result in a y value of 0. The graph reveals two places where the graph crosses the x-axis. The table reveals that the x values of -10 and 3 result in a y value of 0. Evaluation of the expression for each x value results in a calculation of 0, thus verifying the accuracy of both x values.

12. **C.** The square root of 157 must be more than 12 since $12^2 = 144$; it must also be less than 13, since $13^2 = 169$.

13. **B.** Vertical angles have congruent measures. Since angles A and C are supplementary, which means that the sum of their angles is $180°$, and angle C has a measure of $114°$, angle A must have a measure of $66°$. Since angles A and B are vertical angles, angle B will also have a measure of $66°$.

14. **D.** Angles c and g are corresponding angles. When two parallel lines are cut by a transversal, the resulting corresponding angles are congruent. Thus, angles c and g are congruent.

15. **C.** Angles DAB and BAC are supplementary, which means they

form a 180° angle. Since $m\angle DAB = 107°$, $m\angle BAC$ must equal the difference of 180° and 107°. Thus, $m\angle BAC = 73°$.

16. **B.** The sum of the interior angles in any regular n polygon is equal to $(n-2)\cdot 180°$, where n represents the number of sides of the polygon. Thus, the sum of the interior angles of a regular octagon is $(8-2)\cdot 180°$ or $6 \cdot 180°$. The sum of the interior angles is 1,080°.

17. **D.** The sum of the interior angles of a triangle is 180°. Therefore, the following equation can be written: $a + 3a + 90 = 180$. Solving for a gives:

$$4a + 90 = 180$$
$$4a = 90$$
$$a = 22.5$$

The measure of the angle opposite the base of the triangle $3a$ is equal to $3(22.5)°$ or 67.5°.

18. **D.** The number of diagonals found in any regular n polygon can be determined using this formula: $\frac{1}{2}\cdot n(n-3)$, where n represents the number of sides of the polygon. Substituting 6 for n gives $\frac{1}{2}\cdot 6(6-3)$, or $\frac{1}{2}(18)$, which equals 9. Thus, a regular hexagon has 9 diagonals.

19. **B.** An isosceles triangle has two congruent base angles. Since the sum of the interior angles is 180° and angle B measures 40°, each base angle is equal to the quotient of 140° and 2, or 70°.

20. **C.** In a triangle, the side opposite the largest angle is the longest, whereas the side opposite the smallest angles is the shortest. Since angle A is the largest angle, BC is the longest side. Since angle B is the smallest angle, AC is the shortest side. Therefore, the correct statement is $BC > AB > AC$.

21. **C.** Similar triangles have congruent corresponding angles and proportional corresponding sides. Therefore, the following proportion can be written: $\frac{6}{x} = \frac{8}{20}$. Solving for x gives $x = 15$. The length of DE is 15.

22. **C.** The radius of the circle can be determined using the given point on the circle and center of the circle. The radius is equal to the distance from the center of the circle to any point on the circle. Thus, the distance can be calculated as $d = \sqrt{(0-3)^2 + (0-4)^2}$ or $\sqrt{25}$, which equals 5. The area of a circle, with radius of 5, can be written as $A = \pi(5)^2$ or $A = 25\pi$, which is approximately 78.5. The area of the circle is approximately 78.5 units^2.

23. **B.** The volume of a cylinder can be determined by using the formula $V = \pi r^2 h$, where r represents the radius and h represents the height. Substituting the given volume and height gives: $7,385.28 = \pi r^2(12)$, where $r = 14$. Thus, the radius of the cylinder is 14 cm.

24. **A.** The line has a negative slope, so you can eliminate choices A and C. You can calculate the slope of line by choosing two points on the line. The slope of a line is the ratio of change in y values per change in corresponding x values. By choosing the y-intercept and the point $(1, -2)$ the following ratio can be written: $\dfrac{-2-6}{1-0}$, which equals -8. Note that any two points on the line can be used to calculate the slope of the line. The slope of the given line is -8.

25. **C.** The distance representing the base of the triangle is 16, whereas the distance representing the height of the triangle is 12. The Pythagorean Theorem can be used to find the length of the hypotenuse. The following equation can be written and solved: $16^2 + 12^2 = c^2$. Solving for c gives $c = \sqrt{400}$ or $c = 20$. Therefore, the length of the hypotenuse is 20 units.

PART 6: ELECTRONICS INFORMATION

1. **D.** All elements of matter are conductors, semiconductors, or insulators. Matter is divided into categories based upon its ability to conduct electricity. Conductors transfer electrons easily, while insulators do not. Matter that is somewhere between these two classifications is considered a semiconductor.

2. **D.** Valence electrons are attached to atoms, and the ease with which they break free determines whether they are conductors, semiconductors, or insulators. Generally, a conductor has fewer than three valence electrons. Semiconductors have four valence electrons and insulators have five (or more).

3. **C.** Coulomb's law states that bodies attract or repel each other with a force that is directly proportional to the product of their individual charges and inversely proportional to the square of the distance between them. When you hold two magnets together, the electric field of force created either pushes them apart or pulls them together. This is a result of Coulomb's law.

4. **C.** A transformer sends electrical energy between circuits. The core of a transformer allows magnetic flux lines to travel between windings. The primary winding is connected to a power source, and the secondary winding is responsible for power output. The enclosure protects the transformer's main components.

5. **B.** The maximum voltage a winding can handle depends on the type of insulation used, not the type of wire used. Insulation protects the winding and the voltage it holds, so the thicker the insulation, the more voltage that may be applied.

6. **A.** The shells in an atom are groups of electrons, and each group is given a letter designation according to its proximity to the nucleus. The outermost shell of an atom is called the valence shell.

7. **C.** When an external force controls electrons, and they move in the same direction, the result is electrical current. While ions transfer during the movement of electrons, their movement does not result in electrical currents.

8. **B.** Rubber, glass, dry wood, and plastic do not exchange valence electrons because they are bound tightly. This makes them good insulators because they carry very little or no electric current. Since the valence electrons cannot move, they do not conduct electricity.

9. **A.** Low-reluctance materials are easily magnetized by other forces, such as when a screw becomes magnetized by friction and sticks to the tip of a screwdriver. The screw becomes a temporary magnet, and when the friction stops, the screw loses its magnetism. Conversely, high-reluctance materials are considered permanent magnets, such as those that stick to your refrigerator.

10. **C.** The magnetic force on any magnet is weakest at its center. The highest concentration of magnetism exists on the outside edges of a magnet.

11. **C.** A body with extra electrons has a negative polarity, and a body lacking electrons has a positive polarity. As electrons are displaced, an electrical charge develops. No charge can exist if bodies are neutral, and both negative and positive bodies are required to create an electrical charge. Therefore, both A and B are true.

12. **C.** Friction caused by rubbing materials together, squeezing certain substances, heating unlike metals, light hitting photosensitive materials, chemical reactions in battery cells, and conductors moving through magnetic fields all create voltage. Currently, these are the only six methods known to produce voltage.

13. **C.** A fixed carbon resistor is one of the most commonly used resistors, and it is depicted on schematic diagrams as a series of jagged lines.

14. **B.** Heat develops when a current is passed through a resistor. The resistor must dissipate heat; if it does not, the heat will cause a change in resistance or cause the resistor to burn out. A resistor's ability to dissipate the heat it generates is measured in watts. Usually, the larger a resistor is, the higher its wattage rating.

15. **C.** The "k" represents kilohms, the measurement for a thousand ohms. The symbol that represents ohms is the Greek letter omega: Ω. Therefore, 20,000 ohms can be represented by the phrase 20 kilohms or by the notation 20 kΩ.

16. **A.** The first four bands in order of importance are black, brown, red, and orange. Many people use the phrase "Bad boys run over yellow

gardenias behind victory garden walls" to remember; the beginning of each word is the first letter of each color, in order. The colors of the resistor color code are, in this order: black, brown, red, orange, yellow, green, blue, violet, gray, and white.

17. **D**. The fourth band on a resistor is known as the "tolerance" band. When there is no fourth band, you can assume the resistor has a 20 percent tolerance. Different colors represent different percentages of tolerance (a gold band represents 5 percent tolerance, while a silver band represents 10 percent tolerance).

18. **B**. A load changes electrical energy into a different form of energy such as power, sound, or light. An electric motor turns electric energy to mechanical energy; a speaker turns electric energy into sound; and a light bulb turns electric energy into light. A television set produces a picture, but as a whole, a television is not considered a load, but the light bulbs inside are.

19. **D**. When a switch on a circuit is closed, the circuit is considered complete. Electrical currents can flow freely from the power source, around the circuit, and back to the power source. Opening a switch interrupts current flow. For example, a flashlight's "On" switch closes the circuit and allows current to flow to the bulb. When the switch is in the "Off" position, the circuit is open. The flashlight cannot work because its electrical currents do not have a clear path on which to travel.

20. **A**. Ohm's law states, "the current in a circuit is directly proportional to the applied voltage and inversely proportional to the circuit resistance." The correct way to express Ohm's law is $I = E/R$. To determine electrical current, divide voltage by resistance (volts by ohms).

PART 7: AUTO AND SHOP INFORMATION

1. **D**. The air-to-fuel ratio, also known as AFR, in an internal combustion engine should always be 14.7:1 to ensure that enough air is present to burn all the fuel. A ratio lower than 14.7:1 is considered a rich mixture, and a ratio greater than this is considered a lean mixture.

2. **A**. A radiator is a heat-exchange system used for heating and cooling inside an engine. Radiators produce heat that can be used to warm a vehicle or to cool a supply of liquid (like engine coolant).

3. **D**. A mixture of antifreeze and water is piped through internal combustion engines to remove heat. This combination is often referred to as engine coolant.

4. **B**. The shape of a ball peen hammer makes it useful for metal work. This type of hammer can shape copper, cut gaskets, and set rivets. Ball peen hammers are also commonly used during forging.

5. **D**. A splitting maul is a type of hammer. Types of screwdrivers include square, hex, pentagon, thumbscrew, slot, cross, cross-head, Phillips, and Frearson.

6. **D**. A double wishbone suspension is a Y-shaped design with each of its two arms attached to the chassis at two points. On a double wishbone suspension, the coil spring and shock absorber are mounted on the arms.

7. **A**. A miter box is a three-sided, slotted box woodworkers use to cut wood. Each slot is large enough for the blade of a saw, and slots are placed at measured intervals. Wood is inserted into one open end of the box and pushed through until it reaches the appropriate slot. The woodworker places a saw in the slot and makes a precisely measured cut in the wood.

8. **A**. The ground electrode in a spark plug can be bent toward or away from its central electrode, a process called gapping. The space between the two electrodes is known as the spark gap. A properly sized gap is necessary for the spark plug to operate correctly.

9. **C**. A trim carpenter generally specializes in trims and moldings, including ornamental woodwork. A cabinetmaker creates cabinets, dressers, chests, and other storage units. Framers build the framework of buildings, and formwork carpenters generally work with concrete.

10. **A**. A socket wrench allows the user to place individual and

interchangeable heads, called sockets, on the end. Socket wrenches are used to remove bolts of various sizes.

11. **B.** A coping saw's U-shaped frame and thin blade make changing directions while sawing easier. One end of a coping saw's blade can be unscrewed and inserted into a drilled hole so cuts can be made from the inside of a piece of wood.

12. **A.** A flathead screw is used when the head of the screw needs to be deeper than or flush with one of the materials being fastened.

13. **C.** A camshaft works by spinning in time with pistons inside an engine. As the camshaft rotates, its valves are forced open. The open valves release air-fuel mixture into the engine.

14. **D.** Catalytic converters turn toxic emissions into nontoxic emissions. Chemical reactions take place when toxic exhaust enters a catalytic converter; the exhaust interacts with a catalyst inside to produce less harmful by-products such as such as carbon dioxide, nitrogen, and water.

15. **C.** A plane is a sharpened metal plate encased in metal housing. When a woodworker pushes a plane across the surface of a piece of wood while applying downward pressure, the plane shaves away thin layers.

16. **D.** Lawn mowers, motorcycles, and speedboats are generally powered by internal combustion engines. A steam-powered locomotive uses an external combustion engine.

17. **D.** Washers are thin, disc-shaped pieces of hardware used to reduce vibration, prevent corrosion, and distribute a fastener's load. Washers can be made from a variety of materials, depending on their application, and come in a vast array of sizes.

18. **B.** A cross-peen is a type of hammer. Tongue and groove pliers are characterized by serrated jaws that can grip nuts, bolts, and oddly shaped objects. Needle-nosed pliers have long, thin jaws that can grip small objects in tight spaces; needle-nosed pliers also have a sharpened joint that can be used to cut wire. Diagonal pliers are only used to cut wire and other thin metal objects.

19. **A.** A dipstick is used to measure the amount of oil in an internal combustion engine. Different engines require different oil levels, and oil wells vary in depth.

20. **B.** The main purpose of a serpentine belt is to transmit power to auxiliary devices. A serpentine belt is routed through devices such as power steering pumps, alternators, and air-conditioning compressors to supply the energy they need. Serpentine belts are more efficient than multi-belt systems, but when a serpentine belt breaks, all auxiliary devices lose power at once.

21. **D.** The fuel, brake, and ignition systems are all examples of major automotive systems. Other major automotive systems include the drive train, suspension and steering system, computer system, emission control system, exhaust system, cooling system, and lubrication system.

22. **C.** The cylinder head houses the combustion chamber and the intake and exhaust valves and ports. The camshaft opens and closes the intake and exhaust valves. The engine block is the frame for the engine, and the connecting rod connects the piston and wrist pin assembly to the crankshaft.

23. **A.** The best way to tighten a wing nut is by hand. The wings on the nut make it easy to tighten and loosen by hand.

24. **B.** The parts of the suspension and steering system include springs, control arms, shock absorbers, the steering knuckle, the steering linkage, the wheel hub, tires, and ball joints. The drive shaft is part of the drive train system.

25. **C.** A piston is an object in an engine that moves up and down in the engine's cylinders. Hot gases from combustion push a piston up and down.

PART 8: MECHANICAL COMPREHENSION

1. **A.** A load distributing system splits a load between two anchor points. The sharper the angle, the more weight is distributed to the anchors. For

example, a load held by two anchors at a 120-degree angle will receive 100 percent support, while a load held at a 60-degree angle will receive only 60 percent support from each anchor.

2.   **D.** Each tool listed in the answer options is a type of lever, which is a simple machine. A bottle opener is a single second-class lever; tweezers are a pair of third-class levers connected to each another; and scissors are two first-class levers connected to each other. Other first-class levers include pliers, the claws on a hammer, and a seesaw. Second-class levers include wheelbarrows, nail clippers, nutcrackers, and staplers. Third-class levers include fishing rods and tongs.

3.   **C.** Mechanical advantage makes moving loads easier. Pulleys, gears, and anchors are methods of mechanical advantage that reduce the force you need to exert to move something.

4.   **A.** When nothing is attached to a load, there is no mechanical advantage. When one load-bearing device is attached to a load, such as a knot, the advantage is 1:1. A pulley provides two load-bearing devices because both ends of the rope are free, and the advantage is 1:2.

5.   **C.** When you stack two mechanical load systems, multiply the first numbers of each ratio. In the example above, the mechanical advantage is 6:1, because $2 \times 3 = 6$. If you stack one with a ratio of 4:1 and one with a ratio of 2:1, the mechanical advantage is 8:1. Stacking mechanical load systems makes moving the load even easier.

6.   **C.** The formula for work that takes place at an angle is $W = Fd\cos\theta$. F represents force, d represents displacement, and θ represents the angle between the force and distance vectors. In this problem, $W = 100\ \text{N} \times 5\ \text{m} \times \cos 30°$. The answer is 433 J.

7.   **C.** Levers and pulleys both provide mechanical advantage. They reduce the force necessary to move a load or overcome resistance.

8.   **D.** A fulcrum is the point where a lever pivots. Envision a seesaw on a playground. If the bar that holds the two seats is the lever, the center-piece that balances the seesaw is the fulcrum.

9. **D**. Force is measured in newtons, which is abbreviated by the letter N. One newton (1 N) is a force that causes an object with a mass of 1 kg to move at 1 m/s.

10. **B**. The formula for force is $F = ma$. F represents force, m represents the mass of the object in kilograms, and a represents the object's acceleration in m/s^2. Therefore, a 10 kg ball moving at 5.5 m/s^2 requires 55 N of force, because $10 \times 5.5 = 55$.

11. **B**. A larger pulley turns more slowly than a smaller pulley when the pulleys are operating together within the same system. Fewer revolutions are necessary to accomplish the same amount of work because a larger pulley has a larger surface area.

12. **B**. The ratio of gears is determined by the distance from the center to the point of contact. In this example, the second gear is three times larger than the first gear, so the ratio is 3:1. If the gears were 1" in diameter and 3" in diameter, the ratio would be the same, just as it would if the gears were 6" in diameter and 18" in diameter.

13. **A**. Torque tends to rotate, or turn, objects. For example, using a wrench generates torque. To calculate torque, multiply the force by the distance from the center. Torque is measured in pound-feet. This means that a 1-foot long wrench with 200 pounds of force applied to it creates 200 pound-feet of torque.

14. **A**. Newton's third law of motion states that for every action, there is an equal and opposite reaction. Answer choice B gives Newton's first law of motion, and answer choices C and D summarize parts of Newton's second law of motion.

15. **C**. Power is the rate at which energy is converted or work is performed. To calculate power, divide the amount of work (W) by the time it took to perform (t).

16. **C**. The formula for determining the safe working capacity (SWC) of a chain is $SWC = 8D^2$, with D representing the smallest link thickness measured in inches. In this example, $SWC = 8 \times 2^2$. First, square the number

2; the answer is 4. Multiply 8 by 4, and the answer is 32. Therefore, a chain with links 2″ in diameter can safely hold 32 tons of weight.

17. **A.** Friction reduces the efficiency of a machine because it takes energy away from the goal. An example is a tangled rope on a pulley system. If a rope is tangled, it cannot easily glide through a pulley; the force acting on the rope needs to increase just to get it through.

18. **D.** The result of force and movement combined, when both force and movement are in the same direction, is called work. Work is measured in joules. One unit of work is one joule. To calculate work, multiply force (in newtons) by displacement (in meters) using the formula $W = Fd$. For example, if you push a box 10 meters using 20 newtons of force, 200 joules of work have been done because $10 \times 20 = 200$.

19. **D.** There are six types of simple machines, and the machines in the answer options are considered simple machines. A machine is something that makes work easier by either transferring a force between two locations, changing the direction of a force, increasing the magnitude of a force, or increasing the distance or speed of a force.

20. **A.** There are three classes of levers: first-class, second-class, and third-class levers.

21. **C.** To calculate work, use the formula $W = Fd\cos\theta$. The force is 147 N (gravity), the displacement is 5 m, and since force and displacement are in the same direction, the angle is 0°. Therefore, $W = 147$ N $\times$ 5 m $\times \cos 0°$. The answer is 735 J.

22. **C.** It is possible for objects to store energy because of their position. When an object stores energy because of its position, it has potential energy that has not been released. For example, a drawn bowstring holds much more potential energy than a bowstring at its usual position.

23. **C.** To calculate potential energy, use the formula $PE = mgh$. PE represents potential energy, m represents mass in kilograms, g represents the force of gravity, which is 9.8 m/s^2, and h represents height. In this case, since the force and movement are going in the same direction, potential

energy is possible. The cart is 3 kg and the ramp is 0.45 m high, so $PE = (3 \text{ kg})(9.8 \text{ m/s}^2)(0.45 \text{ m})$, and the total potential energy is 13.2 J.

24. **A.** An isolated system has no net external force altering its momentum. In an isolated system, the only forces that contribute to the momentum change of an individual object are the forces between the objects themselves. Choice B is incorrect because the shag carpet creates friction that slows the vacuum cleaner, and Choice C is incorrect because the friction from the dirt road changes the momentum of the cars.

25. **A.** Newton's second law states, "The acceleration (a) of a body is parallel and directly proportional to the net force (F) and inversely proportional to the mass (m)."

This book contains two practice exams. Visit mymaxscore.com to download your free third practice test with answers and explanations.

ASVAB Practice Exam 2

ASVAB

Part 1

General Science

Time—11 minutes

25 questions

Directions: This test assesses your knowledge of general science principles usually covered in high school classes. Choose the best answer for each question and then mark the space on your answer sheet that corresponds to the question number.

1. As altitude increases, air pressure

   A. increases.
   B. decreases.
   C. remains the same.
   D. decreases, and then increases.

2. Coal was formed from

    A. oil.
    B. limestone.
    C. natural gas.
    D. plant material.

3. What happens when water causes a waterwheel to start turning?

    A. Potential energy is converted to electrical energy.
    B. Potential energy is converted to mechanical energy.
    C. Mechanical energy is converted to electrical energy.
    D. Mechanical energy is transferred from the water to the waterwheel.

4. Removing wastes is the main function of which human body system?

    A. Digestive system
    B. Excretory system
    C. Circulatory system
    D. Respiratory system

5. Pascal's principle states that whenever pressure on a closed container filled with a liquid is increased at any point,

    A. there is no change in pressure.
    B. the change in pressure takes place equally throughout the liquid.
    C. the change in pressure in the liquid is greatest at the bottom of the container.
    D. the change in pressure in the liquid is greatest at the point where the pressure is being exerted.

6. Granite is an example of what type of rock?

    A. Igneous

    B. Extrusive

    C. Sedimentary

    D. Metamorphic

7. Which is an example of kinetic energy?

    A. Sound

    B. Nuclear energy

    C. Chemical energy

    D. Gravitational energy

8. The gene for red flowers (R) in a pea plant is dominant over the gene for white flowers (r). If a heterozygous red pea plant is crossed with a homozygous red pea plant, about what percentage of the resulting seeds can be expected to produce plants with red flowers?

    A. 0 percent

    B. 50 percent

    C. 75 percent

    D. 100 percent

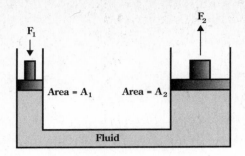

9. The diagram above shows a hydraulic lift. If A_2 is 20 times A_1, and $F_1 = 1$ newton, then $F_2 =$

A. 1 newton.
B. 2 newtons.
C. 10 newtons.
D. 20 newtons.

10. Metamorphic rock can be formed from _____ rocks.

A. igneous
B. sedimentary
C. metamorphic
D. All of the above

11. Which of the following is a unit of mass in the metric system?

A. Liter
B. Gram
C. Meter
D. Newton

12. Healthy parents have an offspring with a genetic disease that is a recessive allele. What can you conclude about the parents?

    A.   No conclusions can be drawn.
    B.   Both parents carry the disease allele.
    C.   They cannot be the offspring's parents.
    D.   Both parents will eventually develop the disease.

13. The distance between identical points on two neighboring waves is the

    A.   pitch.
    B.   amplitude.
    C.   frequency.
    D.   wavelength.

14. Ocean water becomes denser with

    A.   an increase in salinity.
    B.   a decrease in temperature.
    C.   an increase in evaporation.
    D.   All of the above

15. Which of the following is a noninfectious disease?

    A.   Scurvy
    B.   Botulism
    C.   Influenza
    D.   Athlete's foot

16. A kilowatt-hour is a measure of

    A.   charge.
    B.   electric power.
    C.   electric energy.
    D.   potential difference.

17. The rift valley on the ocean floor is

    A.   in the abyssal plain.
    B.   on the mid-ocean ridge.
    C.   on the continental shelf.
    D.   in the submarine canyon.

$$H_2 + O_2 \rightarrow H_2O$$

18. To balance the equation above, the number 2 should go before

    A. H_2 and O_2.
    B. O_2 and H_2O.
    C. H_2 and H_2O.
    D. H_2, O_2, and H_2O.

19. The tilt of Earth on its axis causes a change in

    A.   day length.
    B.   the angle of the sun's rays that hit Earth.
    C.   the intensity of solar radiation that hits a given area on Earth's surface.
    D.   All of the above

20. The green pigment in plants is called

   A.   stoma.
   B.   cytoplasm.
   C.   chlorophyll.
   D.   chromosome.

21. Which of the following decreases the current through a circuit?

   A.   Adding a fuse
   B.   Adding a battery
   C.   Adding a light bulb
   D.   Removing a light bulb

22. The change in the time of the tides is due to the

   A.   rotation of Earth.
   B.   rotation of the moon.
   C.   revolution of Earth around the sun.
   D.   revolution of the moon around Earth.

23. The atomic number of oxygen is 8. If an oxygen atom has 8 neu-
    trons, its atomic mass is

   A.   8.
   B.   16.
   C.   32.
   D.   64.

24. Which of the following has two layers of membrane and an inner layer that is folded to form crista?

   A. Vacuole
   B. Chloroplast
   C. Mitochondrion
   D. Endoplasmic reticulum

25. Visible light with the longest wavelength is seen as

   A. red.
   B. blue.
   C. violet.
   D. green.

END OF PART 1

ASVAB
Part 2
Arithmetic Reasoning
Time—36 minutes
30 questions

Directions: This test assesses your skills in arithmetic. Choose the correct answer and then mark the space on your answer sheet. Use scratch paper for any figuring you need to do.

1. A contractor must tile a floor that is exactly 16 feet across. If one tile is $\frac{3}{4}$ of a foot long, how many tiles will the contractor need to lay one row across the floor?

    A. 12
    B. $21\frac{1}{3}$
    C. 24
    D. $32\frac{3}{4}$

2. If a printer can print 12 pages in one minute, how long will it take to print 26 pages?

    A. 1.5
    B. 1.67
    C. 2.0
    D. 2.67

3. David draws a number out of a hat. It is the 16th odd, positive integer. What number does he draw out of the hat?

    A. 27
    B. 29
    C. 31
    D. 33

4. On Tuesday, Jackson buys 3 coffee cakes and 2 cups of coffee for $10.35. On Wednesday, he buys 2 coffee cakes and 4 cups of coffee for $12.90. What is the cost of a single cup of coffee?

   A. $1.75
   B. $1.95
   C. $2.25
   D. $2.50

5. Kim flips a coin and rolls a regular, six-sided die. What is the probability that she gets heads and rolls a number greater than 2?

   A. $\dfrac{1}{12}$

   B. $\dfrac{1}{3}$

   C. $\dfrac{1}{36}$

   D. $\dfrac{1}{4}$

6. Carla rolls two six-sided dice. What is the probability that both will land on the number 3?

   A. $\dfrac{1}{3}$

   B. $\dfrac{5}{6}$

   C. $1\dfrac{1}{6}$

   D. $\dfrac{1}{36}$

7. Angelica increases her hourly rate by $2.00. If her new hourly rate is $42, what is the percent increase of her hourly rate?

   A. 4 percent
   B. 5 percent
   C. 6 percent
   D. 8 percent

8. Theresa's text-messaging plan costs a flat rate of $7.99 per month, plus $0.07 for each text message she sends. If she sends 132 text messages during the month of December, how much will she pay for the service this month?

   A. $16.88
   B. $17.23
   C. $17.56
   D. $18.02

9. Hannah deposits 25 percent of her weekly paycheck into a savings account. If Hannah earns $350 per week, how much will she have in her savings account after 3 weeks?

   A. $109.38
   B. $116.67
   C. $262.50
   D. $612.50

10. Last year, a local coffee shop charged $3.73 for a small gourmet coffee. This year, the coffee shop is charging $3.95 for the same beverage. The percent increase in the cost of the gourmet coffee is

   A. 4 percent.
   B. 6 percent.
   C. 7 percent.
   D. 8 percent.

11. Mario creates flower beds using stones to enclose each space. He has finished six flower beds this week for six customers. He used 27, 24, 21, 24, 19, and 28 stones, respectively. What is the median number of stones he used?

    A.   22.5
    B.   23
    C.   24
    D.   24.5

12. The price of a half-gallon of orange juice is 150 percent of the price charged 5 years ago. The current price is $3.60. What was the price of the half-gallon of orange juice 5 years ago?

    A. $2.20
    B. $2.40
    C. $2.60
    D. $2.80

13. The probability that Eric will attend graduate school is 0.32. The probability that he will take courses at Texas A&M University is 0.28. The probability he will attend graduate school or take courses at Texas A&M University is about

    A.   49 percent.
    B.   50 percent.
    C.   51 percent.
    D.   52 percent.

14. Judy saves 15 percent of each paycheck. If each paycheck is $1,900, how much does she save per paycheck?

   A. $245
   B. $265
   C. $285
   D. $305

15. Rick's monthly health insurance premium is 6 percent of his monthly salary. His monthly premium is $240. His monthly salary is

   A. $3,800.
   B. $3,900.
   C. $4,000.
   D. $4,100.

16. Armand purchases 5 textbooks for the fall semester. The books cost $172.50, $88.90, $94.50, $75.60, and $56.40. What is the average cost of one of his textbooks?

   A. $96.68
   B. $97.58
   C. $97.68
   D. $97.88

17. The median test score in a class is 85.5. Which data set represents this class?

   A. 92, 84, 93, 78, 71, 70, 98, 83, 91, 7
   B. 89, 92, 78, 81, 96, 99, 94, 82, 75, 77
   C. 97, 72, 81, 97, 68, 86, 66, 74, 69, 77
   D. 76, 92, 93, 87, 91, 69, 100, 85, 92, 87

18. Kate buys some new business clothes, which cost $177.94 including sales tax. If the total cost of the clothes prior to sales tax is $164.00, what percentage is the sales tax?

    A.   8 percent
    B.   8.5 percent
    C.   9 percent
    D.   9.5 percent

19. A bag contains 8 green marbles, 3 red marbles, 2 yellow marbles, and 4 blue marbles. Jacob draws a marble out of the bag, does not replace it, and draws another marble out of the bag. What is the probability that he first draws a blue marble and then a green marble?

    A. $\dfrac{2}{17}$

    B. $\dfrac{11}{17}$

    C. $\dfrac{12}{17}$

    D. $\dfrac{25}{34}$

20. Hannah buys 5 pairs of jeans, priced at $28.95 each, and 3 sweaters, priced at $18.99 each. The average cost of each item of clothing Hannah purchased is

    A. $25.20.
    B. $25.22.
    C. $25.24.
    D. $25.26.

84, 68, 91, 58, 54, 66, 55, 78, 69, 66, 77, 62

21. Which of the following is the greatest in the data set shown above?

   A. Mean
   B. Range
   C. Mode
   D. Median

22. Jon eats $\frac{2}{3}$ of a pie and Darnell eats $\frac{1}{4}$ of it. How much more pie did Jon eat than Darnell?

   A. $\frac{1}{12}$

   B. $\frac{1}{7}$

   C. $\frac{5}{12}$

   D. $\frac{3}{16}$

23. Enrico creates 45 applets in 9 months. If this trend continues, how many applets can he create in 3 years?

   A. 160
   B. 170
   C. 180
   D. 190

24. Brett has $20,890 in his college savings fund. If the funds are to be equally used over a four-year period with the amount used per year equal to an integer amount, how much money will be left over?

    A. $0.50
    B. $2.00
    C. $2.50
    D. $4.00

25. Two consecutive integers have a product of 2,352 and a sum of 97. What is the larger of the two integers?

    A. 44
    B. 45
    C. 47
    D. 49

X	Y
1	3
2	10
3	17
4	24
5	31

26. Given the table of values shown above, which of the following shows the relationship between x and y?

    A. $y = x + 2$
    B. $y = 7x - 4$
    C. $y = 6x - 2$
    D. $y = x + 7$

27. Rachelle can bill 8 customers in 1 hour. Don can bill 12 customers in 1 hour. They must work together to bill 182 customers this week. How long will it take them to finish the job?

    A.   9 hours, 6 minutes
    B.   9 hours, 10 minutes
    C.   12 hours, 48 minutes
    D.   18 hours, 20 minutes

28. Darcy had $585 in his debit card account and spent $697 dollars, resulting in a negative balance. What is the balance on the account?

    A.   −$88
    B.   −$112
    C.   −$585
    D.   −$697

29. Joe read $\frac{3}{4}$ of a book on Monday and an additional $\frac{1}{5}$ of the book on Tuesday. If the book is 360 pages long, how many pages did he read during the two days?

    A.   328
    B.   332
    C.   340
    D.   342

30. A six-sided die is rolled 18 times. How many times will the die be expected to land on an even number?

    A.   3
    B.   6
    C.   9
    D.   12

END OF PART 2

ASVAB
Part 3
Word Knowledge
Time—11 minutes

35 questions

Directions: This test is about the meanings of words. Each question has an underlined word. You must decide which word in the answer choice has nearly the same meaning as the underlined word. Then mark this space on your answer sheet.

1. Nina was known to <u>procrastinate</u> and often did her homework in the morning on the school bus.

    A. Avoid
    B. Delay
    C. Suspend
    D. Intervene

2. <u>Veritable</u> most nearly means

    A. wistful.
    B. zealous.
    C. authentic.
    D. immature.

3. She preferred to knit with the <u>variegated</u> yarn because it created such amazing and random patterns.

    A. Tepid
    B. Matted
    C. Convoluted
    D. Multicolored

4. Subside most nearly means

    A. vanish.
    B. upsurge.
    C. speed up.
    D. quiet down.

5. We were impressed with his endless stamina in the face of such arduous exams.

    A. Attitude
    B. Courage
    C. Endurance
    D. Compassion

6. Somber most nearly means

    A. erratic.
    B. solemn.
    C. innovation.
    D. antiquated.

7. The man's flagrant disrespect toward the speaker made many people angry.

    A. Obvious
    B. Discreet
    C. Restrained
    D. Intermittent

8. <u>Credible</u> most nearly means

   A.   repairable.
   B.   believable.
   C.   susceptible.
   D.   contemptible.

9. The <u>placid</u> lake reflected the summer's bright blue sky and puffy white clouds perfectly.

   A.   Gullible
   B.   Vigilant
   C.   Tranquil
   D.   Fastidious

10. The <u>discrepancy</u> in the accounting records was cause for immediate concern.

   A.   Inflection
   B.   Increment
   C.   Invocation
   D.   Incongruity

11. <u>Jocular</u> most nearly means

   A.   amorous.
   B.   infamous.
   C.   humorous.
   D.   ambiguous.

12. The police officer gave the woman an <u>ultimatum</u>: surrender her license or go to jail.

    A. Penalty

    B. Scolding

    C. Demand

    D. Punishment

13. <u>Fallacy</u> most nearly means

    A. mistaken belief.

    B. conscious decision.

    C. rational conclusion.

    D. illogical assumption.

14. <u>Ravenous</u> most nearly means

    A. candid.

    B. derelict.

    C. famished.

    D. distraught.

15. The <u>dilapidated</u> old house looked like it would fall down if the wind blew much harder.

    A. Pristine

    B. Dubious

    C. Fraudulent

    D. Ramshackle

16. The baseball player used his <u>dominant</u> hand to toss out the game's first ball.

    A.   Inferior

    B.   Primary

    C.   Disabled

    D.   Impaired

17. After studying for more than two hours, she finally <u>formulated</u> a plan on how to approach the final exam.

    A.   Devised

    B.   Discarded

    C.   Contracted

    D.   Overlooked

18. <u>Fluctuate</u> most nearly means

    A.   oscillate.

    B.   generate.

    C.   integrate.

    D.   consecrate.

19. The supervisor was <u>emphatic</u> that workers put on their personal protective equipment before going onto the job site.

    A.   Blasé

    B.   Hostile

    C.   Insistent

    D.   Lackadaisical

20. <u>Passive</u> most nearly means

    A.   avid.
    B.   supple.
    C.   morose.
    D.   submissive.

21. The books were all kept in the <u>archives</u>, so I had to ask a reference librarian to get them for me.

    A.   Annals
    B.   Domicile
    C.   Collection
    D.   Documents

22. <u>Apathy</u> most nearly means

    A.   relevance.
    B.   importance.
    C.   indifference.
    D.   consequence.

23. The room was <u>festooned</u> with brightly colored streamers in preparation for the birthday party.

    A.   Emanated
    B.   Enamored
    C.   Emaciated
    D.   Embellished

24. The freshmen <u>orientation</u> was held the first weekend in August, and it usually attracted hundreds of new students.

   A. Communal
   B. Prospectus
   C. Introduction
   D. Misdemeanor

25. The police officer made sure the crime had been committed in his <u>jurisdiction</u> before he started writing out the report.

   A. Anarchy
   B. Precinct
   C. Conclave
   D. Manifest

26. <u>Benign</u> most nearly means

   A. rancor.
   B. poignant.
   C. malignant.
   D. innocuous.

27. The employee's <u>overture</u> for making the building more sustainable was met with limited enthusiasm.

   A. Prestige
   B. Segment
   C. Namesake
   D. Proposition

28. <u>Skirmish</u> most nearly means

    A. waif.
    B. scuffle.
    C. tangent.
    D. pinnacle.

29. Thanks to the flickering candle, the child's <u>silhouette</u> could be seen through the gauze curtain.

    A. Satire
    B. Solvent
    C. Shadow
    D. Symmetry

30. <u>Tawdry</u> most nearly means

    A. gaudy.
    B. timely.
    C. unerring.
    D. discerning.

31. His grandfather's photograph and <u>obituary</u> were published in the local newspaper.

    A. Notary
    B. Oratory
    C. Funerary
    D. Reformatory

32. Inanimate most nearly means

    A. lifeless.
    B. habitat.
    C. unfounded.
    D. ramification.

33. The cantankerous old man yelled at anyone who stepped on his lawn.

    A. Depraved
    B. Diminutive
    C. Benevolent
    D. Argumentative

34. Contrite most nearly means

    A. reiterate.
    B. repugnant.
    C. remorseful.
    D. reverberation.

35. Irrevocable most nearly means

    A. irrelevant.
    B. irreparable.
    C. irreversible.
    D. irrepressible.

END OF PART 3

ASVAB

Part 4
Paragraph Comprehension
Time—13 minutes

15 questions

Directions: This test assesses your ability to understand what you read. This section includes reading passages followed by questions or incomplete statements. Read the paragraph and select the choice that best completes the statement or answers the question. Mark your choice on your answer sheet.

The loggerhead turtle migrates around a large loop in the Atlantic Ocean for many years before returning home to breed. Scientists wanted to know whether loggerheads have some kind of mental "compass" that allows them to detect variations in Earth's magnetic field, so they constructed special water tanks surrounded by magnetic coils. When placed in the tanks, baby loggerheads swam toward the coils, seeming to confirm the theory. But a compass won't help if you don't know where you are. Researchers surmise that these creatures also may possess "map sense," which tells them where they are relative to feeding grounds.

1. What does the author want readers to know about scientists' studies of loggerhead turtles?

   A. Scientists have presented too narrow a view of the problem.
   B. Scientists have confused researchers with contradictory results.
   C. Scientists have revealed the migratory methods used by the animal.
   D. Scientists have made progress but still face some unanswered questions.

This strange land may resemble the surface of Mars more than any other location on our planet. It is a craggy place, laced with craters, and the soil is predominantly red in color. This is appropriate, because the temperatures can be blast-furnace hot in Australia's Outback, an enormous area which is as large as Italy, Spain, and France put together.

2. Australia's Outback is most likely compared to the surface of Mars because of its

    A. size.
    B. color.
    C. distance.
    D. temperature.

Often called "broncos," or "mustangs," horses were brought to the Americas by Spanish explorers. About four hundred years ago, some escaped and became the first "wild mustangs." Native Americans took to these hardy animals and captured, bred, and domesticated them. In fact, it was from the Cayuse tribe that the horse got another of its nicknames.

3. According to the passage, these animals have been called by all of the following nicknames EXCEPT

    A. pony.
    B. bronco.
    C. Cayuse.
    D. mustang.

It is generally accepted that the game of golf was invented by Scots in the fifteenth century. The game became wildly popular in Scotland, along with "football," or soccer. Historians note that both sports were banned by law in 1457. Evidently, these activities were distracting people from the practice of archery, which was necessary to keep people safe. The law was generally ignored by the Scottish, and golf went on to become an international pastime.

4. It can be inferred from the passage that archery was considered important because it was

    A. less expensive than golf.
    B. preferred by Scottish royalty.
    C. required for military purposes.
    D. thought to be a more competitive sport.

For thousands of years, native villages in Alaska have been supported by permafrost, frozen soil that underlies about 80 percent of the state. However, Alaska's permafrost is melting, and native houses are tilting and sinking. And without a wall of earth to hold it back, the sea is slowly eroding the shoreline and moving closer to coastal homes. The villagers living in these homes have become innocent victims of global climate change caused largely by the burning of fossil fuels in industrialized nations. The solution is for the villages to be moved to higher ground, but this is prohibitively expensive.

5. Which best restates the author's main point?

    A. Permafrost is vital in supporting Alaskan villages.
    B. International pollution is affecting Alaskan people.
    C. Alaskan villagers are facing a crisis that is not their fault.
    D. Residents of Alaska's coast are being forced to move away.

The colorfully dressed dancers twirl weighted strips called *boleadoras*. Their dance celebrates the ancient tradition of the Gaucho, the cowboy of Argentina. These riders of the *pampas* were renowned for their dress. They wore wide-brimmed hats and baggy trousers, and belts of silver coins circled their waists.

For warmth, they used a blanket with slits, called a *poncho*, and for protection they carried a single weapon, the *facon*, a long knife. The weighted *boleadora* was hurled to trap the legs of fleeing cattle.

6. According to the passage, the Gaucho wore all of the following EXCEPT

    A.   silver belts.
    B.   baggy pants.
    C.   woven scarves.
    D.   wide-brimmed hats.

One of the solutions proposed to solve traffic jams is called the "Skycar." Now in the planning stages, this amazing vehicle will have eight rotary engines that will allow it to take off straight up into the air. It will cruise over gridlock at 350 mph, with its flight satellite-controlled. In an emergency, two parachutes will be deployed and allow the craft to float back to Earth. Once on the ground, it won't stall. The Skycar combines gasoline and electric power to cruise along the highway.

7. The author's tone in this passage is

    A.   confused.
    B.   humorous.
    C.   concerned.
    D.   enthusiastic.

Obtaining a job as a ranger in one of America's national parks is difficult and requires dedication. Competition for these jobs is fierce. A good start might be a college major in park management, forestry, or natural history. Even with a degree, an applicant may have to wait until an assignment opens up in a metropolitan park, where he or she will be counted on to work all weekends and holidays. After this basic beginning, the novice can apply to ranger school for advanced training. Without a college degree, a person can try to get started by applying for a volunteer job in a park.

8. The main idea of this passage is that people who want to become park rangers

A. must enroll in ranger school following college.
B. are assured of a job with the right college degree.
C. need to travel a long and difficult road to success.
D. may get started by applying for a volunteer job in a park.

The athlete stood at the foul line and bounced the ball twice, then again. *One more free throw wins the game,* he thought. He rotated the ball slowly in his hands and concentrated on the back rim of the basket. The roaring crowd noise seemed to fade to a murmur in his ears. He barely felt his arms and hands as the shot went up.

9. Which word best describes how the athlete feels about making the free throw?

A. Unsure
B. Scared
C. Anxious
D. Confident

What if trees could talk to us? Would they tell us whether they are receiving enough water or sunlight? Would they issue a warning if they grew too hot or too cold? Teams of researchers have developed a method to communicate with giant redwood trees and monitor their ability to absorb moisture, check their changes in temperature, and measure their sun exposure. They attach mini-sensors to the trees from top to bottom.

Connected to tiny computers, these devices broadcast a continuous stream of information to curious scientists.

10. Which of the following is most similar to the technology described in the passage?

    A. A radar beam indicating a driver's speed
    B. A computer indicating when a dog is hungry
    C. A computer that turns heat on and off in a house
    D. A hidden camera that records animal movements

A member of the Paiute tribe of Nevada, Sarah Winnemucca spent her life working for her people. As a student in convent schools, she became adept at the English language, which helped in her work as an interpreter in army camps. She received praise for her lectures about the problems faced by her tribe. She made more than four hundred speeches promoting them, and in 1880, she presented their cause to President Rutherford B. Hayes. Her book, *Life Among the Paiutes*, became a classic.

11. In this passage, the author's primary purpose is to

    A. inform readers about the Paiute tribe of Nevada.
    B. convince readers to read a book about the Paiutes.
    C. entertain readers with a story about a Paiute woman.
    D. inform readers about a Paiute woman's accomplishments.

The hot dog concession at the county fair checked the usage of toppings and found the following: chopped onions were not selected as often as pickle relish; chili was preferred over melted cheese; and yellow mustard was not used as much as brown mustard.

12. Based on this information, which would be the LEAST favorite hot dog at the fair?

    A. A chili dog with pickle relish and brown mustard
    B. A cheese dog with pickle relish and brown mustard
    C. A chili dog with chopped onions and yellow mustard
    D. A cheese dog with chopped onions and yellow mustard

They called them "Skywalkers." In the old days, ironworkers on skyscrapers were required to walk narrow I-beams at great heights and drive rivets in rain and gusts of whipping wind—with no safety belts or harnesses. It required a certain level of courage to take on this line of work. The Mohawk Indians from Canada's Kahnawake reserve became famous for it. The tradition goes back more than 120 years, when ancestors of current-day Mohawks were hired as day laborers on a huge cantilever bridge being built across the St. Lawrence River. Their agility and fearlessness impressed their employers and started a tradition that flourishes today.

13. It can be inferred from the passage that today's high-steel workers

    A. wear safety belts and harnesses.
    B. are mostly from the Mohawk tribe.
    C. have ancestors who built skyscrapers and bridges.
    D. experience no fear when working at great heights.

A pioneer family in American country music, the Carters began in Virginia's Clinch Mountains and went on to fame with hits such as *Wabash Cannonball, Keep on the Sunny Side,* and *Wildwood Flower.* A.P. Carter and his wife began singing socially at parties. Joined by his sister-in-law, Maybelle, the Carters earned an audition with Victor Records in 1927 and were signed to a long-term recording contract. The Great

Depression of the 1930s slowed their careers, but they were saved by a new outlet—radio. Broadcasting from a station in Del Rio, Texas, their music was heard across the nation.

14. The passage supports the conclusion that the Carters' professional career began when they

   A.   formed a trio with Maybelle Carter.
   B.   sang at social gatherings in Virginia.
   C.   began broadcasting from Del Rio, Texas.
   D.   obtained an audition with Victor Records.

The novels and stories of author John Steinbeck often dealt with the struggle of the poor and oppressed. As a young reporter with the *San Francisco News* in the 1930s, Steinbeck talked to people from the nation's "Dust Bowl" who had come to California seeking jobs to sustain their families. His series of articles about them eventually grew into his Pulitzer Prize–winning novel *The Grapes of Wrath*. Another novel, *In Dubious Battle*, dealt with a strike of fruit pickers, and *Of Mice and Men* told the tragic story of two traveling farm workers.

15. In discussing author John Steinbeck, the author's primary focus is on

   A.   a series of articles by a young reporter.
   B.   the struggle endured by people of the Dust Bowl.
   C.   a recurring theme expressed in the author's work.
   D.   the various jobs sought by Depression-era farm workers.

END OF PART 4

ASVAB

Part 5

Mathematics Knowledge

Time—24 minutes

25 questions

Directions: This test assesses your ability to solve general mathematical problems. Select the correct answer from the choices given. Mark the corresponding space on your answer sheet. Use scratch paper as needed to solve each problem.

1. Which of the following represents the sum of $8\sqrt{48}$ and $5\sqrt{27}$?

   A. $19\sqrt{3}$
   B. $31\sqrt{3}$
   C. $37\sqrt{3}$
   D. $47\sqrt{3}$

2. What is the product of $(4x-6)$ and $(-2x+6)$?

   A. $-8x^2 +36x -12$
   B. $-8x^2 +12x -36$
   C. $-8x^2 -18x -12$
   D. $-8x^2 +36x -36$

3. Which regular polygon has interior angle measures that add up to 900°?

   A. Octagon
   B. Hexagon
   C. Heptagon
   D. Pentagon

4. Given a rectangle with a length of 12 inches and a width of 9 inches, which of the following represents the ratio of the perimeter of the rectangle to the area of the rectangle?

    A. $\dfrac{1}{6}$

    B. $\dfrac{7}{16}$

    C. $\dfrac{7}{18}$

    D. $\dfrac{1}{3}$

5. Which of the following is a factor of the expression $21x^2 + 8x - 4$?

    A. $7x - 4$
    B. $3x + 2$
    C. $3x + 4$
    D. $7x - 6$

6. Which polygon has more than 3 lines of symmetry?

    A. Square
    B. Rhombus
    C. Rectangle
    D. Equilateral triangle

7. A square has a perimeter of 48 cm and an area of

    A. 124 cm².
    B. 128 cm².
    C. 132 cm².
    D. 144 cm².

8. A triangle has a base of $4x$ inches and a height of $2x - 2$ inches. Which of the following represents the area of this triangle?

   A. $4x(x-2)$ in²
   B. $2x(x-2)$ in²
   C. $4x(x-1)$ in²
   D. $8x(x-1)$ in²

9. What does $4^{\frac{5}{2}}$ equal?

   A. 28
   B. 32
   C. 34
   D. 38

$$0.1, 0.01, 0.001, 0.0001, \ldots$$

10. What is the sum of the infinite geometric series shown above?

   A. $0.1000\bar{1}$
   B. $0.\bar{1}$
   C. $0.10\bar{1}$
   D. $1.0\bar{1}$

11. What is the solution to the equation $-50 = -12x + 46$?

   A. $x = 8$
   B. $x = -\dfrac{1}{3}$
   C. $x = \dfrac{1}{3}$
   D. $x = -8$

12. Line l has a slope of 4. Which equation represents a line that is perpendicular to Line l?

   A. $y = 4x + 4$

   B. $y = \dfrac{1}{4}x - 8$

   C. $y = -\dfrac{1}{4}x + 6$

   D. $y = -4x + 2$

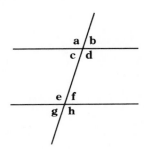

13. Which angles above are congruent?

   A. a and f
   B. c and f
   C. b and h
   D. g and d

14. Which of the following expressions represents the sum of the interior angles in a regular octagon, where p represents the sum of the interior angles in a regular pentagon?

   A. $4p$
   B. $3p$
   C. $2p$
   D. $6p$

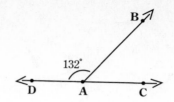

15. What is the measure of ∠BAC in the figure above?

    A.   42°
    B.   48°
    C.   52°
    D.   54°

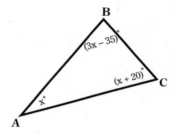

16. What is the measure of ∠B in the diagram above?

    A.   59°
    B.   68°
    C.   74°
    D.   82°

17. Which of the following side lengths represents a right triangle?

    A.   3 in, 4 in, 6 in
    B.   6 in, 9 in, 15 in
    C.   12 in, 16 in, 20 in
    D.   9 in, 16 in, 25 in

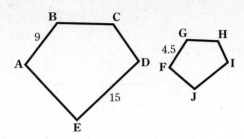

18. The pentagons above are similar. What is the length of $\overline{IJ}$?

    A. 7.5
    B. 8.5
    C. 9.5
    D. 10.5

19. A tree trunk has a circumference of approximately 69.08 inches. The radius of the tree trunk is approximately

    A. 8 inches.
    B. 9 inches.
    C. 11 inches.
    D. 12 inches.

20. Which is the radius of a circle with an area 3 times its circumference?

    A. $r = 2$
    B. $r = 4$
    C. $r = 6$
    D. $r = 8$

21. A box of candy is 6 inches by 4 inches by 8 inches. If each candy takes up 3 cubic inches of space, how many chocolates will fit in the box?

    A. 48
    B. 54
    C. 64
    D. 66

22. A cylindrical pitcher has a height of 9 inches and a radius of 4 inches. How many cubic inches of water can the pitcher hold?

    A. 113 in³
    B. 144 in³
    C. 226 in³
    D. 452 in³

23. Two points are 5 units apart on a coordinate grid. If one point has coordinates of (7, −4), the other points are

    A. (3, −1).
    B. (4, −2).
    C. (3, −2).
    D. (4, −1).

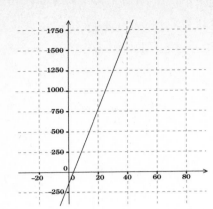

24. The graph above shows the profit of a local flower shop for the month of December. In the graph, *x* represents the number of arrangements sold. The average cost of an arrangement is

    A. $50.
    B. $75.
    C. $100.
    D. $125.

25. Amy needs to construct a triangle. Which of the following sets of lengths will NOT create a triangle?

    A. 8 in, 7 in, 12 in
    B. 12 in, 8 in, 5 in
    C. 11 in, 4 in, 6 in
    D. 5 in, 6 in, 9 in

END OF PART 5

ASVAB

Part 6

Electronics Information

Time—9 minutes

20 questions

Directions: This section assesses your knowledge of electrical, radio, and electronics information. Choose the correct answer and mark the corresponding space on your answer sheet.

1. An atom with more than its normal amount of electrons is called a _____ ion, while an atom with less than its normal amount of electrons is called a(n) _____ ion.

    A. negative; positive
    B. positive; negative
    C. positive; electron-deficient
    D. negative; electron-deficient

2. Which of the following statements about electrons is true?

    A. Electrons in an atom's conduction band cannot be removed.
    B. Electrons found in an atom's forbidden band are excellent conductors.
    C. Electrons found in an atom's valence band move freely to other bands.
    D. None of the above

3. The external voltage applied to a PN junction to aid current flow is known as

    A. diode.
    B. reverse bias.
    C. forward bias.
    D. junction barrier.

4. Which of the following is most likely a good insulator?

    A.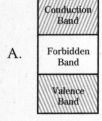

    B.

    C.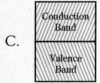

    D. None of the above

5. Which of the following is most likely a conductor?

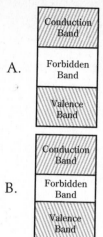

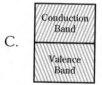

D. None of the above

6. Which of the following statements about atoms is true?

A. A covalent bond holds atoms together in a crystal.

B. When atoms share valence electrons, a covalent bond is produced.

C. An atom must have eight valence electrons for its shell to be considered complete.

D. All of the above

7. A PN junction is formed when

   A. a cathode meets a diode.
   B. AC/DC current flows in all directions.
   C. N-type semiconductor materials are separated from P-type semiconductor materials.
   D. a section of N-type semiconductor material is joined with a section of P-type semiconductor material.

8. The maximum amount of current that can flow in the forward direction is called

   A. maximum surge current.
   B. peak recurrent forward current.
   C. maximum average forward current.
   D. None of the above

9. According to the standard diode color code system, what would the ID number be for a diode with red, yellow, and green bands at one terminal?

   A. 139
   B. 239
   C. 245
   D. 589

10. Increase in current within a diode generates heat, and heat causes an increase in current. This cycle, which eventually destroys diodes, is known as

    A. diode cycle.
    B. heat danger.
    C. thermal runaway.
    D. excessive diode current.

11. The only way to accurately test a diode is to

    A. apply a current surge and measure output.

    B. remove the diode and replace it with a new one.

    C. perform a dynamic electrical test that determines only forward current.

    D. perform a dynamic electrical test that determines forward and reverse current.

12. According to the semiconductor identification system, XNYYY represents important information about diodes, transistors, and other semiconductors. What does "X" represent?

    A. A specific type of semiconductor

    B. The semiconductor's reverse polarity

    C. The number of semiconductor junctions

    D. The semiconductor's registration number

13. The three elements of a two-junction transistor are

    A. emitter, diode, and base.

    B. diode, base, and collector.

    C. emitter, base, and collector.

    D. None of the above

14. Which diagram represents an NPN-type transistor?

A.

PN Junction

Emitter | N | N | P | Collector

Base

B.

PN Junction

Emitter | N | P | N | Collector

Base

C.

PN Junction

Emitter | P | N | Collector

Base

D.

PN Junction

Collector | P | N | P | Emitter

Base

15. What are the four classes of operation for amplifiers?

A. A, B, C, and D
B. A, AB, B, and C
C. AA, BB, and CC
D. 1A, 2B, 3C, and 4D

16. An amplifier that has high fidelity has low

A. power.
B. substrate.
C. distortion.
D. efficiency.

17. The two general classifications of integrated circuits are

    A. hybrid and passive.
    B. substrate and passive.
    C. hybrid and monolithic.
    D. substrate and monolithic.

18. What formula would you use to determine the gain for a CB transistor configuration?

    A. $\beta = \dfrac{\Delta IC}{IB}$

    B. $\alpha = \dfrac{\Delta IC}{\Delta IE}$

    C. $\alpha = \dfrac{\Delta IE}{\Delta IC}$

    D. $\gamma = \dfrac{\Delta IE}{\Delta IB}$

19. When critical voltage has been reached in a PN junction, ruptured covalent bonds allow released electrons to accelerate. This is called

    A. Ohm's law.
    B. the Zener effect.
    C. diode breakdown.
    D. the avalanche effect.

20. The basic purpose of a silicon controlled rectifier (SCR) is to

    A. act as a power switch.
    B. stop electrical current.
    C. measure electrical current.
    D. fix damage caused by the Zener effect.

END OF PART 6

ASVAB

Part 7
Auto and Shop Information
Time—11 minutes
25 questions

Directions: This test assesses your knowledge of automobiles, shop practices, and tools. Choose the correct answer to each question and then mark the corresponding space on your answer sheet.

1. The part of the engine that increases the voltage of a battery to spark a vehicle's spark plugs is the

   A. capacitor.
   B. distributor.
   C. ignition coil.
   D. None of the above

2. Lathes are used for

   A. woodworking.
   B. metalworking.
   C. Both A and B
   D. Neither A nor B

3. Which car accessory uses battery power?

   A. Crankshaft
   B. Gearshift lever
   C. Windshield wipers
   D. Manual door locks

4. The tool shown above is a(n)

    A. joist.
    B. framing square.
    C. carpenter's level.
    D. adjustable ratchet.

5. All of the following statements about nails are correct EXCEPT

    A. 23-gauge nails are called pin nails.
    B. 23-gauge nails do not have a head.
    C. 19-gauge nails are called brad nails.
    D. 15- and 16-gauge nails are called finish nails.

6. A diagonal-peen hammer's head is at a __-degree angle from its handle.

    A. 15
    B. 45
    C. 75
    D. 90

7. What purpose does a piston serve in an engine?

    A. It delivers a spark to the spark plug.
    B. It covers and uncovers ports in a cylinder wall.
    C. It transfers force from expanding gas to a crankshaft.
    D. Both A and B

8.   Which of the following vehicles uses differential steering?

   A.   Tank
   B.   Boat
   C.   Motorcycle
   D.   Lawn mower

9.   The type of saw you would most likely use on metal is a(n)

   A.   jigsaw.
   B.   table saw.
   C.   circular saw.
   D.   abrasive saw.

10. A joist is used to

   A.   section off a floor for concrete.
   B.   section off the foundation of a house.
   C.   provide support for a ceiling, roof, or floor.
   D.   None of the above

11. A support beam used in construction is a

   A.   truss.
   B.   purlin.
   C.   girder.
   D.   Both A and C

12. Which of the following statements is true?

   A.   Frictional brakes cannot exist inside a drum.
   B.   Frictional brakes can be classified as shoe brakes or pad brakes.
   C.   Both A and B
   D.   Neither A nor B

13. Why might a lack of compression occur in an engine?

    A. The air intake might be clogged.

    B. There may be impurities in the fuel.

    C. The piston rings are worn or broken.

    D. None of the above

14. Which statement about an air-cooled engine is true?

    A. It is considered "high-performance."

    B. It is heavier than a liquid-cooled engine.

    C. It runs hotter than a liquid-cooled engine.

    D. Both B and C

15. What is the main difference between diesel engines and gasoline engines?

    A. Diesel engines produce battery power.

    B. There are spark plugs in diesel engines.

    C. There are spark plugs in gasoline engines.

    D. None of the above

16. A chisel that resembles a punch and has a cutting edge shaped like the letter "L" is called a

    A. corner chisel.

    B. mortise chisel.

    C. flooring chisel.

    D. framing chisel.

17. What tool would you use to hold wood steady for finely detailed carving?

    A. Vise
    B. Lathe
    C. Plane
    D. None of the above

18. In a four-stroke engine, the four strokes are

    A. intake, rotation, ignition, and exhaust.
    B. intake, compression, ignition, and exhaust.
    C. compression, carburetion, exhaust, and ignition.
    D. injection, carburetion, compression, and exhaust.

19. What causes an engine to run smoothly?

    A. Cylinders igniting at different times
    B. Electricity running through the alternator
    C. A slow release of energy from the crankshaft
    D. None of the above

20. All of the following are common reasons for engine failure EXCEPT

    A. lack of spark.
    B. lack of exhaust.
    C. bad air-fuel mix.
    D. lack of compression.

21. The part of the engine that reduces toxins in exhaust emissions is the

    A. muffler.
    B. tailpipe.
    C. exhaust manifolds.
    D. catalytic converter.

22. All of the following are part of a radial tire EXCEPT

   A. beads.
   B. springs.
   C. the rim.
   D. the liner.

23. A crosscut saw is designed to cut

   A. fine curves.
   B. with the grain of wood.
   C. across the grain of wood.
   D. aluminum, steel, and copper.

24. Brakes that prevent wheels from locking so that an automobile can stop on a slippery road are called _____ brakes.

   A. disk
   B. power
   C. no-lock
   D. antilock

25. Which statement about a diesel engine is true?

   A. It has a low compression ratio.
   B. It uses a spark to initiate combustion.
   C. It does not have a spark-ignition system.
   D. It is more complex than a gasoline engine.

END OF PART 7

ASVAB
Part 8
Mechanical Comprehension
Time—19 minutes

25 questions

Directions: This test assesses your knowledge of mechanics. Choose the correct answer to each question and then mark the corresponding space on your answer sheet.

1.   What is net force?

A.   The strongest force acting on an object
B.   The sum of all forces acting on an object
C.   The sum of all forces pushed onto an object
D.   The sum of all forces pushed off of an object

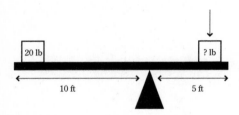

2.   How much weight must be applied to balance the lever above?

A.   35 lbs
B.   40 lbs
C.   45 lbs
D.   60 lbs

3.   Shifting to a larger gear on a mountain bike will make pedaling

A.   easier and increase the bike's speed.
B.   easier and decrease the bike's speed.
C.   more difficult and increase the bike's speed.
D.   more difficult and decrease the bike's speed.

4. Which of the following is an example of a mechanical advantage?

   A. Using a screwdriver
   B. Pouring coffee from a pot
   C. Using a crowbar to open a trunk
   D. Both A and C

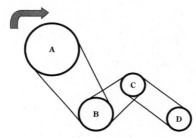

5. If wheel A turns clockwise, what direction does wheel D turn in the figure above?

   A. Clockwise
   B. Counterclockwise
   C. Wheel D can go either way.
   D. Wheel A has no impact on wheel D.

6. How much force is required to move a 1,000 kg vehicle at 50 m/s²?

   A. 50 N
   B. 500 N
   C. 5,000 N
   D. 50,000 N

7. The formula for work is $W = Fd$. In this formula, F represents force and d represents

   A. depth.
   B. distance.
   C. direction.
   D. displacement.

8. 1 joule is equal to

   A. 1 ohm.
   B. 1 watt.
   C. 1 kilowatt.
   D. 1 newton-meter.

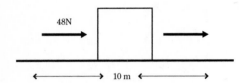

9. Determine the work performed in the figure above.

   A. 4.8 J
   B. 48 J
   C. 240 J
   D. 480 J

10. When the direction of a shaft's rotation needs to be changed, what kind of gears should be used?

    A. Bevel gears
    B. Worm gears
    C. Helical gears
    D. None of the above

11. Which statement about a fixed pulley is true?

    A. It lightens the workload by half.
    B. It creates a mechanical advantage of 1.
    C. It changes only the direction of the force applied.
    D. Both B and C

12. The formula for pressure is

  A. $P = \dfrac{F}{A}$.

  B. $P = F_1 A_1$.

  C. $P = FA$.

  D. $P = \dfrac{A}{F}$.

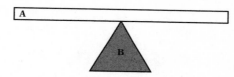

13. What are the components in the figure above?

  A. A: lever; B: fulcrum
  B. A: fulcrum; B: lever
  C. A: torque; B: fulcrum
  D. A: fulcrum; B: torque

14. Which statement about a compound pulley is true?

  A. At least one pulley is fixed.
  B. At least one pulley is moveable.
  C. Both A and B
  D. Neither A nor B

15. According to Newton's first law of motion, objects at rest tend to stay at rest, unless they

  A. act upon a force.
  B. lack momentum.
  C. are acted upon by a force.
  D. have forward momentum.

16. Which is a third-class lever?

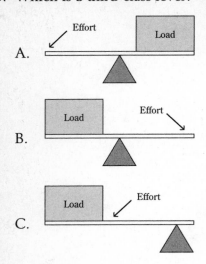

A.

B.

C.

D.   None of the above

17. All of the following are simple machines EXCEPT a(n)

   A.   lever.
   B.   pulley.
   C.   abacus.
   D.   inclined plane.

18. Which surface provides the least amount of friction on an object with a smooth surface?

   A.   Concrete
   B.   Gravel road
   C.   Sheet of glass
   D.   Finely sanded wood

19. When you hit a ball with a golf club, the MOST force is exerted by

    A.   you.
    B.   the golf ball.
    C.   the golf club.
    D.   None of the above

20. All of the following are examples of kinetic energy EXCEPT a

    A.   person running a race.
    B.   bird flying through the air.
    C.   leaf being blown by the wind.
    D.   bicycle in a stationary position.

21. What is inertia?

    A.   The tendency of an object to move forward
    B.   The tendency of an object to change velocity
    C.   The resistance of an object to a change in its state of motion
    D.   None of the above

22. A wedge is a simple machine because it

    A.   can be used to lift an object.
    B.   can be used to hold an object in place.
    C.   converts a force on its blunt end to a force on its inclined surfaces.
    D.   All of the above

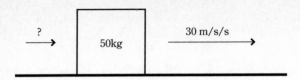

23. How much force is needed to move the object above?

    A.   80 N
    B.   80 J
    C.   150 N
    D.   150 J

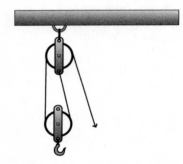

24. What is the mechanical advantage given by the pulley shown above?

    A.   2
    B.   3
    C.   4
    D.   5

25. A pair of scissors is made of

    A.   1 first-class lever.
    B.   2 first-class levers.
    C.   2 third-class levers.
    D.   2 second-class levers.

END OF EXAM

Practice Exam 2 Answers and Explanations

Answer Key

PART 1: GENERAL SCIENCE

1. B
2. D
3. B
4. B
5. B
6. A
7. A
8. D
9. D
10. D
11. B
12. B
13. D
14. D
15. A
16. C
17. B
18. C
19. D
20. C
21. B
22. B
23. B
24. C
25. A

PART 2: ARITHMETIC REASONING

1. B
2. D
3. C
4. C
5. B
6. D
7. B
8. B
9. C
10. B
11. C
12. B
13. C
14. C
15. C
16. B
17. B
18. B
19. A

20. B

21. A

22. C

23. C

24. B

25. D

26. B

27. A

28. B

29. D

30. C

PART 3: WORD KNOWLEDGE

1. B

2. C

3. D

4. D

5. C

6 B

7. A

8. B

9. C

10. D

11. C

12. C

13. A

14. C

15. D

16. B

17. A

18. A

19. C

20. D

21. A

22. C

23. D

24. C

25. B

26. D

27. D

28. B

29. C

30. A

31. C

32. A

33. D

34. C

35. C

PART 4: PARAGRAPH COMPREHENSION

1. D

2. B

3. A

4. C

5. C

6. C

7. D

8. C

9. D

10. B

11. D

12. D

13. A

14. D

15. C

13. B

14. C

15. B

16. D

17. C

18. A

19. C

20. C

21. C

22. D

23. A

24. A

25. C

PART 5: MATHEMATICAL KNOWLEDGE

1. D

2. D

3. C

4. C

5. B

6. A

7. D

8. C

9. B

10. B

11. A

12. C

PART 6: ELECTRONICS INFORMATION

1. A

2. D

3. B

4. A

5. C

6. D

7. D

8   C

9. C

10. B

11. A

12. C

13. A

14. B

15. B

16. C

17. C

18. B

19. D

20. A

PART 7: AUTO AND SHOP
INFORMATION

1. C

2. C

3. A

4. C

5. D

6. B

7. D

8. A

9. C

10. C

11. C

12. B

13. C

14. A

15. C

16. A

17. A

18. B

19. A

20. B

21. D

22. B

23. C

24. D

25. C

PART 8: MECHANICAL
COMPREHENSION

1. B

2. B

3. C

4. D

5. A

6. D

7. D

8. D

9. D

10. A

11. D

12. A

13. A

14. C

15. C   21. C

16. C   22. D

17. C   23. C

18. C   24. D

19. A   25. B

20. D

Answer Explanations
PART 1: GENERAL SCIENCE

1. **B**. Air pressure decreases with altitude. The air pressure at any level of the atmosphere is the total weight of the air above a unit area. At higher elevations, there are fewer molecules above a given area than there are above a similar area at lower elevations.

2. **D**. Coal, oil, and natural gas are all called fossil fuels, because they were formed from the remains of plants and animals that lived millions of years ago. Coal was mostly formed from plants that lived in swamps. The dead plant material was buried and compacted under sediments to form coal. Oil and natural gas were formed when decomposed plant and animal materials were subjected to heat and pressure in the absence of oxygen. Limestone is mostly calcite, which formed as the shells of tiny ocean animals that died and fell to the seafloor.

3. **B**. A waterwheel converts the potential gravitational energy of a height of water into rotational mechanical energy. The rotational energy can then be harnessed to do work or to make electricity.

4. **B**. The excretory system, including the skin, lungs, and kidneys, removes wastes from the human body. The respiratory system, including the nose, lungs, trachea, and diaphragm, exchanges oxygen and carbon dioxide with the environment. The digestive system, including the digestive tract and other organs, helps the body break down food so that it can be absorbed by the body. The blood, heart, and blood vessels make

up the circulatory system, which transports nutrients, gases, waste products, hormones, and other substances to all parts of the body.

5. **B.** Pascal's principle states that an external pressure applied to a fluid in a closed container is uniformly transmitted through the liquid. This means that Choice B is correct: The change in liquid takes place equally throughout the liquid.

6. **A.** Granite is a type of igneous rock that crystallized from magma deep within the Earth.

7. **A.** Kinetic energy is the energy of motion—of waves, electrons, atoms, molecules, substances, and objects. Potential energy is stored energy and is the energy of position. Sound is the movement of energy in waves. Sound is produced when a force causes an object or substance to vibrate—the energy is transferred through the substance in a wave.

8. **D.** The genotype of a heterozygous pea plant is Rr, and the genotype of a homozygous pea plant is RR. If Rr is crossed with RR, then 100 percent of the resulting seeds would receive a dominant R gene and would therefore produce plants with red flowers.

9. **D.** F_2 will be equal to 20 newtons. In a hydraulic lift, an external pressure is applied to a fluid in a closed container. Because of Pascal's principle, the pressure is uniformly transmitted throughout the liquid. Increasing the area of the output piston by 20 times also increases the area of the output force by 20 times. Since work can neither be created nor destroyed, the distance over which the input force is applied must be 20 times the distance of the output force.

10. **D.** Any kind of rock can be "morphed" or changed into a metamorphic rock when it is subjected to heat and pressure deep under Earth's surface.

11. **B.** A gram is a metric unit of mass equal to a thousandth of a kilogram. A milliliter is a metric unit of volume. A newton is defined as the amount of force required to cause a mass to accelerate, or increase in speed. A pound is an English measure of weight.

12. **B**. A recessive allele is only expressed when two genes are present. Each parent has one recessive allele, and, therefore, neither has the disease. The offspring received two recessive alleles, one from each parents, and therefore has the disease.

13. **D**. Wavelength is the distance between identical points on two neighboring waves. The wavelength of sound waves determines pitch. The height of a wavelength is a measure of its amplitude. The amplitude of sound waves determines volume. Frequency is the number of waves passing a certain point per unit of time. A sound with a shorter wavelength or a higher pitch has a greater frequency.

14. **D**. Ocean water becomes denser with an increase in salinity or a decrease in temperature. An increase in evaporation increases the salinity of ocean water and, therefore, makes it denser. All of the answers are correct.

15. **A**. Scurvy is a noninfectious disease that is caused by a vitamin C deficiency. All of the other diseases are caused by pathogens: influenza is caused by a virus; athlete's foot is caused by a fungus; and botulism is caused by a bacterium.

16. **C**. A kilowatt-hour is a measure of electric energy. When you use a thousand watts of electricity in an hour, you use a kilowatt-hour. A watt is the rate of use of electricity at an instant in time. Kilowatt-hours measure the total usage of electrical energy over time.

17. **B**. The mid-ocean ridge is split lengthwise down its crest by the rift valley. The sea floor is spreading outward on either side of the rift valley.

18. **C**. The same number of atoms of each element must exist after a chemical reaction as existed before the reaction. Because there are two oxygen atoms to the left of the arrow, there must also be two oxygen atoms to the right of the arrow; therefore, a 2 must be placed before the H_2O. Now the O atoms are balanced, but there are 4 H atoms on the right, and only 2 on the left. To correct this, a 2 must be placed before the H_2.

19. **D.** All of these answers are correct. In winter, the Northern Hemisphere is tilted away from the sun, which makes the days shorter. The sun's rays hit Earth at a more oblique angle; therefore, the intensity of solar radiation that hits a given area on Earth's surface is less. In summer, the Northern Hemisphere is tilted toward the sun; therefore, the days are longer and the sun's rays hit Earth at a more direct angle. The intensity of solar radiation that hits a given area on Earth's surface at this time is greater.

20. **C.** Chlorophyll, the green pigment in plants, captures the sun's energy to convert water and oxygen into glucose. The cytoplasm is the region of the cell between the nucleus and the cell membrane. A chromosome in the nucleus contains the genetic code that is passed on from one generation of cells to another. A stoma is a pore in a leaf that allows gases to pass back and forth.

21. **B.** The amount of current in the circuit (in amperes) is equal to volts/ohms. Increasing voltage by adding a battery increases the current. Adding a resistance such as a light bulb (measured in ohms) decreases the current. Adding a fuse should not affect the current. It will break the current if it becomes too great.

22. **B.** The moon's gravity pulls the ocean water into a bulge (high tide) on the side near the moon. It also pulls the earth away from the water on the other side of Earth, causing a second bulge of water on the side farthest from the moon. At right angles to these bulges are the low points, or low tide. As Earth turns, the bulges stay lined up with the moon. Because the moon is revolving around Earth, the times of the high and low tides are not the same each day. The times of the tides change with the phases of the moon.

23. **B.** The atomic mass of an atom is the total of protons and neutrons. The atomic mass of the oxygen atom is 16.

24. **C.** A mitochondrion has a two-layer membrane and crista. Chloroplasts have double membranes but no crista. A vacuole is a single

membrane-bound sac. The endoplasmic reticulum is an extensive network of membranes throughout the cytoplasm.

25. **A.** The visible part of the electromagnetic spectrum ranges from red, which has the longest visible wavelength (700 nm), to violet, which has the shortest visible wavelength (400 nm). The order of all the colors on the visible spectrum from longest to shortest is red, orange, yellow, green, blue, and violet. (The name Roy G. BV can be used to help memorize this order.)

PART 2: ARITHMETIC REASONING

1. **B.** To determine the number of tiles needed, divide the length of the floor by the length of each tile. To do this, invert the fraction expressing the length of the tile and multiply: $16 \times \dfrac{4}{3} = 21\dfrac{1}{3}$.

2. **D.** For the printer to print 26 pages at the rate of 12 pages per minute, multiply the number of pages by the rate in minutes per page: $26 \text{ pages} \times \dfrac{1 \text{ minute}}{12 \text{ pages}} \approx 2.67 \text{ minutes}$.

3. **C.** The odd positive integers can be written as the sequence 1, 3, 5, 7, ... Using the term number as the input value and the term value as the output value, the following formula can be derived to find the nth value of any term: $a_n = 2n - 1$. The value of the 16th odd, positive integer can be determined by evaluating the formula for an n-value of 16. Doing so gives $a_n = 2(16) - 1$, which equals 31.

4. **C.** Each sentence can be translated into an algebraic equation. The first sentence can be represented as $3x + 2y = 10.35$, where x represents the cost of a coffee cake and y represents the cost of a cup of coffee. The second sentence can be represented as $2x + 4y = 12.90$, with each variable representing the same value. The x-value and y-value can be determined by solving this system of equations. The method of elimination is one method that can be used to solve the system. Each term in the first equation can be multiplied by 2, giving the equation $6x + 4y = 20.70$.

Each term in the second equation can be multiplied by -3, giving the equation $-6x - 12y = -38.70$. Adding the two new equations gives $-8y = -18$, where $y = 2.25$. Thus, the cost of one cup of coffee is $2.25.

5.   **B.** The probability of event A and event B can be determined using the following formula: $P(\text{A and B}) = P(\text{A}) \times P(\text{B})$. The probability of getting heads is $\frac{1}{2}$. The probability of rolling a number greater than 2 is $\frac{4}{6}$. Therefore, the probability of getting heads and rolling a number greater than 2 is $\frac{1}{2} \times \frac{4}{6} = \frac{4}{12}$, which reduces to $\frac{1}{3}$.

6.   **D.** Because there are 6 possible outcomes for the roll of a die, the probability of rolling the number 3 on a single die is $\frac{1}{6}$. To find the probability of this occurring twice, simply multiply the two probabilities: $\frac{1}{6} \times \frac{1}{6} = \frac{1}{36}$.

7.   **B.** The percent increase of her hourly rate can be determined by setting the hourly increase equal to the product of the original hourly rate and some percent increase, x. If the new hourly rate is $42 and the increase is $2, then the original hourly rate was $40. Therefore, this equation can be solved for x:

$$2 = 40x$$
$$x = 0.05$$

The percent increase of her new hourly rate is 0.05, or 5%.

8.   **B.** The cost of Theresa's monthly text-messaging plan can be represented by the equation $y = 0.07x + 7.99$, where x represents the number of text messages sent and y represents the total monthly cost. Substituting 132 for the variable x gives $y = 0.07(132) + 7.99$, or 17.23. Theresa will pay $17.23 for her text messaging service this month.

9.   **C.** To determine the amount saved after 3 weeks, multiply the weekly paycheck amount by 0.25 to find the amount saved in one week, and then multiply this amount by 3: $350 \times 0.25 \times 3 = $262.50.

10. **B.** To determine the percent increase, first calculate the amount of the increase: $3.95 − $3.73 = $0.22. This amount should be set equal to the product of the original cost and some rate of increase, x. Therefore, solve this equation to determine the percent increase: $0.22 = 3.73x$, which gives $x \approx 0.06$. Therefore, the percent increase in the cost of the coffee beverage is approximately 6 percent.

11. **C.** The number of stones used can be arranged in ascending order, as shown here: 19, 21, 24, 24, 27, 28. The middle two scores are 24 and 24, which have an average of 24.

12. **B.** The price of the half-gallon of orange juice 5 years ago can be determined using this equation: $3.60 = 1.50x$, where x represents the price of a half-gallon of orange juice 5 years ago. Solving for x gives $x = 2.40$. The price of the half-gallon of orange juice 5 years ago was $2.40.

13. **C.** The probability of event A or event B can be determined using the following formula: $P(A \text{ or } B) = P(A) + P(B) − P(A \text{ and } B)$. The probability of event A and event B can be determined using the formula $P(A \text{ and } B) = P(A) \times P(B)$. Therefore, $P(A \text{ and } B) = 0.32 \times 0.28$, or 0.0896, and $P(A \text{ or } B) = 0.32 + 0.28 − 0.0896$ $P(A \text{ or } B) = 0.32 + 0.28 − 0.0896$, or 0.5104. The probability that Eric will attend graduate school or take courses at Texas A&M University is approximately 51 percent.

14. **C.** The amount she saves per paycheck is equal to the product of 15%, or 0.15, and $1,900. Therefore, she saves $285 per paycheck.

15. **C.** Rick's monthly salary can be determined using this equation: $240 = 0.06x$, where x represents his monthly salary. Solving for x gives $x = 4,000$. Rick's monthly salary is $4,000.

16. **B.** The average cost of a textbook can be determined by summing the cost of the five textbooks and dividing by the total number of textbooks, or 5. The average cost of one textbook can be determined by evaluating the expression $\dfrac{172.50 + 88.90 + 94.50 + 75.60 + 56.40}{5}$. Therefore, the average cost of one textbook is $97.58.

17. B. The data set given for Choice B has a median score of 85.5. Arrange the scores in ascending order, as shown here: 75, 77, 78, 81, 82, 89, 92, 94, 96, 99. The middle two scores are 82 and 89, which have an average of 85.5.

18. B. The rate of the sales tax can be determined by first finding the difference in the cost of the clothes prior to sales tax and then finding the cost of the clothes after sales tax. This difference equals $13.94. This amount should be set equal to the product of the cost of the clothes prior to sales tax and some sales tax, x. Therefore, the rate of the sales tax can be determined by solving the equation $13.94 = 164x$, which gives $x = 0.085$. Therefore, the rate of the sales tax is 8.5 percent.

19. A. The probability of event A and event B can be determined using this formula: $P(A \text{ and } B) = P(A) \times P(B)$. The probability of drawing a blue marble is $\dfrac{4}{17}$. Since the first marble is not replaced, the probability of then drawing a green marble is $\dfrac{8}{16}$, or $\dfrac{1}{2}$. Thus, the probability of drawing a blue marble and then a green marble is $\dfrac{4}{17} \times \dfrac{1}{2} = \dfrac{4}{34}$ or $\dfrac{2}{17}$.

20. B. The problem asks for a weighted average. The weighted average can be determined by evaluating the following expression: $\dfrac{5(28.95) + 3(18.99)}{8}$, which is approximately 25.22. Therefore, the average cost of the 8 items of clothing is $25.22.

21. A. The mean, median, mode, and range are 69, 67, 66, and 37, respectively. Therefore, the mean is greatest.

22. C. To subtract the amount of pie eaten by Darnell from the amount eaten by Jon, the fractions must be converted to a common denominator. Multiply the top and bottom of one fraction by the denominator of the other and vice-versa: $\dfrac{2}{3} \times \dfrac{4}{4} = \dfrac{8}{12}$ and $\dfrac{1}{4} \times \dfrac{3}{3} = \dfrac{3}{12}$. Subtracting the numerators of the converted fractions yields: $\dfrac{8}{12} - \dfrac{3}{12} = \dfrac{5}{12}$.

23. **C.** Enrico's situation can be represented with the following proportion: $\dfrac{45}{9} = \dfrac{x}{36}$. Note that 36 is used because there are 36 months in 3 years. Solving for x gives $x = 180$.

24. **B.** The total amount of money in the fund should be divided by 4, which gives a quotient of $5,222.50. Since the amount used per year must be an integer amount, the whole number of $5,222 should be multiplied by the number of years (4) giving a product of $20,888. The amount left over is equal to the difference of $20,890 and $20,888, or $2.

25. **D.** The given statement can be translated as follows: $\begin{matrix} xy = 2{,}352 \\ x + 6 = 97 \end{matrix}$. The equations can be solved for y and rewritten as $y = \dfrac{2{,}352}{x}$ and $y = 97 - x$. The point of intersection of the two graphs will reveal the values of x and y that make the equations true. The point of intersection can be verified using the table feature of a graphing calculator. Doing so shows the point of intersection to be (48, 49). Therefore, the larger of the two numbers is 49. The point of intersection can be checked by substituting the x value of 48 and the y value of 49 into each of the original equations:

$$\begin{matrix} (48)(49) = 2{,}352 \\ 2{,}352 = 2{,}352 \end{matrix} \quad \text{and} \quad \begin{matrix} 48 + 49 = 97 \\ 97 = 97 \end{matrix}.$$

26. **B.** The function represented by the given table can be determined by first finding the slope of the line. The slope can be calculated by evaluating the ratio of the change in any two y-values to the change in any two corresponding x-values. For example, the slope can be written as $\dfrac{10 - 3}{2 - 1}$, or 7. This slope and x- and y-values from any ordered pair in the table can be substituted into the slope-intercept form of an equation. Using the slope of 7 and point (1, 3) gives $3 = 7(1) + b$. Solving for b gives $b = -4$. Thus, the function represented by the table is $y = 7x - 4$.

27. **A.** Together, Rachelle and Don can bill 20 customers in 1 hour. This relationship can be written as a ratio: $\dfrac{1 \text{ hour}}{20 \text{ customers}}$.

The total number of hours it takes to bill 182 customers can be represented by the following expression: $\dfrac{1 \text{ hour}}{20 \text{ customers}} \times 182 \text{ customers}$. Thus, the total number of hours it takes to bill 182 customers is 9.1 hours; 0.1 hours is equal to 6 minutes. Therefore, the total time is 9 hours, 6 minutes.

28. **B.** To find the balance, subtract the amount spent from the starting amount in the account: $585 – $697 = –$112. To subtract a larger number from a smaller number, simply subtract the smaller number from the larger number and change the sign to negative.

29. **D.** The total portion of the book Joe read during the two days is equal to the sum of $\dfrac{3}{4}$ and $\dfrac{1}{5}$. Therefore, Joe read $\dfrac{19}{20}$, or 95%, of the book. The number of pages he read can be calculated by finding the product of 0.95 and 360, or $\dfrac{19}{20}$ and 360. Therefore, Joe read 342 pages during the two days.

30. **C.** The theoretical probability of a die landing on an even number is $\dfrac{3}{6}$ or $\dfrac{1}{2}$. Thus, the number of times the die can be expected to land on an even number after rolling it 18 times is $18 \times \dfrac{1}{2}$ times, or 9 times.

PART 3: WORD KNOWLEDGE

1. **B.** *Procrastinate* most nearly means *delay*. *Avoid* means to shun or evade, *suspend* means to stop or halt, and *interrupt* means to disturb.

2. **C.** *Veritable* most nearly means *authentic*, as in "The veritable truth was that he had not committed any crime." *Immature* means childish or juvenile, *wistful* means hopeful or reflective, and *zealous* means overly enthusiastic.

3. **D.** *Variegated* most nearly means *multicolored*. *Tepid* means lukewarm, *matted* means tangled or knotted, and *convoluted* means complex or confusing.

4. **D.** *Subside* most closely means *quiet down*, as in "The pain will subside as soon as the medication is administered." *Vanish* means to disappear completely, *upsurge* means to suddenly increase, and *speed up* means to quickly gain in strength.

5. **C.** *Stamina* most nearly means *endurance*. *Courage* means brave or heroic, *compassion* means empathy or kindness, and *attitude* means perspective or tone.

6. **B.** *Somber* most nearly means *solemn*, as in "The somber music was fitting on this sad occasion." *Innovation* means something invented or new, *erratic* means irregular, and *antiquated* means old-fashioned or out of date.

7. **A.** *Flagrant* most nearly means *obvious*. *Restrained* means held back, *intermittent* means on and off or interrupted, and *discreet* means subtle.

8. **B.** *Credible* most nearly means *believable*, as in "The witness provided credible evidence of the crime." *Repairable* means able to be fixed, *susceptible* means vulnerable, and *contemptible* means hateful or shameful.

9. **C.** *Placid* most closely means *tranquil*. *Gullible* means to believe almost anything, *vigilant* means to be extra aware of, and *fastidious* means extremely neat or precise.

10. **D.** *Discrepancy* most closely means *incongruity* or *mistake*. *Increment* means a percentage or addition, *inflection* means accent or tone, and *invocation* means a chant or summons.

11. **C.** *Jocular* most closely means *humorous*, as in "The teacher's jocular attitude made the lecture far more interesting and entertaining." *Amorous* means interested in love, *infamous* means notorious or well known, and *ambiguous* means unclear or confusing.

12. **C.** *Ultimatum* most closely means *demand*. *Punishment* means the act of punishing someone for doing something wrong, *scolding* means a verbal admonishment, and *penalty* means a punishment or harsh measure for doing something wrong.

13. **A.** A *fallacy* most nearly means a *mistaken belief*, as in "The idea that Earth is flat is a fallacy of the past." An *illogical assumption* means an assumption that does not make sense. A *conscious decision* means a decision that one makes on purpose. A *rational conclusion* is a conclusion that is logical, or that makes sense.

14. **C.** *Ravenous* most closely means *famished*, as in "The athlete had missed breakfast and lunch, so when the game was over, he was truly ravenous." *Distraught* means emotionally upset, *candid* means honest or blunt, and *derelict* means neglected.

15. **D.** *Dilapidated* most nearly means *ramshackle*. *Pristine* means immaculate or pure, *fraudulent* means false or untrue, and *dubious* means doubtful.

16. **B.** *Dominant* most nearly means *primary*. *Disabled* means handicapped or dysfunctional, *inferior* means less able, and *impaired* means injured or damaged.

17. **A.** *Formulated* most nearly means *devised*. *Discarded* means to throw away, *overlooked* means to ignore, and *contracted* means to sign up with terms as in a contract.

18. **A.** *Fluctuate* means *oscillate*, as in "The temperature fluctuates wildly during the spring." *Generate* means to make or create, *integrate* means to blend or merge, and *consecrate* means to bless or sanctify.

19. **C.** *Emphatic* most nearly means *insistent or absolute*. *Hostile* means extremely angry or violent, *lackadaisical* means lazy, and *blasé* means neutral or casual.

20. **D.** *Passive* most nearly means *submissive*, as in "The protestors were polite and passive, even though they were unhappy about the situation." *Supple* means flexible, *avid* means enthusiastic or eager, and *morose* means depressed or gloomy.

21. **A.** *Archives* most nearly means *annals*. *Documents* means papers, *collection* means a gathering of objects or items, and *domicile* means a home or place to live.

22. **C.** *Apathy* most nearly means *indifference*, as in "The apathy of the crowd was made clear by the silence." *Consequence* means what follows actions, *relevance* means significance or something with bearing, and *importance* means something that is essential, with meaning.

23. **D.** *Festooned* most nearly means *embellished*. *Enamored* means *charmed*, *emaciated* means extremely thin and starving, and *emanated* means radiated or emitted.

24. **C.** *Orientation* most nearly means *introduction*. *Communal* means shared, *misdemeanor* is a type of minor crime, and a *prospectus* is an advance notice about something.

25. **B.** *Jurisdiction* most nearly means *precinct*, which is an area of authority or a territory. A *manifest* means obvious, a *conclave* means a meeting, and *anarchy* means disorder or lawlessness.

26. **D.** *Benign* most nearly means *innocuous*, as in "The medical test fortunately came back with a report of a benign condition." *Rancor* means spite or malice, *poignant* means emotional or touching, and *malignant* means dangerous or deadly.

27. **D.** *Overture* most nearly means *proposition*. *Segment* means a small section or portion, *prestige* means respect or status, and *namesake* means a person with the same name as someone else.

28. **B.** *Skirmish* most nearly means a *scuffle*, as in "The two brothers argued over chores and ended up in a skirmish." *Waif* means an abandoned child, *tangent* means part of a survey line, and *pinnacle* means the highest point or peak.

29. **C.** *Silhouette* most nearly means *shadow*. *Satire* means the use of irony or sarcasm, *solvent* means flush or having money, and *symmetry* means balanced proportions.

30. **A.** *Tawdry* most nearly means *gaudy*, as in "The tawdry outfit she had on looked like she had picked it out while blindfolded." *Discerning* means tasteful and refined, *timely* means punctual, and *unerring* means without any mistake or errors.

31. **C.** *Obituary* most nearly means *funerary*. *Reformatory* means institution, *notary* means a legal representative, and *oratory* means a debate or speech.

32. **A.** *Inanimate* most nearly means *lifeless*, as in "The room was full of inanimate objects that were worth thousands of dollars." *Habitat* means home or place in which to live, *unfounded* means groundless or baseless, and *ramification* means consequence or result.

33. **D.** *Cantankerous* most nearly means *argumentative*. *Benevolent* means conniving and kind, *diminutive* means unusually small, and *depraved* means immoral or corrupt.

34. **C.** *Contrite* most nearly means *remorseful*, as in "The young boy was contrite after accidentally breaking the table lamp." *Reiterate* means to repeat with emphasis, *repugnant* means offensive or disgusting, and *reverberation* means an echoing vibration.

35. **C.** *Irrevocable* most nearly means *irreversible*, as in "The mistake was irrevocable and would haunt him for the rest of his life." *Irreparable* means unable to be repaired or fixed, *irrepressible*, means unable to be kept down or quieted, and *irrelevant* means having little or no relevance or importance.

PART 4: PARAGRAPH COMPREHENSION

1. **D.** The last two lines of the paragraph indicate that scientists still have much to learn about loggerhead turtles even though they seem to have proven that loggerhead turtles swim toward Earth's magnetic field. Therefore, the best answer choice is D: Scientists have made progress but still face some unanswered questions.

2. **B.** The most outstanding feature of Mars is its color, which is why it's known as the "Red Planet." This is the reason the author compares Australia's Outback to Mars; the Outback has red soil.

3. **A.** This question asks about a detail in the paragraph. It asks you to identify the name that is not mentioned in the paragraph. The paragraph does not mention the word "pony," so this is the correct answer.

4. **C.** This question asks you to make an inference. This means that you won't find the answer stated in the paragraph. However, the paragraph says that the games of golf and football were distracting people from archery, which was necessary to keep people safe. This should lead you to infer that archery was probably needed for military purposes.

5. **C.** This question asks you to identify the main idea, or the author's main point. The paragraph explains that the burning of fossil fuels is to blame for the loss of permafrost. It also says that villagers are being harmed by this lost because their homes are tilting and sinking. Choice C incorporates both of these ideas and, therefore, is the best answer.

6. **C.** This paragraph asks you to choose the detail that is not mentioned in the paragraph. The paragraph does not say that the dancers wore woven scarves, so Choice C is correct.

7. **D.** This question asks you to identify the author's tone in the paragraph. The best answer choice is enthusiastic—the author describes the Skycar as amazing and does not say anything negative about the car. The author does not seem confused or concerned about the car, and the paragraph is not humorous.

8. **C.** This question asks you to choose the answer choice that gives the main idea. The best answer is Choice C: People who want to become park rangers need to travel a long and difficult road to success. The other answer choices give details in the paragraph.

9. **D.** The athlete seems reasonably sure he can make this shot. He concentrates on the back rim of the basket and barely feels his arms and hands at the shot went up. This suggests he has made free throws many times before. He is confident that he will make the shot.

10. **B.** The technology in the paragraph uses a tiny computer to indicate the needs of redwood trees. The closest technology is a computer indicating when a dog is hungry.

11. **D.** The paragraph gives biographical information about Sarah Winnemucca, who worked hard to make a better life for the Paiute tribe

of Nevada. Therefore, the best answer is Choice D: the purpose of the paragraph is to inform readers about a Paiute woman's accomplishments.

12. **D.** According to the paragraph, the favorite hot dog was a chili dog with pickle relish and brown mustard. However, you're asked to indicate the least favorite, which is a cheese dog with chopped onions and yellow mustard.

13. **A.** The paragraph says that in the old days, ironworkers on skyscrapers were required to walk narrow I-beams in bad weather without wearing safety belts or harnesses. From this information, you can infer that today's high-steel workers wear safety belts and harnesses.

14. **D.** This question asks you to choose the event that started the Carters' professional career. The answer choices all contain information from the paragraph, but the event that launched the family's professional career was when they earned an audition with Victor Records in 1927.

15. **C.** The paragraph says that when he worked as a reporter, Steinbeck talked to poor families about their lives. The articles he wrote about these people eventually grew into a novel. Steinbeck's other novels were also about unfortunate individuals. Therefore, the best answer choice is C: a recurring theme expressed in the author's work.

PART 5: MATHEMATICAL KNOWLEDGE

1. **D.** The radical expression $8\sqrt{48}$ can be rewritten as $8\sqrt{16}\sqrt{3}$ or $8\times4\sqrt{3}$, which simplifies to $32\sqrt{3}$. The radical expression $5\sqrt{27}$ can be rewritten as $5\sqrt{9}\sqrt{3}$, or $5\times3\sqrt{3}$, which simplifies to $15\sqrt{3}$; therefore, $32\sqrt{3}+15\sqrt{3}=47\sqrt{3}$.

2. **D.** Each term in the first binomial should be multiplied by each term in the second binomial. The product can be written as $-8x^2+24x+12x-36$, which simplifies to $-8x^2+36x-36$.

3. **C.** The sum of the interior angle measures of any regular polygon (n) can be determined using the formula $(n-2)\times180$, where n represents the number of sides of the polygon. Since the sum of the interior angles

is known, the following equation can be written: $(n-2) \times 180 = 900$. Divide each side by 180: $n - 2 = 5$. Then add 2 to both sides, which results in $n = 7$. Thus, a seven-sided regular polygon (or heptagon) has an interior angle measure sum equal to 900°.

4. **C.** The perimeter of the rectangle is equal to 12 inches + 12 inches + 9 inches + 9 inches = 42 inches. The area of the rectangle is equal to 12 inches × 9 inches = 108 square inches. The ratio of the rectangle's perimeter to its area is $\dfrac{42}{108}$, which reduces to $\dfrac{7}{18}$.

5. **B.** The expression $3x + 2$ is a factor of the given trinomial: $(3x + 2)(7x - 2) = 21x^2 + 8x - 4$.

6. **A.** A square is the only polygon with more than 3 lines of symmetry; it has 4 lines of symmetry. A rhombus has 2 lines of symmetry, a rectangle has 2 lines of symmetry, and an equilateral triangle has 3 lines of symmetry.

7. **D.** Since a square has four congruent sides, each side is equal to the quotient of 48 and 4, or 12. Thus, each side length of the square is 12 centimeters. The area of a square can be represented as $A = s^2$, where s represents the side length of the square. Substituting 12 for s gives $A = 12^2$. The area of the square is 144 square centimeters.

8. **C.** The area of a triangle can be determined using the formula $A = \dfrac{1}{2}bh$, where b represents the length of the base and h represents the height. Substitute $4x$ for the base and $2x - 2$ for the height:

$$A = \frac{1}{2}(4x)(2x - 2)$$
$$A = \frac{1}{2}(8x^2 - 8x)$$
$$A = 4x^2 - 4x$$

Then factor out $4x$: $4x(x - 1)$.

9. **B.** The expression $4^{\frac{5}{2}}$ can be written as $\sqrt{4^5}$ or $\sqrt{1,024}$, which equals 32.

10. **B.** The sum of an infinite geometric series can be determined by using the formula $S = \dfrac{a}{1-r}$, where a represents the value of the first term and r represents the common ratio between the value of the terms. Substitute $0.\bar{1}$ for both a and r: $S = \dfrac{0.\bar{1}}{1-0.\bar{1}}$ or $S = \dfrac{0.\bar{1}}{0.9}$, which equals $0.\bar{1}$. Thus, the sum of the infinite geometric series is $0.\bar{1}$.

11. **A.** The equation can be solved by first subtracting 46 from both sides, as shown here: $-50 - 46 = -12x$ or $-96 = -12x$. Then divide both sides by -12: $x = 8$.

12. **C.** Perpendicular lines have negative reciprocal slopes. Thus, a line perpendicular to Line l must have a slope of $-\dfrac{1}{4}$. The equation given for Choice C has such a slope.

13. **B.** If two parallel lines are cut by a transversal, pairs of alternate interior angles are congruent. Therefore, angles c and f are congruent.

14. **C.** The sum of the measures of the interior angles of an octagon equals $(8-2) \times 180° = 1,080°$. The sum of the interior angles of a pentagon equals $(5-2) \times 180° = 540°$. Given that the sum of the interior angles of a pentagon is represented by the variable p, the sum of the interior angles of an octagon can be represented by the expression $2p$ since $1,080°$ is two times the measure of $540°$.

15. **B.** $\angle DAB$ and $\angle BAC$ are supplementary, meaning they sum to $180°$. Since $m\angle DAB = 132°$, $m\angle BAC$ is equal to the difference of $180°$ and $132°$, or $48°$.

16. **D.** The sum of the interior angle measures of a triangle is $180°$. Thus, the following equation can be written: $x + 3x - 35 + x + 20 = 180$. The equation can be solved for x by writing: $5x - 15 = 180$, which gives $x = 39$. Angle B is represented by the expression $3x - 35$. Therefore, $m\angle B$ is equal to $(3(39) - 35)°$ or $82°$.

17. **C.** A right triangle has side lengths that adhere to the Pythagorean Theorem, which states that the sum of the square of the two legs equals the square of the hypotenuse, or $a^2 + b^2 = c^2$. Therefore, a right triangle will have a sum of the square of two legs equal to the square of a third leg, or hypotenuse. A triangle with side lengths of 12 inches, 16 inches, and 20 inches adheres to this theorem: $12^2 + 16^2 = 20^2$ because $400 = 400$.

18. **A.** Similar polygons have congruent corresponding angles and proportional corresponding sides. Therefore, the following proportion can be written: $\frac{9}{15} = \frac{4.5}{x}$. Solving for x gives: $x = 7.5$.

19. **C.** The circumference of the tree trunk can be represented using the formula $C = 2\pi r$. Substitute the given circumference of 69.08 inches: $69.08 = 2\pi r$. Divide both sides by 2π (using 3.14 for π): $r = 11$. The radius of the tree trunk is 11 inches.

20. **C.** A circle with radius of 6 has a circumference equal to 12π and an area equal to 36π; 36π is 3 times 12π. A circle with a radius of 2 has the same circumference and area. A circle with a radius of 4 has an area that is 2 times the circumference. A circle with a radius of 8 has an area that is 4 times the circumference.

21. **C.** The volume of the box is equal to the product of the dimensions. Therefore, the volume of the box is equal to 6 inches × 4 inches × 8 inches = 192 cubic inches. Since each candy takes up 3 cubic inches of space, the number of candies that will fit in the box is equal to the quotient of 192 and 3, or 64.

22. **D.** The volume of the pitcher represents the number of cubic inches of water that can be held by the container. The volume of a cylinder can be found using the formula $V = \pi r^2 h$, where r represents the radius and h represents the height. Substitute 4 inches for the radius and 9 inches for the height: $V = \pi(4)^2(9)$ or $V = 144\pi$. Therefore, the pitcher can hold approximately 452 cubic inches of water.

23. **A.** The distance formula can be used to determine which of the

coordinates could represent the other point. Substitute the coordinates of the given point and the coordinates of the point in Choice A: $d = \sqrt{(3-7)^2 + (-1+4)^2}$ or $d = \sqrt{(-4)^2 + (3)^2}$, which simplifies to $d = \sqrt{25}$. These coordinates result in a distance of 5 from the point (7, −4).

24. **A.** The slope of the line represents the average cost of each arrangement. The slope of the line can be determined by finding the ratio of the change in *y*-values to the change in corresponding *x*-values. Any two points on the line can be used to determine the slope of the line. The coordinates (10, 250) and (30, 1250) seem to be good estimates for points on the line. Substituting the coordinates of these points gives the ratio: $\frac{1250-250}{30-20}$, which simplifies to 50. Therefore, a good estimate for the slope of the line is 50, indicating an approximate average price of $50 for an arrangement.

25. **C.** To create a triangle, the sum of any two side lengths must be greater than the length of the third side. The side lengths of 11 inches, 4 inches, and 6 inches will not form a triangle because the sum of 4 inches and 6 inches is less than 11 inches.

PART 6: ELECTRONICS INFORMATION

1. **A.** An atom that has more electrons than usual acquires a negative charge and is therefore called a negative ion. One with fewer electrons than usual acquires a positive charge and is called a positive ion. Atoms constantly lose and gain electrons.

2. **D.** Electrons in the conduction band are excellent conductors because they can be easily removed by other electric fields. Electrons can pass through the forbidden band but can never come to rest there. Those in the valence band are tightly bound to the atom, making them poor conductors.

3. **B.** Applying external voltage to a PN junction reduces its barrier, which allows current to flow more freely. External voltage that opposes

the electrostatic field of the PN junction is considered forward bias. Applying external voltage to a PN junction in the opposite direction aids the junction and resists current; this is known as reverse bias.

4. **A**. Insulators have very wide energy gaps, so they require a substantial amount of energy to create a current. The figure in Choice A has a wide forbidden band, so it is most likely a good insulator.

5. **C**. In a conductor, valence electrons can move freely using only a small amount of energy. There is no forbidden band, or energy gag, in the diagram in Choice C, so this is a conductor.

6. **D**. Atoms with fewer than eight valence electrons become highly active, seeking to fill the gaps. When an atom finds valence electrons, it binds itself to them. When valence electrons belong to another atom, the connection between the two atoms is called a covalent bond. The arrangement of the molecules in the bond is called a crystal. Choice D is correct because all statements are true.

7. **D**. A PN junction forms when N-type semiconductor material is joined with P-type semiconductor material. The PN junction becomes a diode rectifier; that is, it converts AC into DC by allowing current to flow in only one direction.

8   **C**. Maximum average forward current is the highest amount of current that can flow in the forward direction without structural breakdown. Maximum surge current is the highest amount of current that can flow in the forward direction as a nonrecurring pulse. Peak recurrent forward current refers to the maximum amount of current that can flow in the forward direction as recurring pulses.

9. **C**. As an industry standard, electrical professionals memorize the numbers assigned to each color under the semiconductor diode color-code system, which is as follows:

COLOR	DIGIT
Black	0
Brown	1
Red	2
Orange	3
Yellow	4
Green	5
Blue	6
Violet	7
Gray	8
White	9

10. **B.** Heat within a diode causes electron-hole pairs to form, which allows current to increase. When current increases, heat then increases—and the cycle repeats itself. When too much current runs through a diode, thermal runaway occurs and eventually destroys the diode. Heat is known as the greatest danger to a diode.

11. **A.** Using a crystal diode test set to determine both the diode's forward and reverse current is the only valid way to check a diode.

12. **C.** The semiconductor identification system is an alphanumerical code that helps technicians distinguish between different semiconductors. "X" is a variable letter that represents the number of semiconductor junctions; "N" is a variable letter that represents the semiconductor. "YYY" is a set of three variable numbers that make up the diode's identification number. In practice, the semiconductor identification system produces codes such as "IN486" to let technicians know precisely what they are dealing with.

13. **A.** A two-junction transistor requires three elements. The emitter produces current carriers. The base of a two-junction transistor controls the flow of the emitter's current carriers, and the collector gathers the current carriers.

14. **B.** Transistors are classified according to the arrangement of their N and P materials; in this case, Choice B displays the correct arrangement of the N-type and P-type material. All NPN transistors have two PN junctions: one between the emitter and the base, and one between the collector and the base.

15. **B.** There are four classes of operation for amplifiers, each with a different level of conduction: A, AB, B, and C. Class A amplifiers are biased so that changes in the signal do not affect the collector-current flow. Class AB amplifiers are designed so that the collector current reaches cutoff during one alteration of the input signal. Class B amplifiers are biased so the collector current reaches cutoff during only one-half of one alteration, and class C amplifiers use reverse biasing so very little of the input signal flows through the collector.

16. **C.** Fidelity is defined as the faithful reproduction of a signal, and distortion is a poor reproduction. An amplifier with a significant amount of distortion has low fidelity, whereas an amplifier with high fidelity has low distortion.

17. **C.** The two general classifications of integrated circuits, commonly referred to as ICs, are hybrid and monolithic. Hybrid ICs are made on glass, ceramic, or other insulating material; the passive components are placed on the foundation first, and then the active components are attached. A monolithic IC's active and passive components are both fabricated on one continuous piece of material, usually silicon.

18. **B.** The current gain for a CB transistor is measured with the Greek letter alpha (α). To determine a CB transistor's current gain, divide the product of Δ (the Greek letter delta indicates a small change) and input current by the product of Δ and the output current.

19. **D.** When heat releases electrons, they can rupture covalent bonds (a covalent bond is when two or more atoms share electrons). As the bonds break, more and more loose electrons accelerate and break more bonds. This is called the avalanche effect because it continues as a chain reaction, much like an avalanche.

20. **A.** An SCR functions as a switch with no moving parts. It is designed to turn power on and off quickly—in some cases, SCRs can switch on and off as often as 25,000 times per second. SCRs can be used to control both large and small amounts of power.

PART 7: AUTO AND SHOP INFORMATION

1. **C.** An ignition coil holds the current from the battery and allows it to build up. When the coil reaches its maximum capacity, a contact breaker opens and the stored energy is released. The energy flows between the coil and the capacitor, and the changing magnetic field creates a larger voltage.

2. **C.** A lathe is used in both metal- and woodworking, so Choice C is correct. Lathes are designed to hold an object still while it is being cut with mechanical cutting instruments.

3. **A.** The 12-volt power a battery provides allows everything electrical in the car to run. The windshield wipers, radio, power accessories, and headlights are all powered by the battery. The crankshaft is powered by combustion, manual door locks are pressed up and down by operators, and a gear shift lever is operated by hand.

4. **C.** A carpenter's level, also called a spirit level, is used to determine whether a surface is level. The glass vials in each circular cutout contain liquid and air. Each indicates whether a surface is level by the placement of the air bubble inside.

5. **D.** Nails are measured by gauge, and the gauges above are most common. Nails with high gauges are thinner than low-gauge nails. Differently sized nails serve different purposes.

6. **B.** A diagonal-peen hammer is often used in metalwork to strike forging tools. The head of the hammer is placed at a 45-degree angle to make striking other objects easier.

7. **D.** Housed in a cylinder, a piston is a moving engine part that transfers force from captured gas to the crankshaft. As a piston moves, it covers and uncovers ports in the cylinder as a side effect of motion.

8. **A.** Differential steering is usually used on tracked vehicles, and the tracks move at different speeds to steer. To turn left in a tracked vehicle, the operator applies the brake to the left track while allowing the right track to continue moving.

9. **C.** An abrasive saw uses an abrasive disc to cut extremely hard materials. Circular saws, table saws, and jigsaws are generally used on wood because their teeth can cut through it without breaking.

10. **C.** A joist is attached between walls, between beams, or between a wall and a beam to provide support. Joists work like the legs of a chair in that they help distribute weight evenly.

11. **C.** A girder is a large horizontal beam that supports smaller beams. A truss is a triangular structure made of three separate beams, and a purlin is a horizontal support beam used in roofing.

12. **B.** Frictional brakes use friction to slow a wheel. There are two types of frictional brakes: those that use pads and those that use shoes. Both can be, and often are, contained in a drum.

13. **C.** Piston rings seal the cylinder where combustion takes place. If the piston rings are worn, the air-fuel mix can leak out of the cylinder; as a result, there is nothing to compress.

14. **A.** Air-cooled engines, like the name implies, are cooled when air flows through the moving parts. Liquid-cooled engines generally run cooler than air-cooled engines. Air-cooled engines are usually lighter and less efficient than liquid-cooled engines.

15. **C.** Diesel engines do not contain spark plugs. Diesel fuel is ignited inside the cylinder and does not need a spark plug to create combustion.

16. **A.** A corner chisel is characterized by its L-shaped cutting edge and is used to cut 90-degree angles. Flooring chisels have thin blades. Framing chisels have thin, flexible blades, and mortise chisels have slightly tapered sides.

17. **A.** A vise is an adjustable tool that clamps wood securely when tightened. Vises can be affixed to a worker's bench or held in one's hand.

18. **B.** First, air-fuel mixture goes into a cylinder (intake). Then the air-fuel mixture is compressed (compression) so it can be ignited (ignition). Finally, it releases its exhaust.

19. **A.** Several cylinders are at work in an engine, and they fire one at a time. When the timing is off, the engine runs poorly.

20. **B.** The most common reasons for engine failure are poor fuel mixtures, lack of compression, and lack of spark. The fuel needs to be precisely mixed with air so combustion can occur after compression. However, if there is no spark, there can be no ignition.

21. **D.** The catalytic converter reduces toxins in exhaust emissions before they are released into the air. The muffler reduces sound. Exhaust emissions exit the vehicle via the tailpipe. Exhaust manifolds lead gases into exhaust pipes, which connect the parts of the exhaust system.

22. **B.** Springs are not part of a radial tire. Beads are steel wires encased in rubber. The tire is mounted on the rim. The liner is the sealed surface of the tire. Other parts of a radial tire include body piles, the main part of the tire, sidewalls, and treads.

23. **C.** A crosscut saw is designed to cut across the grain of wood. A coping saw is designed to cut fine curves. A rip saw is used to cut with the grain of wood, and a hacksaw cuts metals.

24. **D.** Antilock brakes (ABS) are controlled by a computer and keep wheels from locking. This allows an automobile to stop in a predictable manner, especially in slippery conditions.

25. **C.** A diesel engine lacks a spark-ignition system. It uses a higher compression ratio to generate heat of compression to start the engine. A diesel engine is simpler than a gasoline engine.

PART 8: MECHANICAL COMPREHENSION

1. **B.** Net force is the sum of all forces acting on an object. For example, when two people are moving an object and one person is pulling while the other pushes, the net force is the sum of their combined effort.

2. **B.** The formula to discover an unknown on a lever is $m_1 \times d_1 = m_2 \times d_2$, where m represents mass and d represents distance. In this case, $m_1 = 20$ and $d_1 = 10$, m_2 is unknown, and $d_2 = 5$. Using mathematics, we know that $20 \times 10 = 200$, so

$$200 = m_2 \times 5$$

$$200 \div 5 = m_2$$

$$40 = m_2$$

Check the math by inserting all the values into the original formula.

$$(20) \times (10) = (40) \times (5)$$

The answer on both sides is 200, so you know each value is correct.

3. **C.** Larger gears require fewer revolutions to accomplish the same amount of work as smaller gears. Although larger gears require more input (pedaling, in this case), they do not need as many turns to accomplish work. Shifting to a larger gear on a mountain bike makes pedaling more difficult and increases speed.

4. **D.** Using a crowbar as a lever to open a trunk demonstrates mechanical advantage, as does using a screwdriver. The screwdriver's handle is larger than its point, so a few turns accomplish more work than unscrewing it with your hand. Pouring coffee from a pot has no mechanical advantage because no matter what you pour the coffee from, you still need to exert the same amount of work.

5. **A.** All the wheels in the diagram will turn clockwise if wheel A is turned clockwise. Follow the bands connecting each with your finger to visualize the motion of each wheel.

6. **D.** The formula to determine force is $F = ma$, where F represents force in newtons, m represents the object's mass in kilograms, and a represents the object's acceleration in meters per second squared (m/s^2). In this problem, $F = (1{,}000 \text{ kg}) \times (50 \text{ m/s}^2)$, so the answer is 50,000 N.

7. **D.** In the formula for work, $W = Fd$, F represents force and d represents displacement. The result, work, is measured in joules.

8. **D.** Each unit of energy, called a joule, is equal to 1 newton-meter. An ohm is a measurement of electric resistance, while watts and kilowatts measure power.

9. **D.** Since the box is moving a distance of 10 meters and 48 newtons of force are being applied, 480 joules of work are being performed on the box. Using the formula for work, $W = Fd$, multiply the force (48 N) by the displacement (10 m). The answer, 480, is the amount of work performed in joules (J).

10. **A.** Bevel gears would be used to change the direction of a shaft's rotation. Bevel gears are generally mounted at 90-degree angles to one another. Helical gears generally work side by side, and worm gears are used to create large gear reductions.

11. **D.** A fixed pulley creates a mechanical advantage of 1. This means that it puts out the same amount of force as is put into it. A fixed pulley can only change the direction of the force applied; it cannot lessen the amount of work needed to accomplish a task.

12. **A.** To calculate pressure, divide the amount of force applied by the area to which it is applied. Force is measured in newtons, and the area in the formula for pressure must be measured in meters^2. The formula for pressure is $P = \dfrac{F}{A}$.

13. **A.** The point on which a lever pivots is called a fulcrum. In this example, the fulcrum is in the center of the lever, like a seesaw.

14. **C.** A compound pulley system contains two or more pulleys, with at least one being fixed and one being movable. A fixed pulley is a pulley that is anchored in place, while a movable pulley has a free axle.

15. **C.** Newton's first law of motion states that an object at rest tends to stay at rest unless it is acted upon by an external force. Simply put, objects that are sitting still will stay that way until something moves them.

16. **C.** On a third-class lever, the effort is between the fulcrum and the load. The illustrations in choices A and B show first-class levers. On a second-class lever, the load is between the effort and the fulcrum.

17. **C.** There are six tools known as simple machines: levers, pulleys, inclined planes, wheels and axles, wedges, and screws. Simple machines are used to change the magnitude or the direction of force. An abacus is not a simple machine.

18. **C.** A sheet of glass provides the smallest amount of friction among the items listed above. Friction slows the progress of work. For example, a box with 10 N of force pushing it will move more easily on a sheet of glass than it will on a gravel road.

19. **A.** You exert the most force. The golf club exerts force on the golf ball, but because of friction, some of the original force you applied is lost. The golf ball exerts no force.

20. **D.** Kinetic energy is the energy of movement. All the answer choices give examples of kinetic energy except answer choice D, a bicycle in a stationary position.

21. **C.** Inertia is defined as the resistance of a physical object to any change in its state of motion or rest, or the tendency to resist any change in its actual motion. Inertia refers to the fact that matter wishes to continue as is, whether it is at rest or in motion, and that it will create some form of resistance.

22. **D.** A wedge can be used to lift or hold an object in place and to separate two objects. Wedges work by transferring force. A wedge-shaped doorstop that prevents a swinging door from moving, a chisel that separates two objects, and a wedge that pries a heavy object up from the ground are all examples of a wedge acting as a simple machine.

23. **C.** The formula to calculate force is $F = ma$, where F represents force in newtons, m represents mass in kilograms, and a represents acceleration in meters per second squared. In this question, the object weighs 50 kg and is moving at 30 m/s². To determine the force needed to sustain this movement, multiply 50 by 30. The answer, 150, is the amount of force needed and is measured in newtons (N).

24. **D.** The number of sections of rope that provide support to the moving block tells you the mechanical advantage of a pulley system.

In this case, the upper pulley is fixed and the lower pulley is moving. There are two ropes supporting the moving block, so the mechanical advantage is 2.

25. **B.** A pair of scissors is made of two first-class levers. In a first-class lever, the fulcrum is between the effort and the load; the fulcrum on a pair of scissors is the pivot point between the two blades. Therefore, a pair of scissors is made of two first-class levers.

About the Authors

Angie Johnston holds a BA in psychology from the University of Texas–El Paso. As a former combat journalist for the U.S. Army and Department of Defense, Angie earned several awards for journalistic excellence from the Secretary of the Army. Angie currently serves in the military and works with National Guard recruiters as a member of the Red Phase cadre. Part of her duties includes preparing potential soldiers for the ASVAB and conducting study sessions for this examination.

Amanda Ross, PhD, is a former lecturer and assistant research scientist at Texas A&M University. She has served as a curriculum developer/instructional designer for various educational publishing companies and as a professional development coordinator for the National Council of Teachers of Mathematics. Amanda is a graduate of Texas A&M University with a PhD in curriculum and instruction in mathematics education. She is currently an independent educational consultant.

Also Available

My Max Score AP Biology
by Dr. Robert S. Stewart, Jr. • 978-1-4022-4315-8

My Max Score AP Calculus AB/BC
by Carolyn Wheater • 978-1-4022-4313-4

My Max Score AP English Language and Composition
by Jocelyn Sisson • 978-1-4022-4312-7

My Max Score AP English Literature and Composition
by Tony Armstrong • 978-1-4022-4311-0

My Max Score AP European History
by Ira Shull and Mark Dziak • 978-1-4022-4318-9

My Max Score AP U.S. Government & Politics
by Del Franz • 978-1-4022-4314-1

My Max Score AP U.S. History
by Michael Romano • 978-1-4022-4310-3

My Max Score AP World History
by Kirby Whitehead • 978-1-4022-4317-2

$14.99 U.S./£9.99 UK

Also Available

My Max Score SAT Literature Subject Test
by Steven Fox • 978-1-4022-5613-4

My Max Score SAT Math 1 & 2 Subject Test
by Chris Monahan • 978-1-4022-5601-1

My Max Score SAT U.S. History Subject Test
by Cara Cantarella • 978-1-4022-5604-2

$14.99 U.S./£9.99 UK